From the author of *I Stand with Christ* & *The Underground Church*

CHASING REVIVAL

A ROAD TRIP BIBLE STUDY

EUGENE BACH

To the men and women who gave their lives
in service of the Great Commission.

CONTENTS

Part 4: Rome and the End of the World

Part 5: Europe: A Continent Changed

Part 6: America: Revival Crosses the Sea

Part 7: China: Revival in the Middle Kingdom

Part 8: The Land Between the Walls

Part 9: Back to Jerusalem

Notes

ACKNOWLEDGMENTS

It humbles me to think of the amazing people God has used to breathe life into this study. I started this adventure of following in the footsteps of revival with no budget, no plans, no script, and no promises, but there were plenty of friends and family along the way. Their support, insight, and self-sacrificing commitment are the real reason why this project is available.

I would especially like to thank my dear friend *Christian*, a man I am unable to refer to by any other name. He played many roles. He was the camera man, editor, script writer, theologian, historian, and sometimes my anger management counselor, but above all, he was my best friend. He traveled with me at a moment's notice to every little nook and corner of the world. He was with me and away from his family on birthdays, holidays, and anniversaries. He never asked for a penny for any of his efforts and felt that he was doing it for the kingdom. For as long as I live, I will look back on his friendship during these years of making this study as an undeserved gift from God.

Christian's brother, who shall also remain unnamed, dedicated so much time to bringing our experiences and personalities to life through his art. His art, which can be found throughout our books and videos, cannot be explained in any other way than anointed.

Thanks also to *Brother Ren* and *Brother Yun*, who were both there in a car on tour in the United States as this dream came about. Brother Ren graciously allowed me to neglect other responsibilities to chase this vision.

Without a doubt, one of the greatest blessings goes to my dear friend *Donald Leow*. It was his encouragement and creativity that led to the name *Chasing Revival* while sitting in the breakfast bar of a small hotel in America. He is much too busy and important to spend his time freely helping people like me, but his humbleness and commitment are unexplainable and unforgettable.

I had mentors along the way like *Pastor Danny Miller*, who helped look over the book in the earliest stages and provided guidance from the perspective of a senior pastor. Pastor Danny has proven to be a source of strength for me during times of uncertainty.

A huge dose of gratitude goes out to my sweet friend *Anna*. I will refrain from using her last name for security reasons, but she has been a constant voice in the back of my head, bringing about both balance and reflection. Her conservative Calvinist background, multilinguistic writing abilities, missionary experience, and amazing skills as a mother have helped me communicate with more clarity and great soberness.

Of course I never would have been able to go anywhere or do anything if it were not for the travel assistance of *Belinda Chadwell* and *Ruth*. They do more than book tickets and arrange visas for me and the BTJ team. They look after me in every single way. Ruth arranges appointments, books taxis, sets up meetings, corresponds with partners, makes dinner reservations, and translates. Belinda doesn't sleep or rest until she makes sure even the smallest details are taken care of.

I want to give a special shout-out to the gifted and talented editor *Julie Breihan*. My writing style is sloppy, lazy, messy, rushed, and run together in a string of mismatched thoughts that make no sense to anyone but me, and this project was the messiest, sloppiest, laziest, and most rushed of them all! I am too ashamed to show my rough drafts to others (especially editors) for fear of judgment and rejection, but Julie has been nothing but graceful and supportive.

I have a big smile on my face as I write a special thanks to the amazing *Mrs. Amy Parker*. Her ideas and enthusiasm for this project even surpassed mine. She brought together editors, printers, marketing plans, designers, artists, and identified a target audience for this project that I never would have dreamed of. I have never met anyone like her in my life and thank God for the privilege of calling her my friend.

More than anyone, I would like to thank my wife and two boys, who have sacrificed more than anyone else for this project. I have spent more than three hundred days a year for the last six years traveling around the world writing this book, filming the videos, and running our ministry projects. My wife has had to run our home as a single mother, and my boys have had to spend their most impressionable years without a father. I have missed many anniversaries, birthdays, and other special events that I will never again have the chance to make up.

My oldest son was twelve years old when I started this project and now, as we go to print, is eighteen and leaving for a military university in America. My youngest was eight and is now almost fifteen. It has not escaped me that I cannot go back in time to tuck them in at night or play pass outside instead of being on the road in another country.

Our family feels called to do what we are doing, but their sacrifice has gone above anything that I can ever repay, though I will spend the rest of my life trying to.

To all of the friends, family, pastors, ministry leaders, missionaries, evangelists, and fellow troublemakers that I fail to mention: I pray that the Lord will repay you in full for your prayers and support while I embarked on this road trip Bible study, *Chasing Revival.*

INTRODUCTION

WHY IS REVIVAL IMPORTANT?

———◆———

"It ain't the parts of the Bible that I can't understand that bother me,
it's the parts that I do understand."

—MARK TWAIN

It was barely past noon when two men sat down together in a small church café outside of a massive Christian conference center. The conference had brought them together. And only the conference could have brought them together, for the two men were so different. Very different.

One was nearly fifty and looked every day of it. He was dressed in khaki pants that could have fit loosely years ago, but now no longer gave his well-fed frame the breathing room it so desperately desired. A traditional white button-up shirt bulged over his belly in the portliest of ways, and his fine, short, thinning blond hair was neatly cut in a manner that would have made any member of the military proud. He was unknown at the conference, a small-town pastor from a fly-over state with few members in his congregation.

Across from him sat the other man, who looked to be about thirty, but it was hard to tell. Fashionable black-rimmed glasses framed his boyish face with a well-trimmed black beard that gave off a heavy metrosexual vibe. The beard, though seemingly frazzled and careless, was as perfectly planned as the ripped jeans, cotton T-shirt, and black-and-white sneakers.

He too was a pastor, but not just any pastor; he was the pastor of legends.

His congregational disciples championed his best-selling books, and the world followed after him singing the modern songs of social justice. Fate brought these two men together when at the same time they had approached the only empty table in the conference center café. They acknowledged each other with pleasantness in their words, but each harbored a painful, awkward discomfort in his heart.

They were from two distinctly different worlds, but on that broody September day, they were in the same place at the same time looking for the same thing: revival.

Both sat in silence at the small round table as boisterous chatter echoed all around them. Though at different levels of the social status, they were united by the same level of emotional and spiritual defeat. Their secret collapse was unknown to the other men in the room, but it was actually shared by many of them.

Spiritually, they were both exhausted, tired, hungry, and thirsty—in desperate need of renewal. They hadn't seen God move in years. They doubted if they had ever really seen Him move at all. They were both a skin sack full of dry bones longing for just a taste of a lonely drop of water from the heavenly finger of Lazarus.

The rural pastor with a small congregation was tired of looking at the same faces every week. He needed fresh meat. His congregation was old and aging. His younger years as a pastor had been spent preaching a weekly lullaby and marching maturing members into the twilight. His church was attended by the mayor, the sheriff, and the superintendent of the school district, but the idea of sinners from far and wide finding salvation at his pulpit had died long ago.

The hip megachurch pastor had a church attended by thousands and a global platform, but the city around him remained largely unaffected. A local politician had never walked through his doors, and the crime rate in his city was embarrassingly high. Truth be told, his church—though impressive and accomplished—had no spiritual influence at all. The line between his church and the lost world outside was so blurry that it was no longer possible to see where one ended and the other began. He could no longer avoid the truth.

It was clear that society was the major source of theology in his church and that it trumped the Bible.

In the early years, the act of making Jesus culturally relevant for a new generation had seemed divinely inspired and spiritually effective, but today it was crystal clear that the social environment dictated standards of morality and that the raw teachings of God's Word were offensive if ever mentioned louder than a whisper and so they were increasingly watered down, avoided.

Both men, sitting in silence at the table together, once dreamed the dream of revival. The mere idea of it had shaken their core, but over time, both men had traded reckless belief for sound security. Past revivals that had once been considered revolutionary had been tamed and oddly had created safe trails that were now widely accepted and marked with certificates, ordinations, salaries, and retirement pensions. Ministry was no longer dangerous. Not even close. It was the epitome of safety.

Where was the rebellious, earthshaking path of revival that created enemies and uncertain earthly futures for everyone involved? Where was the revival that required reckless abandonment?

The true trophies of revival's martyrs have never looked appealing on the walls of a fancy office, and their victories are often never fully appreciated until the storms have passed.

What insanity could have possibly possessed these two men to crave for revival in the first place? They prayed for revival and yearned for it with every fiber of their being, but had history taught them nothing? Didn't they learn how the prophets were treated? Had they not read about the gruesome deaths of the disciples and the torture of the first-century church leaders?

Today, their families were safe and secure. These two pastors had been given salvation—sweet but boring salvation . . . Why not leave well enough alone?

What sadistic heart longs to lead his family out of the cradle of comfort and into the fires of revival? And for what purpose? Revival is a dangerous proposition for those who have grown accustomed to the calm.

For all people, I assume, there comes a time when maintaining a normal Christian life becomes exhausting. Religion by itself is too heavy a burden to carry. The exhaustion is compounded by the many indulging rewards for sin, but the sin that rewards one is a suffering punishment for another.

The sin that rewards one with the secret pleasure of pornography at the same time endorses the never-ending anguish of another who tried to escape poverty by selling her body. The sin that rewards one with temporal wealth for forging identification abuses another with the loss of credit and savings.

The sinful satiation of one part of society eventually imprisons the entire society. Sin is not legislated in isolation, meaning that it is not possible to endorse sin without punishing the innocent.

Communities that suffer in poverty, crime, or moral decay are not simply the result of political mismanagement or bureaucratic ignorance, but rather the collective endorsement of sin. It is the responsibility of Christians to resist the endorsement of evil. If the church is not present or effective, which is essentially the same thing, then the blood of the lost is on the hands of the believers.

So, to alleviate poverty, crime, and moral decay, the church should resist sin, and this will remove suffering—right? Pray for revival and all problems will subside—yes?

Not exactly. Maybe the endorsement of sin *and* the resistance of sin both bring suffering.

The resistance of sin also brings about misery, and sometimes the anguish can be even more intense than that associated with endorsing sin. However, the temporal pain of resisting sin leads to lasting benefits, whereas the delayed pain of sanctioning sin births pains that continue for generations.

For instance, the man who exercises and adopts a healthy diet will experience cravings that will have to be resisted and spend more money for quality food, as well as feel the discomfort of getting up and moving instead of sleeping and watching TV, of pain during exercise, and of aching sore muscles. But the result of such an endeavor can lead to long-term health.

The joys of sleeping, habitually watching TV, and constantly eating whatever your craving mouth desires will give immediate satisfaction, but the long-term ailments associated with such decisions await everyone.

Both paths cause pain, but only one eventually brings reward.

Societies suffer because of the church, because if churches are the salt, then the sin of the world is like an open wound that is agitated by the salt. If churches are not the salt, people suffer because they are not convicted of their sins and thus reap the long-term consequences of those sins.

What a tragedy for those who suffer without gain.

Both Jesus and Satan suffer, but only one suffers for purpose rather than punishment.

Back at the conference table, both pastors sat at the table and pondered the escape of their suffering. Somehow they intuitively knew that their misery was both contagious and generational. If they continued ignoring the sickness in their churches, it would be fatal for everyone. Yes, they could possibly eke out a mediocre existence and escape the by-products of their cowardice through death, but their children and their children's children would inevitably inherit suffering.

Sitting at the table in silence, both men desired something more—more than they could communicate or form into decipherable thoughts. The world they inherited should be better and could be better, but it would take a radical change of diet. It would take sweat and sacrifice. It would be an excruciating exercise of painful self-abandon, but if they could—only for a minute—touch the throne room of God, they might see a spiritual revival of men and women that would change history forever.

DAY 1

ANSWERING THE CALL

———◆———

"The two most important days in your life are the day you are born and the day you find out why."

—Mark Twain

Why does revival matter? Why would anyone want to experience it? Isn't it enough to be saved and know that we have been given eternal salvation? Does revival make us any more saved? Does revival give us bonus points?

Maybe there is something more to be found in revival than mere salvation. Maybe we were meant for something more, but what is it? Why is it important?

Why does revival matter?

Unlike other books about revival, this work is not written with absolute answers. Neither is it written with leading questions that arrive at predestined answers that have been previously mapped out. Instead, it is a delicate quest that lead to a five-year, around-the-world journey tracing the footsteps of revival.

The Bible has been slaughtered by many men as unlearned as I am, and I beg God not to allow me to publicly (or privately, for that matter) crucify it further with zealous ignorance.

I am not an expert on revival, and I do not claim to be able to explain it better than the next man. However, I have been working and serving in the midst of one of the largest revivals in the history of man, and it has left me with an overwhelming desire to know more and share the things I have discovered on my journeys with those around me.

I travel around the world several times a year and work in more countries than I can count, and over time I have seen that there is a clear difference between the nations that have experienced revival and those that have not.

Being involved with grassroots missions in China has thrown me into the fires of cultural immersion and allowed me to experience this revival firsthand as it was happening. Traveling with Chinese missionaries into many closed nations has provided me with a unique perspective of the pain that exists in nations where revival has tarried.

It is in China that I have found my greatest challenges, holding hands with my greatest joys, and it is from here that I will cautiously attempt to share. My journey in search of revival does not start with revival, but with a challenge that can lead to revival.

If you are like me, there is a voice inside you that you have always heard telling you that you were created for something great, and that voice keeps calling your name like a rhythmic chant deep in your soul. It is the reason why you were born.

You might not know what "it" is, but "it" inconveniently interrupts petty celebrations and stubbornly wakes you up in the middle of the night telling you that you were made for more than this. "It" is your mission. "It" is the challenge of your lifetime, and no matter how strong, smart, rich, talented, or famous you become, you will never in your lifetime find any purpose as fulfilling as the mission you have been given.

You were born with a purpose. You were created with a mission.

All of your talents, ambitions, and character traits combined with your experiences, trials, failures, and triumphs have culminated into one person for this time and place in history. You are a part of a long line of history, a link in history's chain. You were not born an hour too late or an hour too early. Your hour has arrived, and the world is calling out.

You might feel like you do not fit in, but you were masterfully created with purpose and carefully designed for a unique mission given to you by your Creator. When you were created, everything about you was taken into consideration—the color of your eyes, the shape of your face, your height, the date and place of your birth, and even your propensity to lose or gain weight were all typed into your DNA since the beginning of time so that you would be prepared for your mission. There has never been another you, and there will never be another you.

You can choose to ignore the voice that is calling you and deny the challenge you were created for, but that road of distractions and denial always ends in disappointment. If you should accept the purpose for which you were created, prepare to have all of your senses overloaded, because there is no greater experience than tackling a task that is impossible to accomplish by anyone other than you, and your faith is the trigger for the world to witness the miraculous intervention of God. There is a lost world of hundreds of millions of people who are crying out for help, and God has called you to help them. He will not abandon you. You were not designed to fail.

God has called you to bring about revival in your generation!

You can choose to answer your calling or let the phone ring. If you do not pick up the phone, you will not be alone. The phone has been ringing unanswered for generations. However, there have been a few brave men and women, a very select few, who have picked up that phone and answered the call.

> **God has called you to bring about revival in your generation! You can choose to answer your calling or let the phone ring.**

What will you do? Will you allow the phone to continue ringing unanswered? Should you roll over and just go back to sleep after awaking with purpose?

In this study we will explore the history of what happens when ordinary people like you and me pick up the phone and answer the call for which they were created. We will follow the history of the Great Commission from the moment it left the lips of Jesus and started a never-ending revival. We will trace that revival all the way around the world and back to you and me.

Hopefully, by following the history of the spread of the Gospel message, we will be inspired to answer our own call.

If we chose to answer, we will not be alone. There is a movement in China today that is ready to join with us. They call their mission Back to Jerusalem.

Back to Jerusalem is more than a vision. It is a continuation of a revival movement that started two thousand years ago in Jerusalem when Jesus gave the command known as the Great Commission. We often call the Back to Jerusalem vision the "Great Commission with kung pao flavor."

In this study we will attempt to follow the movement of the Gospel message from its genesis to the present so we can see how others answered that call. Each section of this study will focus on the historical spread of Jesus' message and how that pertains to what the Bible teaches and what we are seeing in the world today.

I believe that each section in this study will show how Jesus is relevant to answering the basic problems of the past and present, and why it is vital to carry out the command of the Great Commission found in Matthew 28:19–20:

Go ye therefore, and teach all nations, baptizing them in the name of the Father, and of the Son, and of the Holy Ghost: teaching them to observe all things whatsoever I have commanded you: and, lo, I am with you always, even unto the end of the world. Amen.

Along the way I hope to identify characteristics that are found in revivals throughout history. We will attempt to chronologically follow the traces of revivals (though not exhaustively) and walk in the footsteps of the very simple men and women whom God called, men and women just like you and me who accepted their challenge to fulfill God's plan in their lives.

Few have ever tried to trace the two-thousand-year path of Christian revival that began in Jerusalem and moved westward. As far as we know, it has never been broken down for a small-group study. As you read, I'm sure you will have questions, and your initial answers to these questions may not be your final ones.

Mine weren't.

Revivalists often study pockets of revival—specific times, people, leaders, or geographical areas in which revival took place—but we are taking a broader approach than that, following the chain of events that started in Jerusalem and is making its way around the globe, all the way back to the place where it began.

Spoon-fed Bible scriptures, easy-cheesy group questions, quick bumper-sticker answers, and back-to-life-as-usual are not what this journey aspires to produce. Sit down and buckle up as we take an epic journey that has never been made before and follow the revival fires around the world from Jerusalem all the way Back to Jerusalem. It is more than just merely walking in the footsteps of history; it is a no-retreat, no-surrender, hold-nothing-back-in-the-reserve-tank kind of journey that punches you in the face. We will attempt to expose the good, the bad, and the ugly as we go from the burning fires of persecution into the current flames of revival.

> **Sit down and buckle up as we take an epic journey that has never been made before and follow the revival fires around the world from Jerusalem all the way Back to Jerusalem.**

You can check your bleeding-heart feelings used to interpret Scripture, your modern, socially compatible theories, and your culturally tainted theology at the door, because the raw history that will present itself in this study demands that we acknowledge that our God is bigger than our meager concepts and that revival is more powerful and earth-shattering than we can begin to comprehend.

DISCUSSION QUESTIONS

1. Do you feel you are doing what you are made for?
2. Are you giving your all or are there things that are holding you back?

3. What are you prepared to sacrifice to experience a revival in the place where you live or to bring revival to a place where Jesus is not yet known?

4. What do you think is needed to transform comfortable Christians into an unstoppable force for the Gospel?

DAY 2

WHAT IS THE GOSPEL MESSAGE?

---

*"A ship is always safe at shore,
but that is not what it was built for."*

—ALBERT EINSTEIN

It has been two thousand years since Jesus gave His life-giving message to the world and commanded His ragtag band of followers to share it, but after two thousand years, two-thirds of the world still lives in dark regions between China and Jerusalem where His name is not known. How can we anticipate the Second Coming when the majority of the world's population has not yet heard about the first coming?

This compels us to ask inconvenient questions: Why are there so many people who have not yet heard? Has the church done everything that could be done? What is the root failure? Have we misunderstood why Jesus came? After two thousand years, is there really an urgency like the disciples believed there was? Believers have been preaching and waiting

> **Believers have been preaching and waiting for more than two thousand years for the Second Coming, but is He really coming again?**

for more than two thousand years for the Second Coming, but is He really coming again? If so, why is He waiting so long?

13

Studying revival in many ways is a study of the explosive movement of the Gospel. Revival is an event that takes place on earth, not in heaven. Heaven has no need for revival. Too often we can think of it as a carnal experience that illicits an emotional response rather than a cognitive one. At the beginning of my journey I encountered areas where some of my initial ideas not just about revival, but also about Christianity, came from my cultural Christianity and not from the teachings of Jesus. I realized these might be harder to let go of than I previously thought.

To adequately trace the history of revival, I began searching for explosive movements of the Gospel message, but before tracing the movement of the Gospel, maybe we should establish what the Gospel message actually is. Studying the movement of the Gospel is not just a scholastic endeavor or an academic discipline; it has a flow, a life, a moving poetry to it. The Word of God is alive. It does not only exist in a book but makes its mark upon the lives of living vessels and has shaped the world we live in today. To trace the movement of the Gospel message is to follow man and witness God chasing after him over and over again, not as an angry tax collector, but as a hungry lover.

The movement of the Gospel and its impact on humanity may not always be recognizable to the purely academic theologian, because its history might not be contained in institutions ruled by authorized clergy members and documented in moldy library books. Instead, maybe it is more embodied, remembered, and handed down in ritual, art, music, sculptures, dance, poetry, and physical manifestations of love toward one another by those who have been impacted by it the most.

At the onset of this study, we mustn't fall into the trap of stuffing God into boxes of our own making. We must accept that our limited understanding of God is colored and formed by our own culture and experiences. We must understand that the real Jesus of Galilee might have been much different in character and appearance than the image we have created in our mind's eye from movies and paintings.

We know that Jesus was not as rigid as His followers have made Him out to be. We know He wanted man to be saved more than man wanted to be saved. You might want to read that last sentence again, because His love is intense. He first loved us before we even knew to love Him. He moved past the clerical leadership's rigid rules and sanctimonious behavior and

> ## We know He wanted man to be saved more than man wanted to be saved.

embraced ordinary people with common lives, hardships, and yes, failures. He adapted His love to the needs of each person, and the responses of those found were as varied as the ways in which they were first lost.

Our journey must begin in Israel, where Jesus contextualized His message for His audience. He taught foreign ideas and concepts by using cultural examples that were familiar to the listeners. His teachings, though, were more than examples, concepts, rules, systems, or mechanisms of understanding. They were emotional, passionate, and life changing because they contained life. God is not only alive, but He is life (John 1:3–4).

And not only is God life, but His Word is alive. It is never stagnant. It is never finished. It is continually moving and working on the heart of man. The Word of God is contagious, and we call the rapid spread of the contagion "revival."

In his sojourn as a visiting professor to Melbourne's Yarra Theological Union, Stephen Bevans may have opened up an entirely new way of viewing the living God when he wrote,

A few years ago I began to realize that our God—the God revealed to us by Jesus of Nazareth through the power of the Holy Spirit—might be best described as a *verb*, not a noun. What I mean by this is that the God we know from revelation might be best imagined not as a static kind of "person"—sort of like us but wiser and more powerful—who is "up there" or "out there." Rather, in a way that is much more exciting and worthy of our adoration and love, God is a Movement—more personal than we can ever imagine—who is always and everywhere present in God's creation, present in the warp and woof of it, working for creation's wholeness and healing, calling creation to its fullness, and calling women and men on a small planet in a minor galaxy in this vast universe—billions of years old, billions of light years in extension—into partnership in God's work.[1]

The theology of the phrase "God is a verb" is as hard to explain as "God is love," but 1 John 4:8–9 says, "He that loveth not knoweth not God; for *God is love*. In this was manifested the love of God toward us, because that God sent his only begotten Son into the world, that we might live through him" (emphasis added).

John said plainly that God is love. If God is love, then love is a noun, a noun meaning God, for "God is love." If it is true that God *is* love, then we are not able to love without God. This is true even before we know God or accept Him (or reject Him). Our first love, the love of our suckling mother when we are only an infant, is a reflection of God because we are created in His image and He is love. As

> **If I love, then God is in me, because without God, I am not able to love.**

an infant we can't describe love, but we feel it and grow in it. If I love, either wittingly or unwittingly, I am reflecting God in my life because "God is love" and I have been made in His image. If I love, then God is in me, because without God, I am not able to love. This does not translate into my eternal salvation, but it can translate into a temporary salvation of living a more tolerable life in a damned world. Even a damned man who openly chooses to reject God is still chased by God with His love and can reap the benefits of His love for him.

If I hate God but love my child, I am reflecting God even while actively rejecting Him because I am incapable of love without God, because God is love. If I am loved in return, then I am benefiting from God's love, which has been given to me, even if it is only a reflection of Him at a social level. It is how man is made, in His image, and we carry His reflection.

I am not saved by this reflection, but I can benefit from it, and if I continue to reject God until death, then I will finally experience a world absent of His love: hell. The mission of Jesus was to give us a way to be united with His love for eternity. This is the Gospel.

If we are searching for a description for the Gospel, this is it, or at least the beginning of it. God is love, and His message is the supreme message of love. God is life, and the Gospel is the supreme message of life.

DISCUSSION QUESTIONS

1. Can you back up the statement that the Gospel message is the supreme message of life and love with experiences from your own life and journey of faith?
2. Can you share examples of how people you know or maybe even churches or neighborhoods have been changed because they were touched by the life and love that came to them through the message of the Gospel?
3. What would you say to someone who says he doesn't need the Gospel because he is happy with his life?

DAY 3

A WORLD WITHOUT THE GOSPEL MESSAGE?

---

*"I am a polyatheist–there are many
gods that I don't believe in."*

—Dan Fouts

Isn't the very definition of hell to be absent of God? Isn't that what the Gospel message tries to rescue us from—a life away from God? If I reject the Gospel, then don't I reject God, and if I reject God, then don't I reject all that He is? By this rejection of God and His Gospel message, don't I by extension reject both life and love? Then why do those who reject God still have the capacity for both love and life?

Maybe there is no escaping God and His Gospel message until He fully allows it. If we still have both life and love, then maybe that is a sign that we are not able to ever run from Him until He allows it by giving us the choice to reject Him. Even after our rejection, if we still have life and love, maybe that is a sign that we have rejected Him but He has yet to give up on us. "Can any hide himself in secret places that I shall not see him? saith the Lord. Do not I fill heaven and earth? saith the Lord" (Jeremiah 23:24).

When societies do not have God and they do not have representatives who carry Him in their earthly vessel, aren't they then largely absent of all that God is—namely love, life, liberty, justice, and wisdom?

If this is true, then can't we actually measure the tangible lack of God in a society by evaluating legislative disregard of life, liberty, justice, and basic human rights? Perhaps the opposite is true, and the movement of the Gospel can be traced and measured by following societies that legislate life, liberty, justice, and basic human rights.

Can these things be observable and measured in a society?

I think so.

To *truly* have love, there must *truly* be freedom. Love in its truest form requires the freedom to reject it, otherwise it is not love,

> **Love in its truest form requires the freedom to reject it, otherwise it is not love, but only mechanical creation.**

but only mechanical creation. If I cannot reject God, then my love for Him cannot be truly known. If God cannot reject me, then His love for me cannot be truly known. God has the power to reject me and is entitled to condemn me to live without His presence for eternity, but He *chose* to love me instead. God is not obligated to love me.

I can choose to reject His love, because I have been given the freedom to do so. However, His love for me is not dependent on my love for Him. A complete rejection would require a complete abandonment, and since I am incapable of life and love without Him, I must have both if I am able to write this, because even in my state of rejection, I am being sustained. This is His grace, and this grace must be at the heart of the Gospel message.

When societies reject God, they reject life, love, and liberty. So, for instance, we can conclude that North Korea's rejection of God is a rejection of all the attributes and characteristics of God in man, which leads to a lack of love and life that can be measured in human rights abuses. If man is not capable of loving God, then his ability to love man dissipates and eventually disappears.

This allows us to evaluate human suffering imposed by social choices. If God respects a society's wishes to reject Him, then is the lack of love, life, liberty, justice, and wisdom found in that society an actual punishment or only a result of God's absence? This question helps us see where the Gospel is not present and has never been present when tracing the history of revival. This can also help us find where it is present and where it has been.

Saudi Arabia, for example, is a super wealthy country, but their people are forced to leave for medical, education, or even basic leisure activities. Egypt is rich with resources, but their people are dying in poverty. Iran has a long, rich history of culture and freedom, but today their people suffer at the hands of cruel dictators.

Is it fair? The people in North Korea did not chose to be born in North Korea. The Iraqis did not choose to be born into Islam. They are experiencing a life largely absent of God in their society, and only the One their leaders have rejected can save them: "Whosoever shall call upon the name of the Lord shall be saved. How then shall they call on him in whom they have not believed? and how shall they believe in him of whom they have not heard? and how shall they hear without a preacher? And how shall they preach, except they be sent?" (Romans 10:13–15). America is not freer than Iran because Americans have a better system of government or a more efficient economic engine. Brits are not smarter or harder working than the Yemeni.

The difference in those societies is the missionary. And the difference is not the presence of the missionary but what is in the missionary, which has the power to transform. However, the message of the missionary only has power when it is received. Nothing can be forced upon the hearers of the message, because the Gospel message is a message of love, and love gives the freedom of choice.

> **The difference in those societies is not the presence of the missionary but what is in the missionary, which has the power to transform.**

Jonah's message to Nineveh only had the power that was equal to (and not greater than) the willingness of the people to receive it.

North Korea and South Korea are populated by people with the same history, culture, language, and physical features. They live on the very same isolated peninsula, but the two countries could not be more different.

North Korea persecutes and kills their own people. They openly declare war on Christians and have destroyed churches and Christian literature.

They continue to be one of the most abusive countries in the world against believers in Jesus Christ, effectively rejecting Him.

South Korea is the opposite. Christians have freedom and protection. Regular envoys from South Korea are sent to Israel in a show of support and solidarity with the God of the Jewish people. As a result, science, academics, medicine, business, and even leisure activities flourish in South Korea. In North Korea, these things have withered up and are on life support.

The differences between West Germany and East Germany can be used to show the impact of God on society. Periods of relative Christian freedom in China versus the period of intense persecution of Christians can be also easily be compared. The difference of systematic persecution of Christians in Russia versus national support for Christians has even been said to be measured in the length of the soup lines.

"And I will make of thee a great nation, and I will bless thee, and make thy name great; and thou shalt be a blessing: And I will bless them that bless thee, and curse him that curseth thee: and in thee shall all families of the earth be blessed" (Genesis 12:2–3).

DISCUSSION QUESTIONS

1. In many Western countries with a strong Christian legacy, Christianity is now experiencing a time of decline. What do you see as the consequences of this for those societies as a whole?
2. Do you think a Christian legacy will continue to bring the life and love of the Gospel in those countries, or do you think we may revert to pre-Christian immorality within a generation or two?
3. Can you think of other countries that rejected the Gospel after a time of strong Christian influence? What happened in those regions?

DAY 4

INTELLECTUAL COWARDS ON CAMPUS

———◆———

"An offended heart is the breeding ground of deception."

—JOHN BEVERE

Back to Jerusalem missionaries from China have seen firsthand the difference God's truth can make in their nation. The rise of believers in China can be directly connected to the economic, political, and social freedoms they are currently enjoying. The current state of affairs of any given country can also be linked to the choices of the earlier generations.

Imagine if a Western man, whether Christian or not, had lived so long under the umbrella of God's blessing that he was left completely ignorant of the world that had existed prior to the first coming of the Gospel message. Wouldn't he be more susceptible to making choices in life based on the idea that God was meaningless for his everyday life? Wouldn't those choices (made in ignorance) then start a trajectory that would impact his children's lives and maybe even their children and their children's children?

The dark, hideous world that existed prior to revival still exists today, but there are now incredibly influential societies that are beacons of hope because of the spread of Jesus' Gospel message. These societies exist because of sacrifices that others made to present the Gospel message, and those sacrifices benefited their children and their children's children.

Today we call these societies "modern" societies, which seems to imply that they are better due to modernity alone, but that is not the case. They are better because of the positive impact that the Gospel message has had on their societies, and this being true helps us quickly identify where the Gospel message has taken root.

Though many modern societies are going through a secularization phase, Christian values are still stamped into their legislative identity. Christian societies that would rather forget their Christian heritage fortunately still benefit from the very heritage they are trying to dismiss.

Advanced societies have come from the Gospel and not from secular education. Who was better educated than the Nazis? Did education help the Japanese to empathize with the raping, murdering, or pillaging of the Chinese, Koreans, or Filipinos? Modernity did not come from evolution. Who better understood the theory of

> **Advanced societies have come from the Gospel and not from secular education.**

evolution than the regimes of Russia, China, North Korea, and Cuba who implemented and enforced the atheist concepts of evolution?

Modern societies today that bring hope, peace, freedom, and altruistic help to the rest of the world are Christian-Judaic societies. This is both observable and measurable, although many Western universities fail to acknowledge this truth because it might hurt feelings. "The heart is deceitful above all things, and desperately wicked: who can know it?" (Jeremiah 17:9).

Universities in the West have declared war on the very Judeo-Christian values that have given them the freedom of thought they enjoy. Their institutions do not exist in atheist, Islamic, Buddhist, or Hindu societies.

It is not considered nice to say that Judeo-Christian societies are superior to all others in terms of academics, but just because it is not nice does not mean it is not true. Truth does not care about being nice. It is true whether it's nice or not.

There are moments when our ignorance makes truth hurtful, and we have two choices: we can either accept the truth and adapt accordingly, or we can disregard the truth and find a lifetime full of hardships.

Our lack of understanding of God can make His actions seem offensive to us. If I am honest, His seeming silence and absence on so many matters are offensive to me. And few things in modern society today are more egregious than being offensive. On many college campuses it is considered to be the highest of crimes.

To be offended in modern society is such a high crime because the emotional welfare of man reigns supreme, but as Christians we do not have the same privilege. We do not have the right not to be offended.

On university campuses in the West, there is a rising tide of offended people who are demanding the right to safe spaces. "Safe spaces" are places where people can be safe from any trigger words or phrases that would cause offense to their emotional well-being. So university campuses have created "safe spaces" where sensitive students cannot be exposed to anything they might find even remotely offensive and where they can be free from any words that might hurt their feelings.

Compounding the problem is that a casual phrase or even a look can be offensive; those are called micro-aggressions. Micro-aggressive phrases are banned on campus, and students who use them are considered to be violating the safe space of other students.

All of this is completely absurd, given that the entire reason to attend a university in the first place is to stretch your horizons and expand your knowledge. On a university campus, perhaps more than anywhere else, you should be able to challenge the things others believe and have your own belief's challenged, even if those ideas, concepts, and people who peddle them might be offensive at times.

If someone is not willing to be exposed to things that might be offensive, then maybe that person lacks the intellectual integrity to be on a university campus. The first rule of education should be to learn things that you did not know before and to maybe even learn rightly things that you wrongly understood. I am dismayed as I see the idea of safe places sweeping through Western higher-learning institutions and virtually eliminating free speech and thought, which essentially cheats everyone from the right to explore complex and challenging thoughts and to arrive at a wise and thoughtful conclusion.

This idea is also rearing its head in Christian churches. Churches too have succumbed to the idea that they must become safe spaces that attempt to insulate their congregants from things that might hurt their feelings.

How can we rightly evaluate the impact of the Gospel if the Gospel is found offensive by the world and we have insulated ourselves from that which is offensive? It is impossible—which is exactly how the world would like it to be.

When we are evaluating the impact of the Gospel, we cannot put our feelings before revelation. The light is offensive to the darkness; therefore, the teachings of the Bible will be offensive to society. If the church caters to the desires of society's wishes, then the majority of what Jesus taught will be labeled offensive.

Maybe we have already accepted the world's view of who Jesus is instead of the biblical view—so much so that when we read the Bible, we do not see

> **The light is offensive to the darkness; therefore, the teachings of the Bible will be offensive to society.**

what it actually says, but we read it with the cultural lens of our society that is preprogrammed to tell us what we are reading.

But as I read through the story Jesus in the Bible, I see words and phrases being used by Him that are a little harsh. They would be considered triggers and labeled as violations of safe space; they would be considered socially abrasive.

The words of Christ are only comforting to those who are in search of truth, and truth cannot be based on feelings. When I attempt to read the words of Christ without the cultural lens of a secularist society, I realize that maybe I have adopted the world's idea of Christianity instead of the truth.

And as harsh as it might seem, I have come to believe that anyone who requires a safe space and cannot deal with the realities of life cannot participate in the Great Commission and cannot share in the suffering of Jesus that brings about revival, because there are no safe spaces in the Bible, and there are definitely no safe spaces in the calling God has put on your life.

I have additional bad news: Everyone reading this book has been called by God, and being called by God requires you to take up your cross and follow Him. Your walk with Him will entail a degree of suffering, and your service will be offensive to the world.

It is the lack of a safe space that leads us into the will of God and exposes us to persecution, but this is the beginning of revival.

And I get it. It's hard to embrace suffering. And I understand that the Bible is full of love, grace, mercy, etc. Don't get me wrong; this is the central message of the Gospel. But the Gospel message is also truth, and truth is true regardless of how we feel. Truth couldn't care less about our feelings.

God's Word is truth, and it doesn't stop being true just because we might be hurt by the truth. And if our feelings are hurt by God's Word, it is not the Word of God that needs to change to adjust to our feelings, but our feelings that need to adjust to fit the truth of God's Word.

> **God's Word is truth, and it doesn't stop being true just because we might be hurt by the truth.**

Now, do not misunderstand. I am not saying that we should preach truth to intentionally hurt others. I am reminding us all that *we* need to be ready to expose ourselves to pain for the sake of searching out the truth.

We cannot continue to create culturally homogenous environments that cater to the world and neglect the true teachings of Christ because of our fear of offending the very world that we are called to save. Why would a rescuer desire to mimic a drowning man in an attempt to save him? The truth only has power to change societies when it is shared, not when it is diluted, so let us cast off these spiritual prophylactics that keep the Gospel from being productive.

Let us toss in the garbage can of history those verbal condoms of safe spaces that keep the truth from impregnating revival into our society and let us more forward boldly proclaiming the true Gospel of Jesus Christ.

DISCUSSION QUESTIONS

1. We are called to identify with the people around us so they can understand the Gospel in their context. However, the balance can tip the other way, in that we compromise the truth to avoid offense. Do you think your church has the balance right, or do you feel truth is sometimes compromised to avoid offending people?

2. Do you feel that nonbelievers are offended unnecessarily by what the church says? Can you give examples?

3. Do you think you have found the right balance in your own testimony to people around you?

4. Is there anything in the Gospel message that you find personally offensive? If so, how do you deal with that?

DAY 5

QUEER LOVE

---

*"To be or not to be is not a question of compromise.
Either you be or you don't be."*

—ISRAELI PRIME MINISTER GOLDA MEIR

Maybe one of the reasons why it is challenging to see revival in our modern countries today is because forgiveness is not a necessity when sin is acceptable. It seems society has been writing the book on morality, and Christians have been all too amenable to adopt it.

The journalist is writing sermons on morality, and the priest is taking notes. The lost world is shaping the way we read the Bible; take a little of this, toss that, sprinkle a little bit of this . . .

Unfortunately, the truth of God's Word is not really known to the world (1 Corinthians 2:14). Jesus said even the religious elect do not necessarily know Him (John 16:3); therefore, if it is truth we seek, we cannot accept the world's evaluation of Scripture or neglect to evaluate what is preached in a church or by a professing Christian against the Word of God.

The love of Christ cannot be fully comprehended by the world, and this lack of comprehension causes confusion. Somewhere along the line, Satan started a lie that Christians cannot condemn sin because that would not be a loving thing to do. The reasoning goes like this: Jesus loves everyone, including sinners, therefore Christians must be accepting of both the sinner and the sin without the need for repentance.

Therefore, Christians who dare to share verses of the Bible in an effort to clarify truth are considered to be offensive. Keep in mind that many of those who are offended would readily admit that they do not believe in the Bible, even though they could quote scriptures in an argument to keep you quiet.

If, as a Christian, you say something considered offensive, then you are not a very loving person, and Christ was all about love and the Bible is really all about love, so if you follow Christ, then you have to also be about love. This is the logic of the world, which insists on dictating what Christians ought to believe.

In this way the world creates Christian paradigms that shackle believers. They define what love is and what it isn't, and then they attempt to confine us in the straightjacket of their definition.

But love is not really known by the world, so we cannot accept the world's definition.

Many Christians foolishly fall into this trap because they are unaware of what Christ's love truly means. Love is being confused with compromise, and it is not the same as compromise. In

> **Love is not really known by the world, so we cannot accept the world's definition.**

fact, compromising on sin is the opposite of Christian love.

First John 4:8 tells us that God is love, but not just any love; He is agape love, which means that He loves us no matter what. In its very nature it is self-sacrificial. In fact, He loves us so much that He sacrificed His life for us, and we as His followers must emulate that. If we show Christ's love, then we must be willing to give our life for others. We must be willing to be isolated, to be rejected, to be spit upon, and even to be crucified. If Christ loves others and we love Christ, then we love others because we become vessels of His love.

But what the world offers is not the love of Christ; it is compromise. The world insists that we compromise the laws of Christ, which are the things that define why we need His love and grace.

Love and compromise are not the same thing, and the two are often purposefully confused in the world's definitions.

Compromise is not always done out of love; often it is done out of self-preservation. The love of the world says, "I love myself, and because I love myself so much, I do not want confrontation." Compromise desires to remain comfortable. Compromise says, "I don't want to hurt your feelings because that would make me feel uncomfortable. I don't want to be rejected from this society. I don't want to be ostracized from this community. I don't want to be isolated at my job. I don't want to be looked down upon by academics in the university." So we compromise, which renders us impotent.

And this spirit of compromise, this need for a safe space, and the confusion about the definition of love are why we have been sold an egocentric Gospel—a Gospel that is all about us but doesn't give a rip about others around us and compels us to abandon the scriptures that do not fit our socially imposed paradigms.

So we are ignorant of what the Bible actually says, and ignorance breeds ignorance. Sometimes when I am reading a scripture that I have read before, I feel like I already know what it is going to say. I have read the Bible over and over again, so I am not anticipating a surprise ending. I am not on the edge of my seat, ignorant of what is going to happen next. I have read the Bible in three different languages, and there are no stories that have new, surprising twists.

The Bible is basically the same, word for word, in every language I know. I have been reading the Bible for most of my life, and not a word of it has changed during my lifetime.

But today I am hit with the idea that maybe I am reading Scripture with cultural eyes given to me from the world and maybe I have been listening to it with cultural ears. As I evaluate the difference between true love and compromise, I come face-to-face with the very idea of God having been shaped by my culture and my society.

What if God wants to teach me something new about something I am reading in the Bible, but I am unable to receive it because I think I already know everything He has to say to me? What if that which I understand in the Bible has been wrongly understood and that which I wrongly understand I teach to others and then they come to believe what I have wrongly taught?

What if my eyes are so clouded by worldly teachings and so absolutely shaped by my cultural understanding of Christ that I have read the Bible over and over with pre-misconceptions, misconceptions that taint everything I read? Let's take it one more step: What if my pride of being educated makes it impossible for me to humble myself enough to admit that I might not know what it is that God is saying to me in His Scriptures? I read the parts I want to read, and I conclude that it says what I think it says based on what I was taught that it says.

Even worse, what if that which I have read and wrongly understood, I have, in my misunderstanding, boldly taught to others as if it were truth?

For instance, how many wise men were there at the birth of Jesus? We have all seen hundreds of nativity scenes, and there are always three. So how strange would it be to know that there is no mention of the number of wise men who came from the East? We just assume that there were three, and that is what we imagine in our mind's eye when we read the story in the Bible. And did you know that the wise men were not present at the birth of Jesus but arrived much later, when He was a toddler?

My culture taught me that Jonah was swallowed by a whale and that Eve ate of an apple—both of which are not true descriptions of what took place (Scripture says Eve ate of a fruit and Jonah was swallowed by a big fish)—but still I read those scriptures and superimpose my imaginings on those events as if they were true, aware of the distortion but too prideful to change.

When I think about how Christ does everything completely opposite of natural reasoning, I become even more aware of the need to release human pride when reading Holy Scriptures, because certain things go against logic—red blood washes white as snow, leaders must become servants, suffering brings freedom, death brings life, etc.

The world needs Christians to have a grave misunderstanding of Christ's love, because it is the love of Christ that the world finds offensive. The teachings of the Bible are chockful of trigger warnings. There are no safe spaces for those who pick up their cross daily and follow after Jesus. The Bible is an absolute liberal nightmare.

In order to bring about revival, we need to allow ourselves to be both spiritually and intellectually humbled before the cross and admit that we do not understand what it is that we are reading. We need to attempt to look at the

Bible with virgin eyes and allow ourselves to be offended before the throne of God and hear the words of Christ when He said, "Blessed is the one who is not offended by me" (Matthew 11:6 ESV).

As I start this journey of chasing revival, I must be on guard against my pride. I must be cautious when the world announces that I need to toss the parts of the Bible that they presuppose to be the wild mistreatment of women, the glowing endorsement of slavery, and rampant homophobia. I must tread carefully when the world claims to hold a morally superior position to that of the Bible and demands that we agree.

It would be a grave mistake to assume that I can anticipate God or dictate His law. There are fewer sins that are greater than pride, which puffs us up and causes us to think we know better than God.

> **There are fewer sins that are greater than pride.**

God has our best interest in mind. Even if we are unable to explain it. Even if we do not understand it. He has a way of writing the story of our life and making it into something amazing and beautiful. There are no bad endings in the kingdom (Romans 8:28).

A bad ending is only a story that hasn't yet finished.

DISCUSSION QUESTIONS

1. Can you share instances of when you thought the Bible said one thing and later you discovered you were wrong?
2. What are some ways you think your culture may have shaped your view of Christianity and of God?
3. Can you give examples of when nonbelievers have used Bible verses they do not understand to accuse Christians of being unloving? How could you respond to them?

DAY 6

REVIVAL NIGHT: AN OXYMORON

—————◆—————

"Every one says forgiveness is a lovely idea,
until they have something to forgive."

—C. S. Lewis

As soon as Judas had taken the bread, he went out. And it was night"
(John 13:30 NIV).

"And it was night." It was a dark night. It was a dark, thick, heavy, black,
evil night.

There was no revival waiting for Judas. Redemption would be elusive. A
spiritual awakening that could have shined light through the darkest night
was sold for cash.

Jesus' disciples stepped out of the same place on the same evening and
were singing hymns. The other disciples had made the decision to follow
Jesus, and though they did not know it at the time, their death warrants were
signed in blood. But as grisly as many of their deaths would be, they had
found the light.

As F. W. Boreham put it when he pondered the hymns sung by Jesus and
His disciples, "Peter went out to be crucified; James went out to be beheaded;
Philip went out to be hanged; Bartholomew went out to be burned; Thomas
went out to be crucified; James went out to be shot; and John went out to
torture and lonely exile."[2] Jesus also went out that night, to be crucified and
to suffer the sins of all humanity. Yet at no point does the Bible tell us that
Jesus or the disciples walked out into the night.

Judas was the only one who left that room with the promise of worldly riches. In the eyes of the world, he should have been the happiest man to leave, but he was not. He was not with the other disciples singing a hymn in the darkness. A song of salvation did not fill his heart or pour out of his lips.

This was not the first time that Judas had witnessed such darkness.

The only time the verse 6:66 (the number in Revelation 13:17–18 that refers to the mark of the Beast) appears in the New Testament is almost as equally dark as the night that Judas betrayed Jesus. Jesus had just finished teaching profound truths about His relationship to God, His Father, and then Scriptures says, "After this many of his disciples turned back and no longer walked with him" (John 6:66 ESV).

There were many more than twelve disciples of Jesus, but we only really know the twelve who did not leave Him when He spoke words that offended them. The other disciples who had followed Him, heard His teachings, and watched His miracles were deeply offended by the words and teachings and could no longer convince themselves to continue on with Him. They stepped away from the Light—and dare I say that it was night.

In the next verse Jesus asked those twelve who were stunned but remaining with Him, "Do you want to go away as well?" (v. 67 ESV). It must have seemed odd to see their friends and colleagues walk away. How offended they must have been for so many of them to depart in unison.

The shell-shocked disciples stood there in the presence of Jesus, and they were unable to deliver a rational argument for their desire to stay. The response of their colleagues was no doubt heavy on their minds.

Simon Peter answered him, "Lord, to whom shall we go? You have the words of eternal life, and we have believed, and have come to know, that you are the Holy One of God" (vv. 68–69 ESV).

Maybe Peter's answer is the beginning of revival. When we have heard all of the arguments, seen all of the trials, truly exposed ourselves to the offensiveness of God's Word, and come to the inescapable conclusion that there is nowhere else to go—maybe that is when God's people will experience revival.

Revival is found in the condition of the souls of those who are hungry and have nowhere else to go. Maybe it is a result of an attachment to Jesus that is born out of desperation. "Lord, to whom shall we go? You have the words of eternal life."

The sun that sits in the sky day after day cannot turn night into morning for those who choose to leave the truth of the

> **Revival is found in the condition of the souls of those who are hungry and have nowhere else to go.**

Gospel message. Those who are offended walk away and step into the night. Jesus said, "Blessed is the one who is not offended by me" (Matthew 11:6 ESV). So the one who walks away is rejecting His blessings.

When a man leaves Jesus, it is always night, and when a nation collectively forces its citizens to abandon the teachings of Christ, the Light is absent. A million suns, all focusing their energy on your city, cannot rescue it from the night if it has decided to make Judas their ruler.

The Light is only offensive to those in darkness who have not come to terms with their trespasses. A Gospel that is self-serving is not the Gospel at all. The Gospel message requires sacrifice, but not as much sacrifice as when it is neglected.

If we follow an egocentric Gospel, we can only protect ourselves from an uncomfortable truth for a short time before we step out into the long, dark night.

To brace against the night, we must prepare to have our thoughts and ideas violated—not by the world, but by God Himself. If we are to learn anything from John 6:66, it is that exposure to failure and rejection is the first step to growth. If we are to learn anything from the disciples who left with Jesus singing hymns, it is that the lack of a safe space leads us into the will of God and exposes us to persecution.

The very idea of baptism that began the ministry of Jesus reflects the need for being separated from worldly connections. It is actually an act of death and rebirth. We die to the world, and when we are baptized, we are symbolically going into the grave, being crucified with Christ, and coming out as a new man.

It is the ultimate symbolism of a covenant with Christ that in order to be with Him I must be dead to the world and dead to myself—and dead people can't be offended!

Revival is connected to the suffering of Christ and the death of sin, and if I am to learn more, I must allow both.

I think that we forget how beautiful suffering can be. None of us willingly sign up for it. You will never hear me pray for patience or long-suffering because I fear the situations God might put me in to have patience or experience long-suffering. But when I find myself in a situation where suffering is required, that is when I find the songs of life, the poetry of survival, the canvas for the artwork of God's grace and mercy. That is when I identify most with those who stepped out singing hymns with Christ, even as He walked to the Garden of Gethsemane.

As we journey through the history of revival, I would ask you to relinquish the sense that you know God and you understand His Word *completely*.

The famous Mr. Bean, the British comedian, one time read from Isaiah 55:8: "For my thoughts are not your thoughts, neither are your ways my ways, declares the LORD" (ESV). After he read that verse, Mr. Bean rightly stated, "And I think what He basically means by that is—I'm mysterious, folks. Live with it."

DISCUSSION QUESTIONS

1. Have you ever felt you wanted to leave Jesus because some of His teachings were too hard?
2. What were the scriptures or teachings that caused you to question your faith? And why did you choose to still believe?
3. Can you share any personal experience of finding joy and peace in suffering?
4. Are you ready to face ridicule and marginalization by society if the Gospel requires it?

DAY 7

REVIVAL AND THE RISE OF FREE NATIONS

"Rebellion against tyrants is obedience to God."

—BENJAMIN FRANKLIN

A case can be easily made that the acceptance or denial of God can decide the future of families, communities, and even nations. If we accept that idea, then we must also believe that the message of Jesus Christ is the single largest contributor to human rights in the world today and missionaries are the single largest hope for those countries that are habitual abusers of human rights.

Christians have been saying that the Gospel of Jesus Christ is the cornerstone for free societies since the dawn of Christianity. Following the Gospel message up until the book of Acts is simple enough, but if the claims of modern Christians are true, that the Gospel is a major contributor to freedom in societies, then that is where we should look for the history of revival.

Could it possibly be that easy, though? Is it truly possible to use this idea of human rights and freedom to trace the history of revival and the impact of the Gospel message?

According Robert Woodberry, a sociologist currently researching at the political science department of the National University of Singapore, not only is the Gospel message central to free societies, but missionaries are the pivotal change agents in transforming societies for the better throughout history.

Woodberry's research is earth-shaking for those who believe in the life-changing power of the Gospel because it gives conclusive evidence that missionaries in the last three hundred years have been the most significant factors in creating healthy societies.

> **Missionaries in the last three hundred years have been the most significant factors in creating healthy societies.**

According to Woodberry's research, "Areas where Protestant missionaries had a significant presence in the past are on average more economically developed today, with comparatively better health, lower infant mortality, lower corruption, greater literacy, higher educational attainment (especially for women), and more robust membership in nongovernmental associations."[3]

Why would countries that deprive their citizenry of basic human rights be any different? What makes Christians think that they must wait for diplomatic channels to make life better before they can truly start to work? What if the answer is the other way around? What if it is the message of the Gospel in the hands of the missionary that makes the difference?

If Woodberry's conclusions are correct, then as we follow the Gospel message around the world, we will also be seeing positive transformations of societies. Furthermore, if he is correct, then the work of missionaries is not for the salvation of lost souls alone, as we are often taught in Sunday school, but is one of the most significant factors in ensuring the health of nations that will benefit multiple generations.

One morning, in a windowless, dusty computer lab lit by florescent bulbs, Woodberry ran the first big test. After he finished prepping the statistical program on his computer, he clicked "Enter" and then leaned forward to read the results.

"I was shocked," says Woodberry. "It was like an atomic bomb. The impact of missions on global democracy was huge. I kept adding variables to the model—factors that people had been studying and writing about for the past 40 years—and they all got wiped out. It was amazing. I knew, then, I was on to something really important."

Woodberry already had historical proof that missionaries had educated women and the poor, promoted widespread printing, led nationalist movements that empowered ordinary citizens, and fueled other key elements of democracy. Now the statistics were backing it up: Missionaries weren't just part of the picture. They were central to it.[4]

Most studies establish the need for sharing the Gospel message from an eternal perspective, but on our road trip Bible study we will establish that there is a by-product that saves man in the here and now, today. There is a temporary salvation of living to be gained in a society impacted by the Gospel message. The Gospel message, when shared in fullness, gives life, and the life is not restricted to only the afterlife.

This does not mean that becoming a Christian automatically creates financial prosperity and physical freedom. What I learned throughout this road trip is that the opposite is often true. What it does establish, though, is that, like the crucifixion of Jesus Christ, sacrifice is needed by some for the benefit of the whole. The sacrifices of a few can benefit an entire society or a nation for generations.

Leaving the idea for a moment of the eternal salvation that Jesus brings, a murderer, for example, who fully rejects Christ can have an arguably more comfortable existence on earth living in a country governed by Judeo-Christian principles, established by those who sacrificed for them, than, say, an honest banker living in a country governed by atheist, Buddhist, or Islamic principles. Another way to say this is that I would have a comparable, maybe even more comfortable and enjoyable lifestyle as a criminal in Norway than as an honest banker in Yemen.

When tracing the movement of the Gospel and seeing what impact it has on entire societies, it suddenly becomes apparent why it is urgent to share God's message with the whole world and pray for revival to come. It also becomes very condemning for those who have it and have benefited from it but withhold it from others. The Good News is only Good News for those who are able to hear it; otherwise, the bad news of what is happening when Good News exists but is not shared with those who need it seems even more tragic.

Let this study excite you to share with your children and family the need for the Gospel message to continue from generation to generation. Let it compel you to share with family, friends, coworkers, and strangers with even more fervor. May our churches cry out for a fresh revival as has been experienced in the past. And may your calling and the reason why you were created become even more apparent to you than ever before.

> **May the burden of world missions burn with an inextinguishable flame that consumes your thoughts day and night.**

May the burden of world missions burn with an inextinguishable flame that consumes your thoughts day and night.

DISCUSSION QUESTIONS

1. If you are from a country that has cultural roots in Christianity, can you share how people today benefit from this revival legacy?

2. What core values in your society do you think have been directly influenced by Christian thinking?

3. Do you know concrete examples where Christians have challenged evil practices or corruption?

4. If you are from a country where Christianity is a recent arrival or does not yet have a strong presence, what do you think or hope will change as believers influence society?

5. Do you think this "temporary salvation," the improvement of people's living circumstances and human rights, should be a goal of mission work, or is it a natural by-product as people are changed by the power of the Gospel?

6. If we don't see this "temporary salvation" happening in our mission efforts, are we doing something wrong?

PART 1

JERUSALEM

"As the Father Has Sent Me, I Am Sending You"

DAY 8

WHERE IT ALL BEGAN

"The price of anything is the amount of life you exchange for it."

—HENRY DAVID THOREAU

Our road trip Bible study truly begins with one Man, Jesus Christ, and in one city, Jerusalem. Jesus did not come as an earthly king or a religious ruler. He did not come as a spirit hovering above an altar that only the high priests could approach. He came as a man, to earth, to a city, on a mission.

I can remember sitting in a church I was attending in Hong Kong during a particular Sunday morning when the pastor and leadership presented the vision of the church. Their vision included pillars, or primary ideas, that were important to the church and would prove to be the foundation for the future.

As I listened to the pastor and saw the presentation that he and the leadership presented, I noticed that missions was not one of the primary pillars of the church. It was not even mentioned.

The sadness of that moment is hard to explain because my entire life is wrapped around missions. I felt so lonely and isolated in this Hong Kong church. It wasn't only that my family felt left out of the vision of the church we were attending, but that the most essential commission that Jesus gave us was not even on the priority list of the leadership. Our former Hong Kong fellowship was not alone. They are only one of many churches around the world that see mission work as an afterthought. It is sad when a church is not heavily involved in missions, not just because I think missions is important, but because I think missions is the purpose of the church.

Jesus was on a mission, and so are we. Ed Stetzer, a former pastor, said during an interview with *Tabletalk Magazine* in January 2014, "Mission is rooted in the identity of God Himself. God is on a mission, and Jesus is the embodiment of that mission. Jesus identifies Himself as being sent more than forty times in the gospel of John. Then, near the end of the gospel of John, He says, 'As the Father has sent me, I am sending you'" (John 20:21 NIV).

Ed went on to say, "The church is sent on mission by Jesus. *It's not that the church has a mission, but rather that the mission has a church.* We join Jesus on His mission."[5]

This concept could be one of the most explosive and damning for many Christians today. This is a radical change of current mainstream ideology about the role of the church. Instead of the church being about the church, an inwardly focused concept that only circulates nutrients from one believer to another, the church is about missions and is outwardly focused.

The church, or the Body of Christ, is, by design, outward focused: focused on God, focused on the Word, focused on reaching others, focused on training and sending others; and if there is any focus on self, it is only to improve the ability to aid an outward cause.

The egocentric church does not represent the Body of Jesus Christ; it is an impostor. If the church builds up wealth, the wealth buildup should be for outward impact. If a church builds up members, the increase in membership must contribute to more outreach. If the church trains up leaders, the impartation of knowledge should primarily be for outreach to others.

Jesus said to Simon Peter in John 21:15, "Simon, son of Jonas, lovest thou me more than these? He saith unto him, Yea, Lord; thou knowest that I love thee. He saith unto him, Feed my lambs."

You do not prove that you love God by feeding His sheep. You feed His sheep because you love Him. It is a cause and effect relationship. The cause is not work to obtain the effect of Jesus' love, but instead Jesus' love produces the effect of works. Just as the manifestation of God's love for us came through His Son, our love for the Father will be manifest in our actions.

Mission is rooted in the very heart of following Jesus Christ. One could even go so far as to say that mission is so deep in the core of the Christian experience that it can be used as the indicator of the condition of the soul. Your mission may be in, through, or outside of the church, but the experience of your salvation and following after Christ have to have an outlet of expression. This is the Gospel sausage factory of what goes in must come out. A messianic Gospel produces a heart of missions. An egocentric Gospel message only requires an outlet of self-service.

> **Mission is so deep in the core of the Christian experience that it can be used as the indicator of the condition of the soul.**

Imagine what the story of Jesus would be if instead of focusing on serving others we were all to think of our own needs first. What would be the Gospel message of self? A Gospel message of self, regardless of its teachings, would produce self-serving evangelists and eventually die out because of the lack of sacrifice required by its adherents to share with others less fortunate.

God, in His infinite and boundless love for man, chose to come to earth, take on the cloak of man, taste of the bitter suffering of His creation, and sacrifice Himself for our sake. He was not just on a mission—He embodied the mission. He became the mission. He experienced the world of man from the perspective of man.

The family members of Jesus, the local rabbis at His synagogue, and later His disciples realized that Jesus was no ordinary man. He was the Word made flesh and was on a mission, and He gave His mission to His disciples, and His disciples passed that mission on to others. Before long the mission of Jesus had a body of believers and then, just like that, the mission had a church. The story of mission begins with God, and the place of that beginning and ending is Jerusalem.

DISCUSSION QUESTIONS

1. Do you think a church can ever be excused from being involved in the Great Commission? Do you think an individual believer can?

2. How does knowing Jesus has called you to go into the world affect your daily life?

3. Are there ways you or your church could be prioritizing the Great Commission more?

4. Do you agree with the statement, "Mission is so deep in the core of the Christian experience that it can be used as the indicator of the condition of the soul"? Why or why not?

DAY 9

JERUSALEM: THE CITY OF CITIES

"You ought to let the Jews have Jerusalem; it was they who made it famous."

—WINSTON CHURCHILL

The mission of Jesus starts in Jerusalem and is ground zero for revival. In many ways it is the city above all cities. Jerusalem is the world's most holy city and holds more significance than any other location on earth, including Lhasa Tibet, Mecca, or the Vatican in Rome. Three of the world's major religions—Christianity, Judaism, and Islam—put an enormous amount of spiritual significance on this city.

Christians, unlike many Jews, believe that Jesus was the fulfillment of Scripture and that His temple where He resides is now in the hearts of His people, not in a structure in Jerusalem. He was the final sacrifice for all mankind, removing the need for continued sacrifice at the temple. If His people in China, for instance, call out His name, He will abide in them, regardless of geographical location. The Chinese Christians do not have to travel to Jerusalem to find His presence.

For the Christian, Jerusalem holds grand significance, but salvation is not hinged on it.

> **For the Christian, Jerusalem holds grand significance, but salvation is not hinged on it.**

Though a pilgrimage to Jerusalem can have deep meaning for a Christian, it is not required. Christians can spend their entire lives experiencing the power of God and not visit Jerusalem even once, or inversely, people can spend their entire lives in Jerusalem and never taste the power of God.

For the Jew, however, Jerusalem is the land promised by God and holds untold spiritual and historical significance. There is a sacred nature in the dirt that has been promised to them since the days of Father Abraham. In many ways, the Jew is inseparable from Jerusalem.

Today, though Judaism is a major religion practiced all around the world, Israel is the only official Jewish state.

Jerusalem is important to Islam, but in a different way than for the Christian and Jew. In the early days of Islam, when Muhammad was trying to win Jewish and Christian converts, Jerusalem was made the first "Qiblahi" or the city that Muslims faced when praying. That soon changed to the Kaaba in Mecca after Muhammad conquered Mecca, where Muhammad's ancestors profited from pilgrims who traveled from far and wide to pray to the gods of Mecca, a practice that essentially still continues to this day.

Though Jerusalem is considered to be important in Islam and home to one of the holiest mosques, it is never mentioned even one time in the Koran. There is actually no real or reliable historical record of Jerusalem ever playing a major role in Islam. Jerusalem has never been the capital of any Arab state, and even though Muhammad is said to have ascended to heaven from Jerusalem, unlike the claims of the Jews and the Christians, Mohammedan claims cannot be proven, which is a nice way of saying that it never actually happened.

The city that Jesus walked through was much different from the Jerusalem of today. The city center was not that large during the days of Roman occupation; in fact, for much of its history it has only been about a square mile. Even today, the population is smaller than that of Indianapolis, Indiana. At first glance, there is nothing remarkable about the city at all. It is not located on a body of water, doesn't have very fertile land, and has no natural resources to speak of.

It would seem to any rational thinker that the great Jehovah who created the high, reaching peaks of the Alps, the fertile soil of Illinois, the life-giving water of the Nile River, or the oil-rich sands of Saudi Arabia could surely find a better "promised land" than the remote, isolated, arid city of Jerusalem. It would also seem that the world's most grand armies of antiquity could have found better real estate to fight over than Jerusalem.

However, regardless of how Jerusalem is measured, it is the beginning and end of world missions. It has been a city that man has been fighting over for four thousand years. It has been conquered forty-four times and completely destroyed twice. It is the city where God chose to have the temple built that would be used to honor Him, and it is the location where He was crucified so that salvation could be possible for all mankind.

To tell the story of Jerusalem is to tell the story of a living God. Time, as we know it today, is split between BC and AD, divided right at the point where Jesus was born. Jerusalem's history is His-story, so everything about the city has significance, and by studying the city, it might be possible to understand the purpose of missions better.

> **To tell the story of Jerusalem is to tell the story of a living God.**

Today, Jerusalem is a walled city with nine gates (New Gate, Flowers Gate, Damascus Gate, Jaffa Gate, Eastern Gate, Dung Gate, Lion's Gate, Tanner Gate, and Zion Gate), which is interesting to me because I live in China, and nine is a holy number in Chinese because it is the number of the emperor. It is the highest number of yang in yin and yang and represents light and heaven. One can often see nine dragons throughout the Forbidden City, and those nine dragons represent the emperor, who for the Chinese represents divinity.

When studying the nine gates of Jerusalem, one can understand in part the past, present, and future. Like Jerusalem, the Forbidden City (故宫) in China has walls surrounding it with gates. Each of these gates has a meaning. All entrances into the Forbidden City were to the south because the north was considered to be the direction of all attacks. The same is true of Jerusalem. Most of the attacks on Jerusalem were from the north.

Like the Forbidden City of China, every gate into and out of the city of Jerusalem has a purpose. The New Gate is as the name indicates—the newest gate. The Damascus Gate is the northern gate leading to Damascus. The Sheep Gate led to the primary area where flocks of sheep were kept.

Though Jerusalem has seen several gates come and go throughout history, there has never been a more important or controversial gate than the Eastern Gate, or Golden Gate as it is called by many Christians.

The Eastern Gate is the oldest of the current gates in Jerusalem, though it is not really a gate at all. It is closed up and walled with bricks. When under the control of the Ottoman sultan, the Muslims heard the Christians and Jews prophesy about the Messiah who would come, descend down from the Mount of Olives, and pass victoriously through the Eastern Gate.

This messianic prophesy by both the Christians and the Jews concerned the Muslim rulers, so they ordered the Eastern Gate to be sealed up and a Muslim graveyard was placed there, believing that the dead bodies would make a prophet, or certainly a Messiah, unclean, thus restricting His access.

The Mount of Olives and the Eastern Gate play a major role in Back to Jerusalem and the mission movement of the last days. This is the last recorded area where Jesus spoke, and these are among the last known audible words of Jesus to His disciples. They still ring out to us today from Acts 1:8–9: "'But you will receive power when the Holy Spirit has come upon you, and you will be my witnesses in Jerusalem and in all Judea and Samaria, and to the end of the earth.' And when he had said these things, as they were looking on, he was lifted up, and a cloud took him out of their sight" (ESV).

The last known recorded words of Jesus before He ascended into heaven, according to Acts 1:8, were not words of comfort and tearful good-byes, but instead this was the very sentence that would be forever remembered as the Great Commission.

DISCUSSION QUESTIONS

1. What is the spiritual significance of Jerusalem for Christians today?
2. What role do you expect Jerusalem will play in the future fulfilment of end-time prophesies?

3. Does this mean Christians should watch current events in Jerusalem closely or even be involved somehow, or is that not something we should concern ourselves with?

DAY 10

REVIVAL: THE FIRST FRUITS

"The wizard [of Oz] says look inside yourself and find self. God says look inside yourself and find [the Holy Spirit]. The first will get you to Kansas. The latter will get you to heaven. Take your pick."

—MAX LUCADO

The last words of Jesus were delivered from the Mount of Olives, where Jesus had shared with His disciples many times in the past. The place where He ascended at the Mount of Olives is expected to be the place where He will descend when He returns again.

In order to get a better understanding of the significance of this area, I boarded a plane and flew to Israel. On this particular journey I was held up for six hours at immigration because of my frequent travels to Iran. The Jewish authorities were not fond of my passport stamps from many different Middle Eastern nations.

When I was finally allowed through, I traveled with the Chinese evangelist Brother Yun (also known as the Heavenly Man) to the Mount of Olives to read Acts 1 together. I was amazed by the panoramic view of the majestic city of Jerusalem. Anyone standing on the Mount of Olives facing Jerusalem is by default facing the Eastern Gate in a westward direction, which would indicate that Jesus was facing west at the time He delivered His final words in Acts 1:8.

"This is where Jesus gave the Great Commission," I said to Brother Yun.

"Yes, Acts 1:8, but not Matthew 28."

His response shocked me. *Not Matthew 28?* I thought to myself. *Were they not a record of the same event, both taking place on the Mount of Olives?*

Almost as if he anticipated my silent question, Brother Yun immediately followed up, saying, "No, in fact, Jesus tells the women who were worshipping Him in verse 10 to go and 'tell my brothers to go to Galilee, and there they will see me,' then later it says in verse 16, 'Now the eleven disciples went to Galilee, to the mountain to which Jesus had directed them'" (ESV).

Though this was the same message, it was delivered on two different occasions, meaning that Acts 1:8 is the sole record of the last words of Jesus. Each time I read Matthew 28, I had read it with the assumption of what I had always been taught.

The book of Acts is the portion of the Bible that actually records the very last moments of Jesus on the earth, His final words, and what happened after the ascension. Because of that, it is the section of the Bible that I will focus on the most when studying the origins of historical Christian revival.

I stood there on the Mount of Olives, the same location of Acts 1, and looked at the walls of Jerusalem. I read from verses 9 to 11, "After he said this, he was taken up before their very eyes, and a cloud hid him from their sight. They were looking intently up into the sky as he was going, when suddenly two men dressed in white stood beside them. 'Men of Galilee,' they said, 'why do you stand here looking into the sky?'" (NIV).

As I read I thought, *Why are they still looking up at the sky? What kind of question is that that the angel poses to the disciples?* These men, who had never seen a Hollywood film with special effects, just witnessed Jesus fly into the heavens. Of course they were still looking up at the sky! And then, to add to that, two men dressed in white miraculously appeared out of nowhere.

It had clearly been a strange day!

According to the next verse, the disciples left the Mount and returned to Jerusalem. They were most likely on the west side of the Mount facing the Eastern Gate since they were only a Sabbath's day walk from Jerusalem.

The city of Jerusalem is west of the Mount of Olives, so already the disciples were moving westward. This is important because from the beginning we see what will be the primary direction throughout the book of Acts.

The disciples moved westward and waited for the day of Pentecost—the

Jewish holiday of Pentecost, not the Christian Pentecost, because remember, the Christian story of Pentecost had not taken place yet.

The disciples did not know, they could not have known, that they were waiting for what would be seen as the first Christian revival, and it would fall on the day of Pentecost.

Pentecost had a deep-rooted meaning for the followers of Jesus and provided the setting for the massive revival that was about to hit the city of Jerusalem.

> **Pentecost the massive revival that was about to hit the city of Jerusalem.**

When I joined the military, I was asked to mark down my religion so that it could be recorded on my dog tags, a metal identification tag that would be placed around my neck and inside the boot strings of my right boot. I wanted to mark Christian as my religion, but there was no such box to tick. Instead, I was given a list of Christian denominations that I had to choose from.

I did not belong to any denomination, but the military said I had to choose one and they did not give me a lot of time to think it over. I looked at the list and saw Anglican, Methodist, Presbyterian, Baptist, etc., and did not feel comfortable choosing any one of them.

On the list I did see the word *Pentecostal* and remembered that I had visited a small rural Pentecostal church a time or two. I quickly chose the Pentecostal box, and for the remaining time in the military I was labeled as a Pentecostal in all of my records. I had always associated the day of Pentecost with the charismatic expression of Christianity as recorded in the book of Acts. I do not think I was alone. I suspect many Americans associate the term *Pentecost* with the American idea of a Pentecostal Christian. However, when I traveled to Jerusalem and began to look more deeply at the words of the apostle Luke in the book of Acts, I was blown away at what I found.

The day of Pentecost was a Jewish holiday long before the Holy Spirit ever fell upon the disciples, and it marked the end of Passover, a period marked by mourning and bitter sadness. The grain harvest that followed Passover lasted for seven weeks and was traditionally a season of gladness, celebration, and dancing. This season drew Jews from all over the known world to celebrate in Jerusalem. Pentecost was the celebration of the wheat harvest—the last cereal to ripen—and took place fifty days after the Passover. It was a free-will offering and included everyone: the fatherless, widowed, foreigners—everyone. Everyone was to be included in the final harvest festival.

> And thou shalt keep the feast of weeks unto the LORD thy God with a tribute of a *freewill offering* of thine hand, which thou shalt give unto the LORD thy God, according as the LORD thy God hath blessed thee: And thou shalt rejoice before the LORD thy God, thou, and thy son, and thy daughter, and thy manservant, and thy maidservant, and the Levite that is within thy gates, and the *stranger*, and the *fatherless*, and the *widow*, that are among you, in the place which the LORD thy God hath chosen to place his name there. (Deuteronomy 16:10–11, emphasis added)

The day of Pentecost was unlike any other celebration on the Jewish calendar. It was likened to the bridegroom courting the bride, who had been eagerly waiting for the day when the bridegroom would come for her. She knew the day he would come, but not the hour.

The groom entering into a covenant with his bride is a reflection to the Jews of the covenant between God and the nation of Israel, which is why Pentecost is considered to be the birthday of when the Jewish people became a nation, when the Law was given to Moses on Mount Sinai.

Song of Songs 4:11 is recited as the groom calls out to his bride, "Your lips drop sweetness as the honeycomb, my bride; milk and honey are under your tongue" (NIV). Because of this verse, the Jewish people have cheesecake to celebrate the day of Pentecost.

Traditionally, during Jewish wedding celebrations in Jerusalem, bridegrooms would carry their brides across the threshold of the Eastern Gate in anticipation of the day when the Messiah would return to fulfill the covenant of God with His people.

The Jewish people often stay up throughout the night of Pentecost reading and studying the Laws Moses was given on the Mount Sinai. Just as importantly, they read through the story of Ruth, a story that also takes place during the spring harvest. Ruth was not Jewish by blood, yet she decided to enter into a covenant with the God of the Jews.

During the days of Ruth, a covenant was usually brokered with a blood sacrifice, which is where we get the phrase "to cut a deal," meaning that if this covenant was broken, there would be a blood sacrifice to pay.

However, the covenant celebrated on the day of Pentecost became one of words, not flesh. What was given to Moses and adopted by Ruth eventually brought death, because everyone was guilty for breaking the Law of Moses, but now man was being given life through Jesus Christ, who made us righteous before God.

The imagery here is so rich that it is impossible for me to write everything I discovered during that short journey to Israel. *Pentecost* is a word that is based on fifty (the word *pente* means fifty), and time after time in the Torah, fifty is the number associated with jubilee and deliverance.

Jesus was the holy lamb that was sacrificed at Passover, and then fifty days later, the Holy Spirit descended down upon the unexpecting Jews on the day of Pentecost!

DISCUSSION QUESTIONS

1. We can easily connect Passover with Good Friday, as the symbolic link is clear. Jesus was the true Passover Lamb. How about the connection between Pentecost and the birth of the church?
2. Why was the Jewish feast of Pentecost a good backdrop for the events in Acts 2?
3. Do you think Pentecost is properly celebrated in your church?
4. Do you have ideas about how our Pentecost celebrations can become more like the feast of mission it was in Acts?

DAY 11

DISCOVERING REVIVAL ON PENTECOST

> "Coincidence is the word we use when we
> can't see the levers and pulleys."
>
> —EMMA BULL

The psalmist wrote, "Will you not revive us again, that your people may rejoice in you?" (Psalms 85:6 NIV).

Imagine the disciples in Jerusalem. As I read through the first part of the book of Acts, I cannot help but imagine them as a collection of poor saps. I know I should probably think of them as men waiting with great excitement and singing songs of victory, but I am left with the impression that nothing is going the way they had anticipated. I imagine this portion of Scripture being a prayer on the edge of their lips, "Will you not revive us again, that your people may rejoice in you?"

What good is a Messiah when the Jewish people have to continue living under the oppression of the uncircumcised Romans? What good is it to be in the lineage of King David if the enemy isn't obliterated by the sword of the righteous like the armies of old?

How amazing would it have felt to have a Messiah who came to earth with muscles bulging like Conan the Barbarian, busting skulls and taking names? One the "sons of thunder" (the apostles Peter, James, and John) would have approved of?

Humiliating the Romans and their polytheistic gods would have brought life back into the bones of the Jewish people and ushered in waves of pride that would have been the theme of songs for generations to come.

To everyone's surprise, that was not what Jesus did. War was not what needed to be taught. Humiliating the enemy was a skill the Jews had mastered—when they were in power to do so. Punishing people for breaking the Law of Moses or following foreign gods was something the Jewish people were good at.

Instead, the long-awaited Messiah came to earth in the lowliest of ways. He did not sit among kings or ride into battle with the top generals. He did not lead armies or attempt a political coup. He brought a strange and foreign brew of grace, mercy, forgiveness, love, and service to others.

> **The long-awaited Messiah did not lead armies or attempt a political coup. He brought a strange and foreign brew of grace, mercy, forgiveness, love, and service to others.**

To add insult to injury, when it was revealed that He truly was the Messiah they had all been waiting for, He then willingly allowed the Sanhedrin to detain Him and hand Him over to the Romans, and then He suffered the most publicly humiliating death known to man.

It had to have been one of the most striking blows ever experienced by the disciples, but then He came back to life! The stone was rolled away! Death was conquered! The disciples were once again with their eternal leader and all would be great again.

And then He left.

Just like that. He was gone, and they were back in Jerusalem—alone—without Jesus.

I have to believe that they were heartbroken. Surely their spirits were crushed because they wanted to go with Him. They almost certainly did not want to be separated from Him yet again, but there they were in Jerusalem all by themselves. Now what? Jesus had always been there to tell them what to do, where to go, and how to behave. They were sitting in Jerusalem, and like a dog that has been told to stay, they sat patiently waiting, with only the last words of their Master to keep them company.

"Will you not revive us again, that your people may rejoice in you?"

They needed Jesus more now than ever before. They needed to be revived.

And then, fifty days after the crucifixion of Jesus, on the day of Pentecost, the sound of a violent wind came down from heaven above and filled the entire house where they were. "They saw what seemed to be tongues of fire that separated and came to rest on each of them. All of them were filled with the Holy Spirit and began to speak in other tongues as the Spirit enabled them" (Acts 2:3–4 NIV).

The Holy Spirit came down and spoke to His people. *This is revival!*

These two verses are among two of the most important verses in the whole Bible and clearly connect with the first Pentecost in ways I had never seen before. Pentecost, both in the Old and New Testament, is what makes Christianity and Judaism completely different from any other religion in the world.

You see, Buddhism is based on the teachings that were experienced by a single man—the founder, Siddhartha Gautama. The birth of Mormonism relies on the revelation of one single individual—Joseph Smith. The entire religion of Islam is established solely on the visions and experiences of Muhammad. No one else was there to witness what these men claimed to have seen. Each one of them shared revelations from their lonely experiences, but this is not true for Christians and Jews on the day of Pentecost. God spoke, and multitudes were there to witness it.

In Acts 2, everyone present was witnessing the same Holy Spirit speaking directly to them "tongues like as of fire" (v. 3) in many different languages. The Jewish people at Mount Sinai also experienced the voice of God speaking directly to them and giving the Law at Sinai (Exodus 19:16–20:1; Deuteronomy 5:1), also in many different languages (Deuteronomy 4:11–15; Hebrews 12:18–19).

According to Jewish teachings on the Torah, God spoke to the Israelites in seventy different languages represented by fire.

In the occasion of Matan Torah [the giving of the Torah], the Bnai Yisrael [children of Israel] not only heard Hashem's [the Lord's] Voice but actually saw the sound waves as they emerged from Hashem's [the Lord's] mouth. They visualized them as a fiery substance. Each commandment that left Hashem's [the Lord's] mouth traveled around the entire Camp and then to each Jew individually, asking him, "Do you accept upon yourself this Commandment with all the halochot [Jewish law] pertaining to it?" Every Jew answered "Yes" after each commandment. Finally, the fiery substance which they saw engraved itself on the luchot [tablets].[6]

Author Rick Deadmond rightly pointed out that "most Christians would outright reject these Midrashim quoted above as religious fiction, but the New Testament book of Hebrews confirms these Midrashim. In speaking of the signs associated with the giving of the Torah at Mt. Sinai, the writer of Hebrews mentions 'the voice of words.'"[7]

It was no mistake that the power of the Holy Spirit came upon the disciples and all of those present on the day of Pentecost. The disciples did not abandon their Jewish faith on the day of Pentecost but were in fact embracing it; therefore, revival is directly connected to the covenant of God.

The disciples were not alone in their groaning and waiting upon the Lord. The entire earth was ready to burst forth with praise, and the power of the Holy Spirit came raining down.

A similar experience was recorded in the Old Testament. The mountains surrounding the Israelites were ablaze, the supernatural fire consuming everything in sight. Thunder cracked as if the earth were splitting in two. And from the midst of it all, God spoke audibly, in a voice that was awesome and almighty.

Both Pentecostal experiences were followed by confusion of those who were not seeking revival. The witnesses in Jerusalem thought that those speaking in tongues were drunk on wine early in the morning (Acts 2:13), and the people with Moses freaked out and hid, saying, "Speak to us yourself and we will listen. But do not have God speak to us or we will die" (Exodus 20:19 NIV).

The day of Pentecost was the launching pad of the Gospel of Jesus Christ, and for the rest of history the term *revival* would carry with it the presence of God.

Revival cannot happen where God is absent. It is the presence of God that revives those who

Revival cannot happen where God is absent.

seek after Him. It is His presence that lifts His people out of despair and worldliness, convicts them of sin, brings about boldness purity, returns the joy of harvest to the celebration of Pentecost, and renews the commitment for the Great Commission and the lost.

Revival is a revelation of God at the same time or in the same region to a group of people. What He has been doing to work on the hearts of individuals is expanded to the multitudes during periods of revival.

People find salvation in a corporate setting just as they did on the day of Pentecost. Revival is a group experience, not an isolated one. It is not a selfish endeavor to be experienced alone. That is why Buddhism, Hinduism, and Islam can never experience a true revival. Their experiences are individual revelations with a false god instead of a group experience with the living Lord.

Basically, if you want salvation, you can find it as an individual, but if you crave revival, then it must be experienced with others.

DISCUSSION QUESTIONS

1. How do you think you would have felt if you had experienced firsthand the events at mount Sinai? Or the events at Pentecost?
2. Would you have freaked out like the Israelites in the desert? Or would you have looked for an alternative explanation like some Jews in Jerusalem? Or would you have been really excited and wanted in?
3. If your city would experience revival, what do you imagine it would look like? Who would love it? Who would hate it? What would change?

DAY 12

THE RECIPE FOR REVIVAL

"You will never know the true value of moment until it becomes memory."
—SPONGEBOB SQUAREPANTS, QUOTING DR. SEUSS

The book of Acts covers a very exciting time in church history. The revival in Jerusalem on the day of Pentecost became the golden standard for every revival that would ever take place. It was a legend that many have desperately wished to see recreated. It is the greatest revival ever recorded in history, which is one of the reasons why it has been canonized for eternity in the New Testament.

No revival has ever seen such immediate effects and none have been so lasting in its results. The Holy Spirit fell on the festival devoted to harvest, and a harvest of three thousand were saved in the blink of an eye as a result.

The new Pentecost was truly the beginning of a harvest festival that would last for another two thousand years and is still continuing to this day. What was taking place in Jerusalem was the fulfillment of John the Baptist's prophecy, when he said he baptized with water but Jesus would baptize with fire and the Holy Spirit. John was beheaded and Jesus was crucified, but the impact of these two men could not be squelched.

Once Peter was filled with the Holy Spirit, something amazing happened—he began to fulfill the Great Commission, which was the final command given to him by Jesus. The mandate given to Peter and the disciples was pretty clear: "But you will receive power when the Holy Spirit comes on you; and you will be my witnesses in Jerusalem, and in all Judea and Samaria, and to the ends of the earth" (Acts 1:8 NIV).

Just as Jesus said they would become witnesses for Him when the Holy Spirit came to them, Jesus laid out a road map for them that was very much like a ripple in a pond: first Jerusalem, then Judea and Samaria, and then the rest of the world.

The day of Pentecost is often called the birthday of the church because that is the day the apostles were filled with the Holy Spirit and began their task of fulfilling the Great Commission.

The Holy Spirit–inspired revival was never to be contained and restricted to Jerusalem alone,

The new Pentecost was truly the beginning of a harvest festival that would last for another two thousand years and is still continuing to this day.

nor were those who were not apostles or followers of Jesus Christ to be kept from it. It was for everyone who would only believe.

There were many Jews who were in Jerusalem for the festival of Pentecost. They were foreigners and spoke languages that were different from Jesus and the disciples, and it is highly likely that many of them did not have a clue who Jesus was. When the Holy Spirit came down, Peter was filled with passion and began to preach, but his message did not have mass appeal in the way that mainstream Christian messages today seek to have.

Peter didn't waste any time trying to win people over by telling stories of sugarplums and cotton candy. It could even be said that he was being a bit rude. After all, Peter was disturbing pilgrims who had traveled to Jerusalem for a festival, called everyone sinners, insinuated that they were all guilty for the death and crucifixion of Jesus, and demanded that they repent for their transgressions.

He was not trying to win popularity awards and went straight to the heart of the Gospel message.

When the people heard this, they were cut to the heart and said to Peter and the other apostles, "Brothers, what shall we do?"

Peter replied, "Repent and be baptized, every one of you, in the name of Jesus Christ for the forgiveness of your sins. And you will receive the gift of the Holy Spirit. The promise is for you and your children and for all who are far off—for all whom the Lord our God will call."

With many other words he warned them; and he pleaded with them, "Save yourselves from this corrupt generation." (Acts 2:37–40 NIV)

The power of the Holy Spirit convicted the people of their sins, and Peter immediately let them know that this message was for their "children and for all who are far off," and that they should "save [themselves] from this corrupt generation."

In the book of Acts, we have our first recipe of the ingredients involved in making a revival soup.

First, it was not planned by man and could not have been planned by man. It was all in the Lord's hands. Peter and the disciples, with all of their knowledge of what Jesus had taught them and told them, could not have planned for it. The only thing that was in their power and control was to pray and wait as the Lord had told them to do. That was it. There was nothing else they could do.

> **Revival was prompted by the supernatural visitation of the Holy Spirit.**

Peter and the disciples were completely vulnerable to the timing of the Holy Ghost. If they had disobeyed and not waited or prayed, then who knows what would have happened.

Furthermore, revival was prompted by the supernatural visitation of the Holy Spirit. He was the yeast that gave rise to the bread. Without Him there would have not been a revival at all.

Peter could easily be the focus of Acts 2, but this was the same Peter who only a few weeks earlier had denied that he even knew Jesus—not once, mind you, but three times! This same man, who would be considered a coward by his own standards of measure, was transformed from a timid Christ-denier to a roaring lion. He was suddenly filled with supernatural authority that was well beyond his own ability.

The Holy Spirit changed Peter completely. It transformed him from a man who denied Jesus into one who boldly stood in front of thousands of people he did not know and proclaimed a very strong message of sin and salvation.

Peter's spirit-filled message flowed both naturally and unnaturally. It did not seem that Peter had to search for the words; they came to him in an instant. However, it also did not seem that Peter had previously planned to address the crowd while he was in the Upper Room praying with the disciples.

This would mean that God gave Peter the words to say for this event that Peter could not have anticipated. As far as we know from Scripture, Peter was aware that they were to wait on the Lord in Jerusalem, but from what we read, Peter was unaware of when it would happen or who would be there.

Peter could not have planned for thousands of pilgrims to be present in Jerusalem from all over the world when the roaring sounds of wind came swooshing in from the power of the Holy Spirit. Peter never could have imagined that the Holy Spirit would give power to supernaturally share the Gospel message in foreign languages by speaking in tongues. It was a miracle, and that was sandwiched on each side by miracles.

Jesus operated in the miraculous, and now the disciples were doing the same. The miracles of Jesus were happening before their eyes just as Jesus had prophesied to them, and if we are to use this event as our future measure for revivals, then miracles must be a central part of it.

God's Word was being proclaimed by Peter and accompanied by miracles.

Peter gave evidence to this when he declared, "Men of Israel, hear these words: Jesus of Nazareth, a man attested to you by God with mighty works and wonders and signs that God did through him in your midst" (Acts 2:22 ESV).

But notice that Peter did not draw the attention of miracles for the sake of wonderment and amazement. This was not a spectacle of entertainment at a circus. Everything in the revival had a purpose. Every ingredient had a means to an end.

It is clear from the beginning that when the people witnessed the power of the Holy Spirit and heard the preaching of Peter, they were convicted of their sins. Peter laid out the options for them. If they were baptized, repented, and shared their faith with others, then they had a chance to save their children and themselves from the wicked and corrupt generation.

> **Everything in the revival had a purpose. Every ingredient had a means to an end.**

This is the outline for revival that impacts a society for generations. Everything we need to know about revival is found here in the book of Acts. This is the blueprint I want to follow as we look at how and where revival continues.

This is the starting line, and the connections go out from here and in many different directions.

Since Luke, the author of Acts, follows Peter, I will also follow Peter.

DISCUSSION QUESTIONS

1. The revival in Acts was unplanned. Why do you think revivals cannot be planned by us?

2. Is there anything we can do to make revival happen?

3. Do you agree that miracles would especially happen during a time of revival? Why or why not?

4. If you agree, does that mean that many miracles are proof that a revival is indeed happening?

5. If great supernatural things started happening in your town, how do you think people would respond?

6. If lots of miracles started happening today, how would things be different now that everything can be recorded and instantly streamed?

PART 2

ASIA MINOR: LAND OF THE GENTILES

DAY 13

LEAVING JERUSALEM

———◆———

"You have one business on earth–to save souls."

—John Wesley

The book of Acts can be referred to as "The Fifth Gospel," "The Gospel of the Holy Spirit," or "The Gospel of the Body of Christ," and it gives an amazing chronological history of revival and the founding of the church in a way that no other document on earth does.

Many overlook the significance of the book of Acts, but it is priceless and irreplaceable because it details the earliest years of the founding of the church and the spread of revival immediately following the ascension of Jesus.

The book of Acts is where the training wheels came off. Everything that Jesus said, taught, and did in the company of the disciples was going to be desperately needed. Immediately after the ascension of Jesus, the disciples headed westward to the city of Jerusalem. It was here that the Holy Spirit came upon them, causing them to speak in other languages—languages

> **The book of Acts details the earliest years of the founding of the church and the spread of revival immediately following the ascension of Jesus.**

that were heard and understood by other nationalities and ignited revival fires.

Peter preached to the crowd and offered the first altar call where three thousand people responded and became followers of Christ, and he became the focus for Luke in the beginning of the book of Acts. Back in chapter 9 of Luke's gospel, Luke recalled a moment when Peter supernaturally discerned who Jesus really was.

Matthew actually has one of the most detailed accounts of this event.

> When Jesus came into the coasts of Caesarea Philippi, he asked his disciples, saying, Whom do men say that I the Son of man am? And they said, Some say that thou art John the Baptist: some, Elias; and others, Jeremias, or one of the prophets. He saith unto them, But whom say ye that I am? And Simon Peter answered and said, Thou art the Christ, the Son of the living God. And Jesus answered and said unto him, Blessed art thou, Simon Barjona: for flesh and blood hath not revealed it unto thee, but my Father which is in heaven. And I say also unto thee, That thou art Peter, and upon this rock I will build my church; and the gates of hell shall not prevail against it. And I will give unto thee the keys of the kingdom of heaven: and whatsoever thou shalt bind on earth shall be bound in heaven: and whatsoever thou shalt loose on earth shall be loosed in heaven. (Matthew 16:13–19)

Two things happened here for the first time. First, Jesus was recognized by His disciples as the Messiah, the Son of God. Second, this is the first time we see the word *church* in the Bible.

Peter was not a scholar or a theologian. He was a fisherman, so his confession to the true nature of Jesus was a revelation that must have sent shockwaves through the ranks of the other disciples. The location of Peter's revelation could not have been by mistake either.

This is actually one of the most foundational scriptures in the entire Bible for the existence of the Catholic church. According to their interpretation of this event, Peter was anointed as the head of the church and became the forerunner for every pope who would follow in his footsteps.

Even the standard for the Vatican, where the pope is seated, is marked with two keys, gold and silver—one for binding and the other for loosening—based on this portion of Scripture. Protestants believe that the original language here is important, so they point out that Jesus used two different words that are recorded in the Greek language. One is the name for Peter—*Petros*—which can mean small rock or small pebble. The other is *petra*, which means big rock.

So in essence, Jesus said, "And I say also unto thee, That thou art *Petros*, and upon this *Petra* I will build my church."

According to most Protestant Christians, the *Petra*—the big rock—is actually Peter's confession that Jesus is the Christ. It would be this confession that would be uttered on the lips of everyone who would eventually enter into the eternal kingdom of God.

The Catholic church has a very strong argument for their interpretation of this scripture, as do Protestants, but their conclusions have led them down completely different paths to fulfill the call of God on their lives.

Regardless of the debate, the meaning is clear that Peter was being prophesied over in the shadow of Caesarea.

It is, however, not only the language that is important in understanding the significance of this passage. The location of this conversation also sheds some light on what is really going on here, as I found when I first visited Caesarea Philippi.

Caesarea was still within the area of Judea, but it had a much larger Gentile influence than Jerusalem and was dedicated to false gods.

The primary landmark in Caesarea Philippi is a large mount known as the "Rock of the Gods." It is an imposing site that still stands today. It is called the Rock of the Gods because the Greeks had built numerous shrines to the gods into the rock face. This large rock formation would have loomed large in the minds of the disciples when Jesus claimed that He would build His church upon "this" rock.

It is important to know that Caesarea Philippi could arguably be called the darkest region in all of Judea for the Jewish people during this time. No respectable Jew would have been caught dead there. Polytheism was the primary focus for the many temples, massive orgies took place for the worship of the nymphs, and it is possible that human sacrifices were made there.

Caesarea Philippi was a spiritually dark pit and was an odd place for the Messiah to reveal who He really was. In my simple mind, I would think that a place like Jerusalem—the city of the kings—would be a much more appropriate location for such a huge revelation.

But Jesus spoke with imagery in His words to Peter, and the Rock of the Gods provided a backdrop to this imagery when Jesus said that He would build His church on *this* rock.

In the center of the Rock of the Gods was a cave that was believed to be the gateway to Hades, which added even more to the imagery here. In the cave is a water spring that was considered to be bottomless because it was the barrier between earth and hell. So when Jesus said that the "gates of hell" will not prevail against His church, the disciples would have connected His words with the image of this spring.

It is important to note that Jesus used the term *church* for the first time in this passage. He did not use the more familiar terms of *temple* or *synagogue*. He was recorded using the Greek term *ekklesia*—which is not a term necessarily linked to a structural building at all, like temple and synagogue would be, but instead is connected to the idea of people or a flock of followers.

Jesus had often used sheep in His illustrations to convey heavenly ideas, and that imagery is also connected to Caesarea Philippi. In ancient times, as well as today, the area is referred to as Paneas, named for the primary god that was worshipped there—the god of Pan.

Pan was a half-man and half-goat Greek god that was the lord of the shepherds. So there is even more imagery here, as Jesus is revealed as the Messiah in the presence of the god of the shepherds.

As I stood there in the shadow of the Rock of the Gods, a place that was dedicated to the gods of the world and represented every dark and hideous thing that repelled me, I couldn't help but see another side of Matthew 16.

What if the church of Jesus Christ was not necessarily to be announced behind the safety of the walls of Jerusalem? What if the message of the Messiah is really to be revealed in the darkest locations on earth where other gods are praised and worshipped?

What if Jesus had chosen to plant His church, not in the cathedrals of holy sites, but instead in the strongholds of dark oppression?

In other words, could it be even remotely possible that the Gospel message was never meant to dwell forever in the safety of those who agree with the light, but it was to be boldly proclaimed instead in the darkest locations on earth?

It seemed to me that Jesus was saying that even though the Gentiles put their trust in the gods of the rock of Caesarea, He was planting His church into the living stones of the disciples, namely Peter, who bore the name Simon Petros—whose name meant rock—and even the most ferocious adversaries of hell would not overcome it.

"Thou art Peter [Petros], and upon this rock I will build my church; and the gates of hell shall not prevail against it." The idea of the location of Peter's revelation being a result of happenstance must have faded when Jesus made this announcement.

The primary temple here for the stone god of the shepherds is now shadowed by the living stone of Peter, who vocally acknowledged the deity of Jesus and was then later prophesied to be a shepherd in the church of Jesus Christ.

Luke, the author of Acts, wrote about this event in his gospel, and in the early chapters of the book of Acts he followed the timeline of Peter fulfilling his role as a leading shepherd of the church of Jesus Christ that was being built by the Holy Spirit.

DISCUSSION QUESTIONS

1. When revealing His identity at the Rock of the Gods, Jesus did so in direct confrontation of the darkness of polytheism. If Jesus had come in our time, where do you think He would have chosen to reveal His identity as Messiah?

2. Do you think we should expose or shield church members from the darkest places of our world?

3. Among the twelve, would you have picked Peter as the leader of the first church? Why or why not?

5. What do you think Jesus saw in him?

DAY 14

ABANDONED

———◆———

"Thanks for helping me with my abandonment issues by abandoning me."

—FACEBOOK MEME

In the initial hours after the ascension of Jesus, the disciples must have felt terribly alone. Their leader had been with them every day for a few years and now He was suddenly gone. None of it really made sense. What were they supposed to do now?

They had walked in the warmth of His presence and grace on a daily basis, which is the envy of every single generation of hungry believers who reads the details contained within the canonical writings. Whether the disciples were fully aware of it at that time or not, they were living the dream! They were walking with the Master.

They were not merely reading His words in red letters on a piece of paper. They were hearing His voice crack the air with their own ears. They were watching Him change the very immutable laws of nature in the most miraculous way right in front of them.

There was no one like Him. There had never been anyone like Him, and there would never be anyone like Him ever again. Unbelievably, they were witnessing it all with their own eyes.

Imagine the moment when the disciples realized that they had indeed been walking with the Son of God for more than a couple of years and now . . . He was gone. Poof. Like a vision. All of His words, teachings, and miracles were now only in their memory.

He was gone, and they were alone.

It must have been the world's worst hangover, going from the highest of highs to the lowest of lows. They had walked with the King of kings and were now back in the land of mere mortals. Few could have felt the heaviness of His absence more than the three amigos who were in the inner circle: James, John, and Peter.

Just as we said earlier, Jesus gave them a very simple road map—they (the disciples) would become witnesses for Him when the Holy Spirit came to them—first in Jerusalem, then Judea and Samaria, and then the rest of the world. This was a simple three-phase ministry plan, and Peter had just witnessed phase one in Jerusalem.

They would not be alone for long. In fact, they would never really be alone again.

The Holy Spirit came to them, and they became witnesses for Him in Jerusalem. Several thousand new souls crying out for salvation were the result of the first revival post resurrection, but what happened behind the walls of Jerusalem would not remain behind those walls for long. The ancient walls of Jerusalem were not able to contain the spiritual explosion that had just erupted.

The promised Comforter had arrived.

Peter, either knowingly or unknowingly, made a prophesy that would challenge his beliefs in Judaism to the core. I am not sure if Peter recognized it at first, but if he did, he did not fully understand the implications of what it truly meant, because it would change his life and view forever.

He stood up before the crowds and quoted from the prophet Joel:

> In the last days, God says,
>   I will pour out my Spirit on *all people*.
> Your sons and daughters will prophesy,
>   your young men will see visions,
>   your old men will dream dreams.
> Even on my servants, both men and women,

> I will pour out my Spirit in those days,
>   and they will prophesy.
> I will show wonders in the heavens above
>   and signs on the earth below,
>   blood and fire and billows of smoke.
> The sun will be turned to darkness
>   and the moon to blood
>   before the coming of the great and glorious day of the Lord.
> And *everyone* who calls
>   on the name of the Lord will be saved.
>   (Acts 2:17–21 NIV, emphasis added)

I often wonder if Peter really knew he was prophesying that this latter-day revival would include non-Jews? If he did know it, he sure did act surprised later on when he was tested on it.

The book of Acts details the many miracles that began to follow the disciples, but Peter is a central focus. Peter healed the lame beggar (Acts 3), Peter preached to onlookers (Acts 3), Peter preached to the leaders of the Sanhedrin (Acts 4), Peter led the new Christians into a community of common sharing (Acts 4–5), and even Peter's shadow had miraculous powers (Acts 5).

> **"*Everyone* who calls on the name of the Lord will be saved."**

Next, Peter found himself in Samaria ministering to the Samaritans (Acts 8), the very people many Jews had considered to be unclean.

If Peter considered himself radical for including the Samaritans in the salvation of this Good News, he was about to learn that this would be mere child's play compared to what God had for him next.

If you leave Jerusalem through Jaffa Gate, you are automatically facing westward toward Joppa. Jaffa Gate was like a highway marker that gave travelers a freeway sign to tell them which highway lead toward Joppa, the oldest active seaport in the world.

Peter next found himself in Lydda, a town on the road between Jerusalem and Joppa. He was bolder than ever. He saw a man who had been handicapped for eight years and, according to Scripture, boldly told the man to get up and walk!

He was on a roll, like a wild cowboy with pistols that shoot laser beams of supernatural healing in the wild west of Judea. As readers of the book of Acts, we are seeing the character and power of Christ all over Peter.

Not only is the power of Christ all over Peter, but what happens next is almost a carbon copy of what Peter saw in Mark 5:35–43 when Jesus took Peter with him to see a young girl who had died. Peter, like Jesus had, asked everyone to leave the room. Peter then, almost with the same exact words of Jesus, who said, "Little girl, . . . get up" (Mark 5:41 NIV), said to Tabitha, "Tabitha, get up" (Acts 9:40 NIV).

The imagery here of Peter walking in the footsteps of Jesus is crystal clear, but there is another storyline at play: revival is following Peter. Wherever Peter went there were miracles and healings, but they were not for the sake of proving the skeptics wrong or astonishing the curious crowds. They do not even seem to be present in the story to prove the apostleship of Peter, because that seemed to have been firmly established already.

The miracles and healings continued to follow Peter, it seems, for a much bigger purpose. That purpose was to bring more people into the church.

People continued to repent of their sins, turn from their wicked ways, and give their lives to Christ.

The revival fires were not just contained in the walls of Jerusalem but had now ventured to the border areas of Judea, including the port city of Joppa.

Like a virus, the Gospel message was growing and reaching more people in more areas. The further it spread, the more difficult it would be to destroy.

But for now, there was no great need for the enemy to panic because this revival flame was only growing among a small Jewish sect, and they were surrounded by the conquering Gentiles who were far too superior to listen to the simpleminded religious ramblings of a nomadic Jewish slave culture.

The Jews were not evangelistic to those outside of their race. They did not put any effort into converting non-Jews to Judaism. Why would they? In their mind, they were the chosen people, which would kind of make everyone else—well . . . not chosen people.

So if the Gentiles had no desire to convert and the Jews had zero desire to convert the Gentiles, then it was a guaranteed recipe for the revival to not move past the Jewish communities.

However, what is impossible for man is possible for God.

DISCUSSION QUESTIONS

1. Why do you think Peter may not have realized that the Gospel was going to spread outside of the Jewish community (which was scattered around the Roman world)?
2. Can you think of places in the Old Testament where God clearly stated His intention that His plan of salvation includes all nations? How do these passages challenge the church today?
3. Do you think a "chosen people" mentality is something Christians in your country may suffer from?

DAY 15

PETER, "SON OF JONAH"

"Three times measure, one time cut."

—SERBIAN PROVERB

I flew into the Tel Aviv airport hoping to walk in the footsteps of Peter, and instead found myself in a small upper room being rigorously interrogated by Israeli immigration officials. Israeli authorities did not like the fact that I had so many stamps in my passport from Muslim countries, so they put me in secondary immigration, where I was questioned by several different officers for more than four hours.

I used the extra time in immigration to read through the book of Acts, knowing I was only a stone's throw away from where chapter 10 took place.

I find it fascinating that if Luke, the "beloved physician," was indeed a Gentile, then the book of Acts was written by the only Gentile author in the entire Bible. As a Gentile, I couldn't help but laugh out loud when I came to Acts 10, where Peter found himself in the city of Joppa, not far from where I was stranded in the Tel Aviv International airport.

It might not seem noticeable at first, but there is a very strong parallel here between what was about to happen to Peter and what happened to Jonah in the Old Testament.

Acts 10 might very well be the single most important chapter in the entire

Bible if you are like me and are not Jewish by birth. Maybe this is the reason why the writings of Luke speak so strongly to me.

According to Luke, revival had only started among the Jewish population, but by chapter 10, it was about to spill over into the Gentile world too. It seems fitting that this next stage of stretching Peter would take place in Joppa, because this was the same port that Jonah fled to when he was running from the calling of the Lord to go and preach a message of repentance to the Gentiles!

Like Jonah, Peter was called to the Gentiles by God. Like Jonah, Peter was given a command that he was reluctant to accept (Jonah 1:3; Acts 10:14). Like Jonah, Peter protested and was unwilling to accept the task that God was giving him. God kept Jonah in the belly of the fish for three days and nights (Jonah 1:17), and Peter saw the same vision and heard the same command three times over (Acts 10:10–16).

In chapter 3 of the book of Jonah, the Word of God came again to Jonah and said, "Go to the great city of Nineveh and proclaim to it the message I give you" (v. 2 NIV), which is like the command that was given to Peter (Acts 10:20).

So Peter could be referred to as "Simon bar Jonah" or "Simon son of Jonah" in a cheeky way that had a double meaning. Simon Peter was walking in the footsteps of Jonah.

Peter had a revelation in Acts 10, and I am not talking about the vision that he saw in the trance. In verse 28, he realized that salvation for all mankind was a story throughout the Word of God and was the reason for the covenant with Israel. God chose Israel as a people to share with the entire world the Good News of salvation; salvation was not for the Jews alone. Calling the Jewish people and making a covenant with them was not a racist game of ethnically homogenized salvation, but instead was a grand honor and a vessel to reach every nation.

Peter's vision was a sign that this message of the Good News was for all people. At the same time that Peter was experiencing the vision, God was also working in the heart of a Roman centurion named Cornelius. Cornelius was a Roman Gentile, considered to be religiously unclean by the Jews, but he was clean when he was washed with the blood of Christ (1 John 1:7).

This movement westward brought the Good News to an entire continent of Gentiles, and for the first time Gentiles in the West could find hope in a Jewish Savior, receive the Holy Spirit, and join the Body of Christ.

From this point on, God was no longer viewed as just the Savior of the Jewish people. He was now the Savior for all mankind.

This was the beginning of something horribly amazing. It was horrible in the sense that persecution of Christians from this point on came not only from the religious Jewish community but would also come from the entire Western hemisphere as the enemy tried to contain and stop

> **From this point on, God was no longer viewed as just the Savior of the Jewish people. He was now the Savior for all mankind.**

the spread of Christianity. But it was beautiful in the way that this was the launching pad of the Gospel message to the Gentiles.

The persecution was only the beginning for the Jewish followers of Jesus Christ, but now they would share the burden with their Western brothers and sisters.

The Gospel message traveled eastward as well, eventually as far east as China, but for whatever reason, Luke did not follow it eastward. The church of the East would one day be overshadowed by an evil that few could have predicted. Six hundred years after the disciples left Jerusalem to preach the Good News, a new religion was born in the East that would terrorize the entire eastern front of Jerusalem for more than a thousand years and today is the biggest obstacle to completing the Great Commission.

A man by the name of Muhammad sparked a demonic march that eventually hit every town and city east of Jerusalem, and even spread into Jerusalem itself. This entire territory between Jerusalem and China eventually became Islamic.

DISCUSSION QUESTIONS

1. Why do you think it took a direct and repeated vision from God to break down Peter's resistance to go to a Gentile?
2. How do you think other Jews who did not have this vision would have felt?
3. Have you ever felt like you were called to share Jesus with people you had good reason to keep your distance from? What happened?
4. Are there social or ethnic barriers that you feel Christians in your country need to break through to spread the Good News?

DAY 16

THE GENTILE SEED

———————

"I had been warned about Jews by my gentile friends—they did terrible things with knives to boys."

—PAUL ENGLE

If it is true that Luke was a Gentile, then Luke would not only be one of the only authors of the Bible not to be Jewish, but if the two books accredited to him were actually written by him that would mean that he wrote more of the New Testament than any other author, including Paul and John.

I thought about this when I was walking in the footsteps of Peter and following the timeline from the book of Acts. This means that the Lord entrusted the majority of the New Testament authorship to a Gentile who carefully documented the movement of the Gospel message westward to the Gentiles.

As he wrote about Peter, Luke would have been privy to some of the more private moments and thoughts of the apostle and would have been acutely aware of Peter's reluctance to reach out to the Gentiles.

Luke wanted to make sure that his audience was aware of the significance of what was happening in Joppa; that is why he slowed down the timeline and shared in detail about the events that eventually led to the first Gentile conversion.

Joppa is not only one of the oldest ports in the world, but since it is located on the Mediterranean, it would have been a bit like home for Peter.

The old seaport of Joppa had more historical significance than the Sea of Galilee where Peter lived, but it was still a bustling place for fishermen and tradesmen.

Back in the day, Joppa was used as the port to bring in materials needed for the building of Solomon's temple as well as to bring in goods for the rebuilding of the temple during the reign of Persia. It continues as an active seaport to this day, and it was here, in the comfort of Peter's environment, that God gave him a vision that would require faith and guts.

The vision, according to Luke, led to an encounter with a man named Cornelius who was not only a Gentile but also was a Roman military commander. A scrappy, full-blooded Jew like Peter would have nothing in common with such a man. The people from Peter's neighborhood would have detested Cornelius because the Romans were seen as occupiers. Let's not forget that Peter was actually a disciple of Jesus, the very man the Roman soldiers, like those commanded by Cornelius, crucified and nailed to a wooden cross.

> **Peter preached with power and conviction about the universal salvation offered through Jesus Christ.**

Peter, a Jew, forbidden to socialize with Gentiles, said to Cornelius, "Truly I understand that God shows no partiality, but in every nation anyone who fears him and does what is right is acceptable to him" (Acts 10:34–35 ESV). For the non-Jewish reader, and certainly for the Gentile author, this had to be one of the most beautiful things to hear.

On the day that Cornelius met with Peter, he became a follow of Jesus. Cornelius was only the beginning of a massive flood of Gentiles who were about to be grafted into the vine of Christ. Peter continued and preached with power and conviction about the universal salvation offered through Jesus Christ.

While Peter was still saying these things, the Holy Spirit fell on all who heard the word. And the believers from among the circumcised who had come with Peter were amazed, because the gift of the Holy Spirit was poured out even on the Gentiles. For they were hearing them speaking in tongues and extolling God. Then Peter declared, "Can anyone withhold water for baptizing these people, who have received the Holy Spirit just as we have?" And he commanded them to be baptized in the name of Jesus Christ. (Acts 10:44–48 ESV)

This was a major shift in how man saw God. God did not change. He has always remained the same, but now the gap that divided man from his Creator was bridged by the crucifixion of the most holy Lamb.

It is not possible to know how the book of Acts would have been interpreted without the telling of this story between Peter and Cornelius. Peter did not recall it in his writings. The writers of the Gospel did not include it in their writings. Paul, an advocate of reaching the Gentiles, did not point to this event. It is Luke and Luke alone who recorded these events.

Assuming Luke was indeed a Gentile, how exciting it must have been for him to write down this exchange between Peter and Cornelius. If Cornelius was the first Gentile saved after revival broke out in Jerusalem, then Luke's own salvation would have followed when the message of the Good News arrived at the doorstep of the very person who is accredited with leading Luke to Christ: Paul.

DISCUSSION QUESTIONS

1. As a Gentile, how does this story make you feel?
2. Do you find it offensive to have been called "unclean"?
3. Note this mini-revival in the house of Cornelius was also orchestrated by the Holy Spirit; He initiated and confirmed it. Have you ever been in a situation where God prepared the hearts of people before you met them?
4. Have you ever been surprised by someone's positive response to hearing the Gospel?
5. What does that say about our role in bringing people to Christ?

DAY 17

GO!

"The roof is not my son, but I will raise it."

—ANONYMOUS

T he message of Jesus in His final command to His disciples was extremely simple. The Great Commission command of Matthew 28:19 can kind of be broken down into just one word—*go*.

As modern-day Christians, it can be easy to forget that the message of the Gospel must have seemed absolutely ludicrous. From the beginning of the disciples' lonely journey after the ascension of Jesus, everything seemed to be going wrong. To the professional event organizer, nothing could have been more poorly planned.

> **The Great Commission command of Matthew 28:19 can kind of be broken down into just one word—*go*.**

There wasn't a distinctive Christian message; it was actually a Jewish message shared among a Jewish population that largely considered it to be heretical.

Jesus was a Jew who kept the Law, recognized the Sabbath, abided by the dietary laws, and could trace His Jewish family heritage to Father Abraham, but He was rejected by the highly respected Jewish leaders and was betrayed by one of His own close friends. His followers were indistinguishable from the Jews who despised them, because they were, well, Jewish. The followers of Jesus did not see Him as the founder of a new religion, but instead as the fulfillment of Jewish scripture; scripture that none of the new followers were well versed in.

As a Messiah and Savior of the universe, it would have been nice if He had found the time to write a few words of instruction. It would have been helpful if He had come at a later time so that He could have posted an instructional video on YouTube.

Instead, He left the Good News in the hands of His followers who were questionably competent and did not exactly inspire hope. They were a ragtag group of men prone to violence and petty arguments. Surely the Creator of mankind could have found a better group of men to carry the message of the most important story ever to be told in the history of the universe. I personally would have found a great king or general who had proven himself in battle. A businessman with great wealth and influence, a scholar, or an author would not have been bad choices either.

If I had a message I wanted to share with the rest of the world, I would find someone with a marketing background, a wordsmith, or at least a camel salesman, but Jesus chose fishermen? Not just fishermen, but fishermen fishing in the Sea of Galilee, which is more of a lake than a sea. That is not even a real sea! The only thing to compete with their lowly position in society was the message they preached.

They did not trumpet the message of a man who had conquered armies, led nations, or left any inheritance of monetary wealth. The Man they followed had the crazy notion that He was God. If He was a god, He was a very unsuccessful god. He was born homeless, brought up in a world ruled by superior Romans, and crucified like a despised murderer at the behest of an angry mob that chose to save the life of a common criminal instead of Him.

This hopeless message of a failed God was left in the hands of gloriously unvirtuous men, and yet it did exactly what it should not have done—IT CHANGED THE WORLD.

How it happened still baffles the most learned of men.

The unassuming message of the Gospel story and the incompetence of the men who carried it is what makes it even more amazingly miraculous—as if a virgin woman giving birth to a miracle worker who later raised from the dead and ascended up into the heavens was not already amazing enough. The audacity displayed by the most unlikely of men made a mark that changed the course of history forever.

They saw something and experienced something that impregnated them with boldness and passion, and it was infectious.

The disciples and early converts became passionate rebels with a message that could not be ignored. They could not be silenced. They were history makers who were convinced that the end of the world was immanent and their role was crucial. They were radically washed in the baptism of fire from the Holy Spirit. On the day of Pentecost they saw and experienced something that had the power to make the most boring person an addicted spiritual adrenaline junky.

When evaluating the acts of the early disciples, one can't help but ask, "When did Christians stop being rebels?" At what point in history did we become jelly-spined wussies with an incessant need to be normalized and accepted by others?

DISCUSSION QUESTIONS

1. Do you think Jesus choosing lowly men to represent Him instead of forging powerful political connections was a model for us to follow? In other words, do you think mission is usually more effective when it comes from below versus from above? Why or why not?
2. Do you think churches have a tendency to be too "worldly" in their approach to mission, too much strategy, planning, and marketing? Or do you think these things are good?
3. What do you think are the biggest differences between how churches in your country do mission and the early mission of the apostles?

DAY 18

REVIVAL'S CONTAGION—PERSECUTION

———◆———

"The blood of the martyrs is the seed of the Church.
When she ceases to bleed, she ceases to bless."

—L. E. MAXWELL

Peter was no doubt a pioneer of missions to the Gentiles and the clear leader of the solidified band of disciples Jesus left behind. The scared group of disoriented disciples were now organizing into a powerful force of bold and fearless evangelists.

Not too far away was another man who was not a part of the group of disciples that Jesus left behind. He was not one of the original followers of Christ, but that would not stop him from forever changing the landscape of future revival. His name was Paul. Paul was as radical and outspoken as Peter, and even though he was an educated man instead of a raw tradesman or a fisherman, he could be quite crude and abrasive.

Paul was born into a Jewish family in modern-day southern Turkey in the town of Tarsus. Paul inherited Roman citizenship, which would prove to be valuable to him during his lifetime. Even though Paul lived in a Roman and Greek society, he was educated by some of the most prominent rabbis of his day (Acts 22:3).

Paul was unapologetically Jewish and was well versed in its dogma, ceremonies, and apologetics. Rumors had started to reach him about a man many people were calling Christ, or the promised Jewish Messiah. There were stories about His authority, His miracles, and His teachings. The news of His crucifixion had also been shared, but not in the way the Jewish leaders had intended it to spread.

Instead of killing the leader and scattering the sheep, the One who was crucified seemed to grow in both fame and popularity. His death did not prove His claims wrong; it proved Him right. In death, He was victorious, and the report of His resurrection meant He had conquered death as the one and true living God.

These rumors were blasphemous in the eyes of Paul! He developed a hatred for the followers of Jesus and set out on a crusade to eradicate them from among the Jewish population.

It was not necessarily Paul's job to keep order among the Jews. He was not exactly deputized to seek out the followers of Christ and bring them to justice. Instead, he took the initiative and sought out the followers of Christ and confronted their teachings.

As I studied Paul, I saw him as a passionate and zealous man who was not about to allow low-rent, uneducated disciples of a carpenter to pollute a pure faith. They had to be stopped. Every day that went by gave strength to the Jesus movement. Day by day His followers grew bolder and more numerous.

One day a Jewish posse of zealots who were like-minded with Paul were able to find one of the men who was in the inner circle of troublemakers. His name was Stephen, and he was a follower of Jesus. Stephen was apprehended in Jerusalem and dragged before the high priest to answer for his teachings.

There must have been many stories from the days of Paul's early persecution of the Christian church, but Luke found it important to share this specific story of Stephen's martyrdom. Stephen was a young man who did not fear the anger of the Jews. He stood boldly before his accusers and began to preach from the Jewish scripture.

As I read this story, I have to admit that I find it to be very odd, because the Jews who were accusing Stephen were the most respected teachers of the Jewish scriptures in the world. If anyone had any questions about the Torah or rabbinical teachings, these men were the ones to go to—not Stephen.

Who was he to lecture them about the teachings of Moses or the history of the Jewish people?

Where did Stephen find the audacity to attempt to teach the teachers? Those who were accusing Stephen, like Paul, had been groomed from the time of birth to be dedicated to the teachings of God and were faithfully committed until the day they died.

They wore the holy robes, offered the blood sacrifice, performed the holy ceremonies, deciphered the great mysteries of the Torah, chanted the holy prayers, and had the authority to enter into the holiest parts of the temple.

Stephen was a nobody. They held his life in their hands like a cat with a trapped mouse. There was nowhere for him to run, and yet he did not tremble in their presence. When Stephen pleaded his case, he could have begged for mercy and apologized for his grave misunderstanding. He was surrounded on all sides by a hungry pack of wolves, but Stephen refused to play dead to avoid being attacked.

A calmness that surpasses understanding came upon Stephen, and he did not fear. His accusers were not able to refute his teachings, so they, being full of anger, dragged him outside of the city with murderous hearts. Each one angrily clutched stones and hurled them at Stephen. Acts 7:55 says that Stephen was full of the Holy Ghost and a great glory seemed to shine on his face. He could see the heavens opening up as the stones broke his bones and crushed his flesh.

The faithful servant of God no doubt suffered a crushing blow to the head that impacted his skull with such force that it knocked the life out of his body, causing him to breath his last.

That was the end. His lifeless body lay on the ground, and the shadows of the angry crowd hovered over him. Blood-splattered stones were all around, and the dust started to settle again. The lust for death was satisfied.

Paul witnessed the death of this follower of Jesus, and it must have seemed well deserved. Peace and calm now rested on Stephen's limp body, but inside Paul's tumultuous heart brewed a storm that wanted to bring every follower of Jesus to the same end.

DISCUSSION QUESTIONS

1. Can you relate to the rage Paul felt in seeing how his beloved Jewish religion was perverted by the followers of Jesus?
2. When your faith is attacked, can you feel so angry that you want to hurt somebody? What does that say about our hearts?
3. Is it ever justified to use violence to protect truth? How was the death of Stephen a testimony to the truth?
4. Peter was miraculously freed from prison, but Stephen was killed and not raised to life again. Do you think the death of Stephen caused theological struggles or doubts in the new believers? Why or why not?

DAY 19

THE CONVERSION OF PAUL

———————

"Conversion is not the smooth, easy-going process some men
seem to think. . . . It is wounding work, this breaking of the hearts,
but without wounding there is no saving."

—JOHN BUNYAN

Paul searched high and low for the Christians who followed the teachings of Jesus. He hunted them day and night and pulled them out of their hiding places, forcing them further underground.

Like a bloodhound locked on the scent of a fresh trail, he gave chase till he overcame them. The gruesome scene of the murder of Stephen was fresh in his mind as he sought the blood of more Christians. Little did he know that Stephen's fate would one day reflect his own. Just as he witnessed Stephen willingly give his life as a martyr outside of the city walls of Jerusalem, so too would Paul in the city of Rome.

> **The very One he hated became the One whom he came to love more than life.**

What Paul did not know was that while he was hunting Christians, Christ was hunting him.

In only a flash of a moment, while Paul was on the prowl for Christians, Jesus came to him supernaturally and changed his life forever (Acts 9). The very One he hated became the One whom he came to love more than life. The men and women he hunted were now the ones he sought out for mentoring.

At first, no one would believe it. It was too incredible. Christians who had gone into hiding would not believe that someone as horrible as Paul could now be their friend and be a trusted brother in Christ. They did not know that Paul would spend his entire life sharing the Good News of Jesus Christ. His place in history would not be marked by the number of Christians he persecuted, but instead would be marked with the untold number of believers who received Christ at the price of his own persecution.

Paul did not know it then, but Jesus had already set his path. When Jesus said in Acts 1:8, "You will receive power when the Holy Spirit has come upon you, and you will be my witnesses in Jerusalem and in all Judea and Samaria, and to the end of the earth" (ESV), Jesus had put the western path in motion.

> **"There is neither Jew nor Greek, there is neither slave nor free, there is no male and female, for you are all one in Christ Jesus" (Galatians 3:28 ESV).**

From Jerusalem to Judea and Samaria—and then to the end of the earth. This was the very path that Luke would follow Paul on.

Jesus called Paul, but his calling was not inevitable. Paul did have a choice, just as we all have a choice. God called Paul to be His witness from Jerusalem, Judea, Samaria, and to the end of the earth just as He called Israel to be a light to the nations of the world, however, over and over again Israel rejected it.

Paul did not reject the calling upon his life. He radically embraced it.

When reading about the life and works of Paul, we should carefully evaluate him in his own Greek and Jewish Mediterranean setting in the first century. Paul was not the founder of Christianity, and he actually never ceased being a Jew. Paul did not see Christianity as a Gentile religion that stemmed from Judaism. Instead, he saw the Gentiles as being accepted into the covenant that God had made with the Jewish nation and that was fulfilled through the sacrifice of Jesus.

"There is neither Jew nor Greek, there is neither slave nor free, there is no male and female, for you are all one in Christ Jesus" (Galatians 3:28 ESV).

This teaching, this idea was revolutionary in a world rife with religious and social division during the days of Paul, and it was about to turn the known world upside down.

Paul was more than likely responsible for the spread of Christianity westward before he even became a believer in Jesus Christ, because many believers were fleeing from the persecution Paul was participating in.

That persecution also led to the lesser Jews, or the half-breeds, being accepted into the fellowship. Philip, one of Jesus' disciples, preached to the Samaritans, who were considered to be unclean because they were not fully Jewish, and he also preached to an African and led him to Christ (Acts 8).

The term *Christian* did not actually come about in Jerusalem. The followers of Christ who were persecuted by Paul did not see themselves as something other than Jewish. The term *Christian* was actually first used in Antioch (Acts 11:26) and became the common name for Gentiles who believed in the deity of Jesus, the Jewish carpenter.

Acts 11:26 marks the beginning of a movement that would forever change history. The church of Jesus Christ was no longer confined to Jerusalem or Israel. It was spreading throughout the entire world. His name was being praised in other languages and foreign countries. Nations with no connection to the Jewish people were starting to hear His name and find hope and peace in their lives. The Creator of the universe brought salvation to all mankind, and He was using His people, the Jews, to spread the Gospel.

Paul was more than a carrier. He was a smuggler. He smuggled the message into the darkest regions on earth and unleashed the power of the Holy Spirit in nations that had never before witnessed His awesomeness. He smuggled the Gospel into areas that had leaders on the lookout for it in order to stop it.

This was the Great Commission of Jesus Christ. He came on a mission to Jewish people, and now He was sending out the Jews on a mission to the rest of the world. As the Jews embarked on this mission, they began to cross the boundaries that their forefathers prophesied about. They were bringing healing to the world.

This is a completely different picture of the church from what we have today. Denominations did not exist. There were no Catholics, Lutherans, Pentecostals, Apostolic, Baptists, Methodists, Eastern Orthodox, Coptic, etc. The deeper one dives into the history of the church, the less likely we are to find denominations.

There was one body, one church, one Savior, and one Lord.

In the beginning Christianity was practically indistinguishable from Judaism. Both had the same set of ethical teachings, met in the synagogue, recognized the Sabbath, refused to worship idols, etc. The traditional Jewish support system provided the first network of communities from Jerusalem to Rome that made it possible to share the message of Jesus Christ.

The synagogue was Paul's launching pad in each new region to the west of Jerusalem. Though the land, language, customs, and laws were different in each new county, Paul was able to establish initial familiarity through the Jewish communities. Paul was a Jew's Jew. He was trained in the best rabbinical teachings available at that time, and as such he brought a certain prestige with him. It was easy for him to find a warm welcome in these circles, but it was almost impossible for him to keep that warm welcome for long once he taught about Jesus Christ.

Paul was locked on to moving into areas where the Gospel had never been preached. He did not want to take the safe route and go to areas where others had been sharing or planting churches. He wrote in Romans 15:20, "Yea, so have I strived to preach the gospel, not where Christ was named, lest I should build upon another man's foundation."

Paul embraced the path that Jesus spoke about: from Jerusalem to Judea, Samaria, and to the ends of the earth. Luke used his letter to follow this movement. Acts 1–10 starts in Jerusalem and moves to Judea and Samaria. Acts 10 introduces the Gentile phase, with chapter 12 following the westward movement of Paul to the rest of the world, which ends tragically in Rome.

In the beginning of Acts, Peter, James, and John conducted their outreach from their base in Jerusalem, but a major shift took place when Paul began launching his outreach from Antioch.

Though Antioch had Jews, it was not a Jewish city. Antioch was the third largest city in the world during the days of Paul, with more than a quarter of a million people. The Olympic Games were established there during the days of Paul.

It was here in Antioch where followers of Jesus began to be called Christians on a regular basis. The fellowship established in Antioch provided aid to the church in Jerusalem when they were experiencing extreme persecution and going through famine.

Persecution in Jerusalem increased, and the mantel of leadership was passed from the apostles to the elders. This further fueled the westward movement of the Gospel of Jesus Christ.

With Paul launching missions from Antioch and the Gospel moving westward, some real, practical challenges started to surface. The farther westward the Gospel moved, the fewer Jews one would encounter, meaning that the majority of converts were Gentiles.

Jews were quickly becoming the minority in their own promise! Luke recorded the question that quickly rose among the apostles as to whether Gentiles had to convert to Judaism in order to be saved.

Peter and Paul found themselves on different sides of the debate regarding this issue, and it led to a heated confrontation.

DISCUSSION QUESTIONS

1. What do you think Paul thought when Jesus told him he was going to be an apostle to the Gentiles?
2. What particular gifts and experiences do you think made him suitable for this mission? Do you see Christianity as a separate religion, or do you see your faith as an extension of Judaism?
3. How do you relate to Jews spiritually: religious Jews, Messianic Jews, and secular Jews?
4. Do you have experience with ethnic division in your church? How is that dealt with or should it be dealt with in your opinion?

DAY 20
THE DISAGREEMENT

—————◆—————

"Ask two Jews and get three opinions."

—OLD SAYING

Should Gentiles convert to Judaism to be saved? This dilemma split the new church. Peter was a disciple who had been around Jesus more than most and was the leader left behind by Jesus Christ. He believed that new converts must be brought into the fold of Judaism. Even though God gave Peter a vision in Joppa that prepared him for ministry to the Gentiles, the idea of God accepting those who were not circumcised, did not keep the dietary laws, and did not attend synagogue was still very difficult for Peter to accept.

Paul, on the other hand, was a hungry missionary who wanted to bring in as many new believers as possible in preparation for the return of Jesus Christ. He was teaching about a God who was so drastically different from the ones that were imagined by the Greeks and Romans.

The Greeks and Romans were experts in religion and took pride in knowing more about the different religions of the world than any other people group, but there was one God they had not heard about. This God gave His life for His people. This God loved mankind so intensely that He gave His only Son so that we could be with Him forever.

The God Paul brought to the non-Jew was a God who did not have to be appeased in His anger but who sacrificed Himself for the purpose of love. This was revolutionary, and the time was right, because the Gentiles were hungry for the love of a heavenly Father.

However, these new converts were not Jews and did not follow Jewish law. They were Gentiles and were considered to be unclean, but Paul brought them into fellowship as they were. Many felt that Paul's methods were too accommodating and compromised what it meant to be Jewish. Jesus was the fulfillment of the Jewish writings and teachings, not an opponent to them.

> ## Jesus was the fulfillment of the Jewish writings and teachings, not an opponent to them.

Paul challenged the current beliefs about salvation by making Jesus Christ the center of salvation. Paul did not put an emphasis on the Law, which the Jewish Christians felt was necessary. And for Peter, the idea of new converts obtaining salvation outside of Judaism was scandalous.

The disagreement between Peter and Paul was fierce. Even Paul's own partner on the field—Barnabas—abandoned Paul and joined Peter's side. In response, Paul wrote that "there is neither Jew nor Greek, there is neither bond nor free, there is neither male nor female: for ye are all one in Christ Jesus" (Galatians 3:28).

Paul was blessed and sent out by the Jewish Christian elders in Jerusalem to go and preach among the Gentiles, but few really thought about what that meant in practice. When Gentiles began to accept the deity of Jesus Christ, the Jewish Christian church was suddenly faced with an overwhelming number of uncircumcised heathens who were considered to be so dirty that the Jews, the Christian Jews, did not even want to sit at the same table and eat with them!

Later, a group of respected elders traveled to Antioch to insist on circumcision even for Gentiles (Acts 15:1–2). The situation was intense. Paul was summoned to return to Jerusalem. The elders needed to talk with Paul and maybe settle his ambition a bit. Paul needed to be set straight about the new converts not submitting to Jewish law.

However, when they all heard the amazing things that were happening through Jesus Christ among the Gentiles, they were blown away, and the Holy Spirit's presence was being confirmed by signs and wonders. After a lot of debate (Acts 15:7), Peter stood up and joined together with Paul, saying that a yoke should not be put on the necks of the new believing Gentiles.

It was proclaimed that Gentiles could come directly to salvation through Jesus Christ without becoming a Jew. Every Christian alive today and not actively a member of a local Jewish synagogue can look back on this chapter as one of the most important to their hearing the Good News of Jesus Christ.

DISCUSSION QUESTIONS

1. If you try to picture yourself as a Jewish elder, would you have chosen Peter's or Paul's side of the argument about whether Christians first had to become Jewish? Why?
2. If you hear of Christians who practice faith very differently from you, do you find it easy or difficult to accept them as brothers and sisters?
3. What biblical reasoning would convince you to accept believers who are very different from you as members of your spiritual family?
4. Do you find it encouraging or disappointing that there were such arguments in the early church? Why?

DAY 21

REVIVAL CONTINUES WESTWARD

———◆———

"If God were our one and only desire we would not be so easily upset when our opinions do not find outside acceptance."

—Thomas à Kempis

Paul must have been a very opinionated individual because, even though he blazed a trail of revival, it seemed he was the center of more than one disagreement. When it came time for him and his old friend and mentor Barnabas to leave out on their next mission journey, Barnabas wanted to take his cousin John-Mark with him.

Paul would have no discussion of Mark joining them because he had abandoned them on the first mission journey.

No reason was really given for Mark's departure, but as Luke's audience, we know that it couldn't have been good because Paul was not happy with the prospect of being abandoned again, so much so that he split with Barnabas and partnered with Silas, a friend of Paul's who was selected as a leader by the early church in Jerusalem, instead.

Paul and Silas left, and though they did not necessarily have the desire to head westward, that was the direction they were forced to go. It might not make sense to say that God forced them to go a particular way, but there is really no other way to explain it.

Paul and Silas obviously wanted to share the Gospel in Asia, but the Holy

Spirit forbid them to (Acts 16:6). For the next phase of revival recorded in the book of Acts, this is of supreme importance.

This is honestly a very odd juncture for those reading the Bible with a critical eye. If all men were to hear the Good News, Asia would have seemed like just as good of a region as any. But it is clear that God, in His omniscience, has His timing for everything.

God, in His omniscience, has His timing for everything.

Paul was not given a map and was not told where to go, but when he attempted to go into the areas that were not in a western direction, he was stopped.

Could this western movement have already started during the days of Jesus' birth, when wise men from the east followed the star that led them westward to Jerusalem? Could the shining light that led the wise men across some of the most unforgiving territory still be calling out to men and women today?

After acknowledging that God purposefully planned the movement of the Gospel message westward from Jerusalem, one is forced to ask the difficult and sensitive question of whether or not some people are more predisposed to believe the Gospel than others. Why can two people with the same background and the same family hear the same message and have different responses to it?

Jesus once taught,

Behold, a sower went forth to sow; and when he sowed, some seeds fell by the way side, and the fowls came and devoured them up: Some fell upon stony places, where they had not much earth: and forthwith they sprung up, because they had no deepness of earth: And when the sun was up, they were scorched; and because they had no root, they withered away. And some fell among thorns; and the thorns sprung up, and choked them: But other fell into good ground, and brought forth fruit, some an hundredfold, some sixtyfold, some thirtyfold. Who hath ears to hear, let him hear. (Matthew 13:3– 9)

Is there a generational wave of rebellion and submission that flows through the nations as it did throughout the Old Testament? Are there periods when the people have open hearts to embrace the truth and periods when they are hardened? Was this the case in Asia and Bithynia?

Whatever the reasons, this was one of the most important moments in Christian history. Before this point, the entire story of God's people had been in the Middle East and Persia. Luke was about to follow the Gospel message to a place it had never been before.

"And when they had come up to Mysia, they attempted to go into Bithynia, but the Spirit of Jesus did not allow them" (Acts 16:7 ESV).

News flash! When both the Spirit of Jesus and the Holy Spirit stop you from going somewhere, it is pretty certain that you will not be making your journey there. Paul was stopped from going east, and he was stopped from going north. He only had two choices left: west and south.

It was then that Paul had a vision of a man from Europe calling to him and saying, "Come over into Macedonia, and help us" (Acts 16:9). God was obviously leading him along the route that He wanted them to go. Paul was not at the Mount of Olives when Jesus gave the Great Commission. He was not

> **News flash! When both the Spirit of Jesus and the Holy Spirit stop you from going somewhere, it is pretty certain that you will not be making your journey there.**

there when Peter had his vision preceding the conversion of the first Gentile. Yet somehow God kept Paul in line with the very parameters that were laid out when He gazed upon the Eastern Gate and sent the disciples out to the nations of the earth.

DISCUSSION QUESTIONS

1. How do you imagine the Spirit of God "blocked" Paul and Silas from going where they had planned?

2. Have you ever had a comparable experience in your life where you made a good and godly plan, and then it seemed like God blocked the way? What happened after that?

3. If all nations needed to hear the Gospel, why do you think God specifically wanted Paul to cross into Europe?

4. Do you think the spiritual climate in a place can make it easier or harder for the Gospel to find inroads?

5. Should the spiritual climate of a place be a determining factor in whether we go somewhere or not to share the Gospel? Why or why not?

DAY 22

PASSING THE BATON

———◆———

*"Oh, East is East, and West is West, and never the twain shall meet,
Till Earth and Sky stand presently at God's great Judgment Seat."*

—RUDYARD KIPLING

Once Jesus set Paul in a westward direction, Paul was locked on. In his letter to the Romans, Paul told them that he would see them as he passed through on his way to Spain (Romans 15:24).

Why did he want to go to Spain?

In the days of Paul, most believed that the world was flat and that Spain was the end of the known world in the west. If Paul was to complete the Great Commission in his lifetime, he would have to make it all the way to Spain. He wanted to see revival cover the entire earth, and Spain was thought to be the end of the world.

He fought hard to make it to Spain, but there is no confirmed evidence that he ever made it. But it was not for a lack of trying. Just before his death he wrote, "I have fought the good fight, I have finished the race, I have kept the faith" (2 Timothy 4:7 ESV).

During the time that he took the Gospel message westward, he would experience more imprisonments than anyone else he knew of (2 Corinthians 11:23). He endured countless beatings and almost lost his life on several occasions.

After being arrested by the Romans, Paul would have received severe public floggings in front of huge crowds who had nothing better to do than to enjoy his humiliation. Paul would have been first stripped naked like an animal before his beating. In the eyes of his punisher, he was to be dehumanized so that he would find no sympathy with the crowd, only disgust.

After his public flogging, he would have been dragged off and thrown into prison and chained up without any treatment for his open flesh wounds. None or few of his clothes would have been returned to him after his flogging. The prison would have most likely been filthy and full of communicable diseases, making infection of his open wounds almost inevitable.

The food he would have received, if he received any, would have lacked any nourishment to help nurse him back to health. In his naked pain, Paul would have been shackled and chained with extreme restriction of movement, allowing the bugs and insects to feast on every open sore. The chains would have forced him to endure the heat of the summer sun or the freezing stone floor of the harsh winter cold.

Some of the prisons, like one I visited in Rome, were cold and damp and had almost no light. The prison was underground like a water well. Paul would have been lowered into the cell by a rope and pulled out when they wanted him. If you are weak and wounded, being pulled up through a hole in the floor by a rope could have been excruciating.

With the lack of light, many prisoners would fall into deep depression and beg for death. Roman guards would be severely punished if they assisted in suicide. The Romans had a strong desire to maximize the suffering of prisoners like Paul. Unless food was provided by family or friends, then there was little hope of having anything edible. Romans took pride in giving prisoners the exact amount of food needed for survival but no more.

Bathing and toilet facilities were not available, so lack of hygiene was a constant problem.

Paul endured this humiliating life for several years so that he would have the opportunity to see revival in areas that had never heard the Gospel message.

Paul was a great enemy of spiritual stagnation. Everywhere he went he was able to see churches planted and people saved. To retrace his steps is not an easy task because he covered so much ground in his attempt to complete the Great Commission before the end of his life. Paul's

Paul was a great enemy of spiritual stagnation.

insatiable desire to share the Gospel with as many people as possible before his death seemed to consume his every thought. Could it be possible that the faces of the early followers of Jesus he persecuted stayed with him later on in life? Did he carry the haunting image of Stephen with him as he too marched to martyrdom? Did something about the sacrificial love and devotion of the early believers minister to Paul in a way that drove him to be one of the great authors of missiology?

Paul once took refuge in his Jewishness but gave it up to cling to his identity in Jesus Christ (Philippians 3:5–7). To the Jew he was a Jew. To the Greek he was a Greek. Paul spent the later part of his life attempting to be all things to all people so that some might come to the knowledge of Jesus Christ (1 Corinthians 9:20–23).

The writings and teachings of Paul predated the writings of the Gospels by decades and were held by Gentiles throughout the Greek world as guidelines to their initial introduction to the Gospel faith.

All these different people groups that Paul ministered to were united by the Roman infrastructure of language and roads.

Roman roads were superior in design to any other roads during that time. They were initially built for the Roman soldiers, but their long-lasting impact would be the tales they could tell from the Christian soldiers who traveled westward.

The Roman roads were originally designed to carry people, goods, and soldiers from country to country in a fast and efficient manner, but their most precious cargo leading to and from Jerusalem was the Gospel message carried by Paul and his colleagues.

As Paul traveled on these roads, he never chose the easy destinations. On one occasion, the road led him to Ephesus, the largest city in Asia Minor, and there he stood before the largest temple in the world and openly challenged the god of Artemis, the most important goddesses in Ephesian society. This was the same temple of Artemis, one of the seven wonders of the world, that was minted on the currency of the powerful Roman Empire and took more than 120 years to build.

Though Artemis is often considered to be the same Greek goddess as Diana, she is actually referred to as the "mother of all things," known to the ancient Canaanites as Asherah, the idol found in Judges 6:30. Once again, a servant of the living God was combatting a spirit from the land of Canaan.

On this occasion, Paul stood in the arena where gladiators fought for their life, and he began to make a plea of salvation to the largest audience of his life. The open theater seated twenty-five thousand people and allowed his voice to be carried with clarity to the ears of the unbelievers. His message put his life in danger, since Artemis worship was one of the main sources of income for Ephesus. His provocative words to such a crowd seemed like a death wish.

Paul did not stop there. Armed with the saving power of Jesus Christ, Paul took the Gospel message to the footsteps of the capital of the western world: Rome.

Paul had several gifts, but none was arguably greater than his ability to make enemies everywhere. He could not have made more enemies if he tried. His persecution and arrest actually made it possible for him to travel to Rome. The church did not have to pay for it because it was being paid for by the Roman government as he invoked his right as a Roman citizen to be tried by a Roman court.

But even during the darkest hours of his incarceration, when his certain execution was drawing closer, he was able to convert people to Jesus Christ and build the timeless model of prison ministry. Paul was using every breath to preach the Gospel to as many people as possible.

In the beginning days after the resurrection of Christ, there were not many disciples. Paul knew that it was a race to evangelize the entire world. It was a race against a society that wanted to kill them. If the Jews and Romans who wanted to snuff out Christianity were able to quickly kill every known believer of Jesus Christ, they could stop the spread of the Gospel before it really got started.

The end of the book of Acts is the beginning of one of the darkest periods of the church. Paul was beheaded, Peter was executed upside down, James was tossed to his death from the temple mound, and the elders of the church were being hunted down at every turn.

The Jewish temple, one of the most amazing buildings in the ancient world, was destroyed, and Jerusalem was burned to the ground. The church scattered. Every government that heard about the followers of Christ created laws to make their proselytizing illegal, and the punishment was often death. For the next one hundred years, any leader of the church had to live life as a criminal and go underground with their message.

This is one of the most dire periods of persecution, but instead of destroying the church, it grew. Within the secret walls of the catacombs, Christians reached out to the lonely and hopeless. Lives were changed. In the diaspora, independent forms of worship evolved; things that helped one group of people get through the hard times were different from that which helped another. What remained constant was the deity of Jesus Christ and the emphasis of love for one another. Sacrificial faith proved to be a very strong thing.

> **The church grew leaps and bounds, and it did so without government legislation in support of their activities, official clergy, or sanctioned training schools.**

The church grew leaps and bounds, and it did so without government legislation in support of their activities, official clergy, or sanctioned training schools.

This was the first-century church that blazed the path for everything that Christians do today two thousand years later.

DISCUSSION QUESTIONS

1. What are ways we can see how persecution aids the spread of the Gospel from the stories of Paul and the early church?
2. Do you see any similar circumstances and outcomes in recent church history?

3. Do you think persecution is essential to keep a church pure? Why or why not? Can you give examples?

4. Do you know instances where persecution destroyed rather than strengthened a church?

5. Do you think it is God's will that Christians face persecution? Why or why not?

PART 3

AFRICA AND THE EARLY
DAYS OF REVIVAL

DAY 23

THE OVERLOOKED CONTINENT

"My favourite animal is the koala, but his life would be boring. I would rather be a giraffe so that I could contemplate the beauty of Africa."

—CATERINA MURINO

On the evening of November 10, 2014, the sound of whooshing blades cut through the dark night as two smoke-black military helicopters flew low to the ground over the knobby ridgeline of Ethiopia. Flying from the direction of Djibouti, their flight pattern was not known by anyone controlling Ethiopian airspace.

Two groups of six-to-eight-men teams were in each of the choppers. They had already received their orders, and they were anticipating the moment when they would hear the order "go" come across their radio.

They were not on a mission to kill Osama bin Laden. They were not on a mission to save a POW or kill a high-value target. Their destination was the Church of Our Lady Mary of Zion. None of the men were wearing insignia, so if any of them were caught, it would only be speculation as to whether they were paid thieves or from Israeli's highly skilled Mossad.

Coming over the ridgeline outside of the small Ethiopian town of Axum, the helicopters finally touched down about five hundred meters from the church. Immediately, the team of men moved tactically through the night wearing their night-vision goggles to give them the advantage.

Within the compound of the churchyard were eleven untrained Ethiopian armed guards and volunteers. Most of them were drifting in and out of sleep. They were not prepared for a military-style attack. The clergy members believed that trained guards were not needed.

Light shuffling of the feet could be heard as the team moved silently to breach the fence of the church compound. Only a short moment later, they were through, and one by one they dropped grenades that released a rare opium-based soporific gas.

The lead team navigated their way into the church while the rear team carried the bulk of equipment needed in the deep catacombs under the church. With jackhammers and explosives, they were able to widen the corridors and remove locked doors leading into the crypt.

After breaching the parameter and getting past the guards, into the church, through the maze of catacombs, and finally inside the main chamber of the underground vault, the team was able to feast their eyes on one of the world's most prized and sought-after treasures—the ark of the covenant. Their viewing pleasure was brief, as less than an hour later they had the ark loaded up on one of the two helicopters and were gone in the same stealthy manner they arrived.

This is not the opening scene of a new Indiana Jones movie, but it is a story that has been told about one of the most famous relics in Ethiopia—the ark of the covenant. The story is said to be as real as the ark being in Ethiopia in the first place.

I traveled to Axum Ethiopia to see for myself.

The Ethiopian Orthodox Church claims to have possessed the ark of the covenant for three thousand years and has guarded it with a succession of virgin monks who, once anointed, are forbidden to ever set foot outside of the chapel until the day they die.

These dedicated monks are said to be the guardians of the ark, and if it is true, they have been the only ones to have ever seen the ark in modern age. Not even the patriarch of the church is allowed to view it.

Was it really stolen? Was the ark ever really there to be stolen in the first place? For the skeptics, seeing is believing, and since no one has ever actually seen the ark, it is really hard to believe that the Ethiopians ever really had it.

But it is not impossible.

Walking among the ruins of the ancient Axumite Empire, where the Queen of Sheba had her throne, it appears that the idea of the ark of the covenant being in Ethiopia is not as far-fetched as some might think. Ethiopia, and indeed Africa, is closely connected to the lost tribes of Israel and is one of the earliest areas to embrace the Gospel message. Many believe that the first Christian king of the Axumites was baptized in Israel by John the Baptist after he arrived to give gifts to the Messiah.

Reading the book of Acts, we are taken on a westward march from Jerusalem, Judea, Samaria, Antioch, Asia Minor, and then to Rome. The dominant Roman culture of Jesus' day, as well as the awesome preservation of the ancient city of Rome, leads to a strong emphasis of ancient Rome as the center of Christian history.

However, there is an entire continent that is often grossly overlooked and forgotten in the westward march of the Gospel, though it is still clearly westward: Africa.

After the resurrection of Jesus Christ, Christianity went about completely reshaping the African continent, and in turn the African continent helped shape the future history of Christianity. Sadly, few know the real story of Africa's pivotal role in shaping Christian history, mainly because of the rise of Islam. Christianity was a part of Africa long before the European missionary movements or colonialism of the seventeenth or eighteenth century. It was largely Christian six centuries prior to the terror of Islamic jihad.

> **Christianity was a part of Africa long before the European missionary movements or colonialism of the seventeenth or eighteenth century.**

The earliest translations of the Gospels were African, and the oldest Bible in the world can be found in the Ethiopian language. Latin, the language of Western Christianity, was mastered by the theological fathers of Africa when much of Europe was still using Greek.

Bible commentary and textual criticism were both invented in Africa and were only later adopted by the church in Europe.

The first non-Jewish convert to the Gospel was arguably not a Roman centurion named Cornelius but a eunuch from Ethiopia (though it is argued that the eunuch was an African Jew). Though the eunuch could have been an African Gentile, he was obviously a God-fearer or someone who followed the Jewish teachings when Philip happened upon him (see Acts 8).

The book of Acts does not mention the impact of this eunuch when he traveled back home to Ethiopia, but it can be assumed that his position in the royal court of the queen, which had allowed him to travel to Jerusalem with an official convoy, gave him great influence.

The foreign convert might very well have been the first from the continent of Africa, but if so, he would not be the last.

DISCUSSION QUESTIONS

1. Can you name any important people in church history who were from the African continent?
2. What do you know about them or their influence?
3. Jesus said, "Go and preach the Gospel"; however, before any of the apostles left their country, the Ethiopian eunuch came to them to learn more about the God of Israel. Do you have experiences like this, when people clearly have been searching and are ready to receive Christ before you even start?
4. Many people claim that Christianity is a "white" religion? How could you answer them?

DAY 24

A FAILED MISSIONARY TRAVELS TO AFRICA

"Success is simply a matter of luck. Ask any failure."

—Earl Wilson

T he eunuch did not make the journey back to Africa alone. Though they might not have traveled with the eunuch, some of Jesus' disciples eventually went to Africa to share the Good News. The disciples were first-generation missionaries, and several of them were able to reach the shores of Africa immediately following Jesus' resurrection.

Philip the apostle traveled to the North African port city of Carthage.[8] It was here—tradition holds—that Philip was tortured and killed for leading an official's wife to Christ.

Matthew also traveled to Ethiopia. Like his colleague Philip, Matthew, also known as Levi, was a Galilean who had the distinctive privilege of being one of the first to be called a disciple of Jesus (Mathew 9:9). However, that did not make him very popular with the Jews because Matthew was a tax collector. Tax collectors worked for the Roman government and were hated by the Jews.

Only a few years after Jesus gave the Great Commission, Matthew made his way to Ethiopia, where he became a friend of Candace the Queen, whose eunuch was baptized by Philip.[9] It is believed that when he was preaching in

Ethiopia, he was martyred by being stabbed to death, but not before seeing many members of the royal family decide to follow Christ.[10]

Even still, Bartholomew was also known for his work in Ethiopia.[11] Ethiopia, for reasons unknown, was given a large number of first-generation witnesses. God used His very own disciples to preach His word in Ethiopia, and many people received salvation. Ethiopia was burning with the very first flames of revival, and embers of those flames remain even today.

> Only a very select few people knew the message of Jesus Christ, and most of them were going to Africa!

Think about this: only a very select few people knew the message of Jesus Christ, and most of them were going to Africa!

What was so special about Africa? There were only eleven original disciples left on earth—why send the majority of them to Africa? Whatever the reason, with that many disciples carrying the power of Jesus, it only makes sense that Africa would be set aflame.

When most people write about the history of Christian revival, few, if any, ever think twice about the continent of Africa, but in Africa we can discover the motherload of revival history.

As amazing as the stories of the Ethiopian eunuch, Philip, Matthew, and Bartholomew are, few disciples from the first generation of believers are as famous for taking the Gospel message to Africa as the apostle Mark.

Mark was the most unlikely of characters to be a missionary to Africa because he had failed the first time he went out to spread the Gospel. Mark had the opportunity of a lifetime when he was asked to join the apostle Paul during his first missionary journey. Mark might not have known it then, but he was on a mission trip that would eventually change the known world.

Mark's mother, Mary, was the cousin of Barnabas, the man who looked after him as they traveled together with Paul. However, for reasons that are not completely clear, things became too difficult for Mark while he was traveling as a missionary with Paul.

Maybe Mark was missing his mother's cooking. Maybe Paul's vigorous evangelism of Gentiles without requiring adherence to Jewish law was too different from the teachings that Mark remembered from his mentor, the apostle Peter. Maybe he was tired, scared, or just became frustrated by living in a non-Jewish area. Who really knows?

But one day Mark just up and left and abandoned Paul and Barnabas on the mission field.

Although the demons of Mark's failure during the first mission journey must have tried to haunt him, Mark believed in the mission and was willing to sacrifice his life for the purpose of the kingdom. He looked to the future and left his past failures behind.

With the commission to take the Gospel to the world, the disciples were sent to different areas. The Holy Ghost appeared to Mark and told him to go to the city of Alexandria, to sow the good seed, which is the Word of God. Mark made his way to North Africa, which is where historians say he had been born, and found himself in the metropolis of Alexandria, where he preached the Good News to everyone who was willing to listen. The language of the common people was known as Coptic, and so many people were eventually saved that even to this day the language of the common people is associated with Christians. *Coptic* means "common," and the term is used to refer to Egyptian Christians because so many people became Christian that they were "common."

The Coptic Christians have kept a careful historical record of the one who brought the Gospel message to them, and they hold that when Mark entered into the city, the strap on his sandal broke. Mark took his sandal to a local man named Ananias to have his shoe mended. Mark shared about the one true God with him, and he became the first convert.

It was not long before many others were coming to salvation. Mark preached the Good News, healed the sick, and cast out demons. The miracles surrounding Mark's ministry were touching the hearts of the common people throughout the city.

Soon, the population of Alexandria was turning their hearts away from the ancient Egyptian gods and the Greek gods, and this was not good for those who held power.

Not everyone is excited about revival.

Almost nineteen years after Jesus' death, Mark established a church in Alexandria that was growing by leaps and bounds. On Easter Day in AD 68, Mark was preaching to the church against the local pagan celebrations of the Alexandrian god Serapis. The loyal followers of Serapis attacked the church, captured Mark, tied him up, and dragged him through the streets of the city.

He was killed the next day, but his martyrdom encouraged many others to follow after Jesus Christ in Africa. Even though he was killed, it was not before he was able to write what is arguably the oldest Gospel story in the Bible. After Mark's death, it was not long before the entire country was evangelized and Alexandria became the Egyptian capital of Christianity.

Several hundred years afterward, Muslims invaded Egypt and took over the city of Alexandria, where Mark was buried. Under the nose of the authorities, a couple of clever Venetian merchants were able to steal Mark's body and take the remains to the northern Italian city of Venice. Today hundreds of thousands of people from all over the world travel to Venice to catch a glimpse of a city built around St. Mark's Basilica, built to remember the life of this simple disciple of Jesus Christ.

DISCUSSION QUESTIONS

1. Have you ever failed in ministry?
2. What does the story of Mark teach about ministry failures?
3. The first Christian in Alexandria is believed to be the person who fixed Mark's sandal. Do you have examples of how God used ordinary encounters to bring people to Him?
4. Mark was allegedly killed because he spoke a strong confrontational message against a local idol. What kinds of issues can get Christians into trouble if they speak against them where you live?
5. In such cases do you think Christians should be confrontational or diplomatic?
6. What if the price for speaking up could be your life, as was the case for Mark?

DAY 25

THE HOLY GHOST WELCOMED IN AFRICA

"The early Celtic Christians called the Holy Spirit 'the wild goose.' And the reason why is they knew that you cannot tame him."

—JOHN ELDREDGE

As Christianity grew in acceptance throughout the Roman Empire, the philosophical culture of the Greeks began to make and shape new Christian practices. As Europe's influence of Christianity grew, less emphasis was placed on the gifts of the Spirit and more was placed on the rational aspects of faith.

Speaking in tongues, healing of the sick, casting out demons, prophetic dreams, and the supernatural signs and wonders that followed the first disciples were things of the past and found less of a home in the Greek mind-set of Europe.

That was not the case in the early African church.

An understanding of the spiritual world was deeply entrenched in African thinking, so it was not difficult for the common African believer to accept the supernatural.

Before the European push of institutionalized Christianity, the Holy Ghost caused an African revival that mimicked the day of Pentecost.

In fact, the Christian faith that is sweeping Africa today is not so much the result of European missionaries as it is from the Holy Spirit's return to one of the places where He originally had such a vibrant presence.

The early church in Africa must have made the first-century missionaries excited because it experienced a massive revival movement—one of the first revival movements that we know about. Large numbers of African men and women began to seek after Christ. They were so hungry that many of them began to travel to the desert to get away and be closer to God in their prayers.

Christianity had largely been an urban religion prior to the revivals in Africa, but many Africans had a need to get away from the crowds of people and drink from the wisdom of God in solitude. They were known as the "desert fathers."

Because of the monastic, isolated life that many of these desert fathers led, a deep, guiding philosophy emerged that would one day influence all of Christendom. Things can get a little messy when digging deep into the ancient religions of the world, but if it is true that all men descended from Shem, Ham, and Japheth, then it should be possible to find roots of monotheism in every culture if one is able to trace it back far enough.

Maybe the initial revivals in Africa had something to do with the teachings that came years before Christianity. Many believe that the ancient Egyptians actually paved the way for revival a thousand years before the disciples came to Africa.

An ancient Egyptian pharaoh, Akhenaten, possibly influenced by Joseph and the tribes of Israel, preached monotheism and a God who created all living things. He supported the abandonment of all other gods in the entire Egyptian Empire and attempted to eradicate polytheism. Interestingly, the same pharaoh who introduced the idea of one true God to Egypt also made the Jewish enemies his enemies. He was known to actively engage in aggression toward the Hittites and the Canaanites and imprisoned those who partnered with them.

Even more intriguing, centuries before Jesus died, Egyptians used the symbol of the cross, called an ankh, as a sign to represent eternal life after death.

There are often comparisons made between the ancient Egyptian gods Osiris, Isis, and Horus and the Holy Trinity. While of course those comparisons have their limitations, it is possible that there were enough conceptual similarities that early Christians were able to use them to explain the Gospel and connect with the people.

While the reasons are largely unknown, what is undoubtable is that Christianity spread in this part of Africa with great speed. The rapid acceptance of Jesus as Lord was amazing. The Gospel

> **Out of Africa came some of the world's greatest and most treasured theologians.**

message went straight into the heart of Africans, and out of Africa came some of the world's greatest and most treasured theologians.

One of those great fathers was known as Tertullian. Tertullian was from the North African city of Carthage (in modern-day Tunisia). Carthage was a booming port city and the second most populated city in the west. As the first generation of disciples died off, the next generation began to carry the torch. Tertullian was one of those torchbearers. Tertullian not only produced the earliest Latin Christian writings but is considered to be the founder of Western Christian theology. He is the earliest writer to use the term *Trinity* to refer to the relationship of God.[12]

Trinity is not a word you can find in the Bible, but it is often used by Christians today to explain the relationship between God the Father, God the Son, and God the Holy Spirit. Tertullian laid the framework for the understanding of the Triune God that was eventually adopted at the Council of Nicaea.

Tertullian was in the company of many Africans who became well-known orators in the second and third century.

Because of Tertullian's writing style, passion, reasoning, and use of legal terms when dissecting theology, it is widely believed that he was a litigator. His beautiful Latin influenced Western Europe so strongly that it became the language adopted by the European church, which divided it from the Greek-speaking Eastern Orthodox church.

Tertullian was the first to jump into the murky waters of pneumatology and write extensively about the power of the Holy Spirit. His writings make him one of earliest Pentecostals, along with the disciples.

Tertullian was a champion of Scripture and held off the heretical jackals as they attacked the teachings of Christ with twisted theology. Without uniform, canonized Christian teachings, the early church of the second and third century was vulnerable to heretical teachers who had the charisma to lead. Christian Africans became the first line of defense against those who tried to pervert theology.

Tertullian was angry at the compromises creeping into the church and by the unwillingness of believers to be martyred for the truth. Some church leaders really did not like him because he wrote things that were not easy reading for those who preferred compromise and ambiguity.

Tertullian defended the teachings of Jesus with tenacity and did not give the enemy any shelter to hide. He believed in the power of Scripture alone. According to him, if a thinker does not seek wisdom from the Scriptures, then their destination is not truth. And he believed that skillful heretics who do not believe in the Scriptures but use them for their arguments should not even be allowed to have their argument heard. They only confuse believers out of their ignorance of God's Word, which cannot rightly be understood by those who do not believe. "What has Athens to do with Jerusalem?" he asked, pointing out that the philosophical mind of man cannot possibly fathom the spiritual truths of the Scriptures.[13] Tertullian believed that Scriptures have authority that points to truth and justice but that truth and justice are not universally understood in the polluted, sinful state of man's mind. A defender of Scripture will sacrifice the human will for that which cannot yet be understood, while the defender of self will sacrifice Scripture for temporal benefits that come with eternal damnation.

> **The philosophical mind of man cannot possibly fathom the spiritual truths of the Scriptures.**

To Tertullian, one's life should be spent seeking truth, and the Scriptures were the only thing that mattered in understanding truth. The key to revelation of Truth in Scriptures is faith, and without faith one cannot understand, so why listen to the understanding of Scriptures according to one without faith? The ignorance of those without faith will only give birth to more ignorance.

But how can one know which faith is the right faith? This was a debate in the early church of Africa, which was struggling to hold on to the original message brought to them by Mark and other disciples. Tertullian's answer was to search the Scriptures and give total authority to its teaching.

Like the early disciples, Tertullian was considered to be a rebel. While the church in Europe was slowly silencing the role of women, Tertullian was working together with a sect that became known as the followers of Montanism, which radically employed women as the key prophets. During a time when Romans found it inappropriate for women to carry out roles of authority, Africans were sending out women as the main leaders of the revival movement.

Because of the leadership of Tertullian, the fourth century saw Carthage become the spiritual capital of the Western world.

DISCUSSION QUESTIONS

1. What do you think about the idea there are remnants of God's truth in every religion that can help a people understand the Gospel? Can you give an example from your culture?
2. What do you think about Tertullian's refusal to let nonbelievers use Scripture in their arguments against Christians?
3. Do you agree that only believers led by the Spirit can properly understand Scripture?
4. In your experience, what kind of Bible verses are used against Christians by nonbelievers to justify their arguments? How do you answer them?

DAY 26

CAN GOD ACTUALLY MOVE MOUNTAINS?

———◆———

"Cupcakes are muffins that believed in miracles."

—ANONYMOUS

Today in the southeastern part of the city of Cairo there is an area that tourists do not like to travel to. It is the most disgusting part of the city. It is known as "garbage city" because it is where the refuse from the entire city is taken and dumped. Anyone driving by "garbage city" can smell the putrid stench from far away, even when the windows are up.

The Muslims of Egypt see Christians as unclean and have designated this area, where the majority of Christians live, to be the location for all the waste that comes out of Cairo. The garbage is piled several feet high in front of the homes, and children play all around as their parents search through the garbage to find anything of value to sell at the local market.

Egypt is an Islamic country, but there are roughly thirty thousand Christians living in "garbage city." And the persecution of the Christians in Egypt has intensified in recent years since the rise of the Islamic Brotherhood. However, near "garbage city" there is a secret that is waiting to be told. Up the mountain on the far side of "garbage city" is a historical treasure for those who are willing to make their way through the piles of garbage that block the road.

I wanted to go there after hearing about a church in the mountain that is the largest Christian church in both Africa and the Middle East. It is a sanctuary that seats thousands of believers in a cave carved out in the side of a mountain.

One morning while staying at the Novotel Hotel by the ancient Nile River, I decided to hire a taxi to take me there. The taxi driver was a Muslim born in Cairo. He had been a driver in the city of Cairo all of his adult life, but he had never been to "garbage city."

"You do not want to go there," he said. "It is unclean," he continued as he tried to convince me to go and see a more typical tourist site like the pyramids or the museum. I assured him that was where I wanted to go and that we could find our way together. I pulled up a map on my phone and used it as a guide to get to the mountain.

We drove through the small alleyways of the Christian village in the shadow of garbage heaps more than twenty feet high, but it was worth the trip. The road to the mountain that was hiding in piles of garbage was fascinating.

As we drove up the side of the mountain, we saw a man walking, so I got out of the car and joined him. I asked him if he had heard about the story of the mountain, and he responded by saying that he had and he could give me a tour if I wanted one.

The young man was a believer at the church and spent every day telling people about the story of the mountain so that it will never be forgotten.

The story I discovered in "garbage city" started with a powerful Muslim by the name of Al-Mu'izz who ruled the caliphate in Egypt during the tenth century. Al-Mu'izz often amused himself debating, and nothing pleased him more than participating in religious debates.

He often brought together the local Jews, Christians, and Muslims to debate in his presence. During one such discussion, Pope Abraam, the sixty-second Coptic pope following in the lineage of Saint Mark (Rome's pope follows in the lineage of Saint Peter), was able to get the upper hand during an argument. Instead of convincing anyone to convert, his argument actually made the others upset, and they looked for a way to get revenge.

The pope was then asked by Al-Mu'izz, "Is it true that in your Bible it says that if you have faith as small as a mustard seed you will be able to move mountains?" referring to Matthew 17:20.

The pope answered that it was true.

"Well then, it should be no problem for you to pray to your God and move Mokattam Mountain. Right?" Mokattam Mountain was a prominent mountain in the center of Cairo.

And just like that, a trap was set for the pope and the Christian church in Egypt. Everyone looked at the pope, waiting to see what his response would be.

Before the pope could reply, the caliph commanded the Christians to pray and move the mountain. He gave them three days to make it happen, and if they could not move the mountain, then it would be proof that their religion was false. And if it was proven that the Christians were followers of a false religion, the caliph would order their execution.

The pope gathered all the bishops and priests together and begged them to fast and pray for the entire three days to move the mountain. He knew the lives of all the Christians in Egypt depended on whether Jesus would answer their prayer to move the mountain.

Immediately the pope, all the leaders, and all the Christians were fasting and praying. The pope went into the church to pray, and he did not leave. He sat in the church and cried out to God. Either God would move the mountain, or the caliph would remove their heads.

The pope prayed and prayed until he was no longer able to stay awake. He drifted off to sleep in the middle of his prayers, and while he was asleep, the Virgin Mary came to him and showed him a vision of a one-eyed poor man who was a common leather worker carrying a leather sack of water over his shoulder. The man the pope saw in the vision was named Simeon.

Simeon was the exact opposite of the pope. The pope dressed in elaborate ceremonial robes, but Simeon wore the rags of a beggar. The pope was educated in the theological teachings of the Coptic Christian tradition; Simeon was an uneducated leather worker. The pope carried the responsibility of the clergy, and Simeon carried water to those who were old, sick, or handicapped and unable to fetch water themselves.

When the pope woke up on the third day, he went out to the mountain where he found Simeon carrying water to the sick and lame like he did every morning. The pope recognized him as the man he had seen in his dream. The pope, priests, and all the people came out to the foot of Mokattam Mountain, and the caliph came to meet them. Simeon was there too.

When Simeon spoke, the pope listened intently. Simeon told the pope to lead the believers of Jesus Christ in prayer and to cry out to God in unison, *"Kyrie eleison! Kyrie eleison!"* which means "Lord have mercy! Lord have mercy!"

When the people cried out to God in prayer, the most amazing thing began to happen.

The ground beneath them began to shake violently. The caliph and all the royal members of his court who had come to witness the Christians praying stood in awe as the power of God started to move.

A rumble shook the earth, and the mighty mountain of Mokattam detached from the ground and lifted into the air, and the sun could be seen shining under it as it moved!

Simeon told the pope to make the sign of the cross with his hands and to drop to his knees before God. He and all the Christians followed Simeon's instructions. When they fell to their knees, the mountain violently came crashing down to the ground.

Again, the ground shook!

The Christians cried out to God and stood up, and again the mountain raised off of the ground and began to move again. When the Christians dropped back to their knees, the mountain again came crashing back down to earth.

This happened three times, and the awesome display of God was in plain view of everyone there.

The mountain literally moved several kilometers to where it is today, which is a few kilometers outside of Cairo.

"God is great!" came a shout from the caliph. When the crowd turned to look at him, he was physically shaking. Nothing else was needed. No further debate could be had. The discussion was over. The power of God had moved the mountain, and the entire crowd could not deny what they had just seen.

The caliph received Jesus Christ as his Lord and Savior and was taken to St. Mercurius Church, where he was baptized at a location that is known to this day as Maamoudiat Al-Sultan, which means the baptistry of the sultan.

To remember this day forever, it was declared that three days of prayer and fasting were to be held every year.

How are the Christians in Cairo able to endure abuse and neglect day after day? What gives them the strength to keep going?

Their homes are in the valley of the mountain that declares their amazing history and God's mighty work. Today the mountain that casts its shadow over the Christians living in "garbage city" is a reminder of the living God who provides. The church built into the side of the mountain reminds all of the actions of one simple believer of Jesus.

The testimony of God's miraculous power sits in one of the strongholds of Islam to this very day.

DISCUSSION QUESTIONS

1. When you read the story of the moving mountain, what were your thoughts? Do you believe God can work in this way?
2. What would be some arguments for and against believing this story?
3. If you had been a believer at the scene of the challenge in Egypt, do you think you would have continued to believe in God if nothing had happened?
4. Can you think of passages in the Bible where the power of God was challenged? What happened?
5. Have you ever experienced a direct challenge to your faith like this pope did? How did you handle it?

DAY 27

THE BASTARDIZATION OF A CONTINENT

"Shame may restrain what the law does not prohibit."

—LUCIUS ANNAEUS SENECA

Africa, like the rest of the world at the time of the disciples, was a dangerous place for the new believers. Christians were often blamed for calamities and natural disasters. The mob mentality in Africa exploded with anger against Christians during times of hardship, and that led to some of the most brutal Christian deaths in recorded history.

A person familiar with Arab Africa today would not recognize the North Africa of the second and third century as the Gospel swept westward. The Arabic regions of North Africa were populated with Nubians and Cushites as well as Greeks. The seaports were bustling with people from around the world, and the port cities were world-class metropolitans. The traders who came into the port cities of the African continent did not just peddle their goods, they also peddled their ideas. The wealth of knowledge that lingered in these cities and danced in the air led to deep thinkers who pondered the great questions of life.

These questions led to persecuted Christian theologians dissecting the nature of Christ and developing ideas that still shape the thinking of biblical teaching today. African preachers began to contemplate the dichotomy of the body and soul, noting how it was the soul and not the body that reflected the image of the Divine. It was the flesh, not the soul, that aged, decayed, died, and essentially blocked the image of the Father. They pondered the complex idea of Jesus being fully man as well as being fully God. If Jesus were not fully man, then the temptation would have been pointless; and if He were not fully God, then the crucifixion would have been worthless.

The early African preachers found truth in the words of John and argued that Jesus was God's only Son and that He was, in fact, Logos—the Word of God—and was eternal as the Father is eternal.

None of the African voices played a more prominent role in the shaping of early Christian thought than Saint Augustine of Hippo. Saint Augustine was able to communicate to the hearts of the people with the voice of a sinner, and his struggle with sin connected many people to the ideas of grace and faith.

He believed and taught that salvation cannot be earned but is free in Christ for those who will accept it. Augustine helped set Christianity apart from the mainstream religions in Africa at that time by teaching that man is completely unable to save himself from eternal damnation. It is only because of God's active role in saving man that there is salvation. Grace is not a rope to be tossed down for man to grab on to and be pulled up out of the pits of hell, but instead it is Jesus descending and pulling man up out of damnation. Man is helpless to even hang on to the rope of salvation if it were not for Christ. Man is free to accept grace only because God played an active role in saving man from his sin. Man is even too weak to be pulled out without being carried by Jesus. Augustine gave birth to a new system of thinking that would later be extremely influential in the Western church. It was this new thinking that influenced medieval philosophy and theology.

> **Man is free to accept grace only because God played an active role in saving man from his sin.**

Outside of the Bible, Augustine's writings are said to be the single most resourced document used during the Reformation and have "been regarded as the most consequential patristic source for the Reformation."[14]

Augustine's influence spread through North Africa and southern Europe. By the fifth century, many African countries were seeing the fruits of revival, and the African continent had several cities, like Carthage and Alexandria, that acted as centers of Christianity for the rest of the world.

Some countries, like the Nubian kingdom of Makuria in modern-day Sudan, reached a "golden age" during the days of their Christian identity, and saw relative peace, wealth, and stability for several hundred years. Most people have never heard of the achievements of this great kingdom, as they were almost completely erased from the annals of history after the Muslim invasion.

Most Christians who have visited North Africa or witnessed the violence in Egypt during the Arab Spring could not imagine that the world's best biblical institutions had once thrived there.

By the early seventh century, North Africa was almost totally Christian, so the question arises: What happened?

There was a wind blowing from the east that was about to change everything in Africa. That wind started in the Middle East. On the Arab Peninsula, a military leader by the name of Muhammad started a new religion, and his disciples were helping him establish a new kingdom based on his teachings.

What took Christians a few centuries to accomplish through sacrifice and martyrdom, the followers of Muhammad were able to do in a matter of decades through military conquest. Africa was key to Muhammad, because Christians in Ethiopia provided a place of refuge during persecution in Mecca. When Muhammad was kicked out of Mecca and was pursued by the angry polytheists who were losing money, Muhammad's followers ran to Ethiopia, where the Christians protected him.[15] Little did the African Christians know that the kindness they paid to Muhammad would one day be repaid with their death.

Africa was one of the first places, outside of Arabia, that Islam spread to. Muslim armies, believing that they had a command from Allah to convert the entire world to Islam or destroy them, set their sights on Africa and attacked.

The armies of Islam were swift and powerful. Only a hundred years after the first battle with Muhammad, Islamic armies controlled 50 percent of the world's Christian population, much of which was in Africa.

In the year 643, Alexandria fell, and by 698, the Muslim armies secured their military and political dominance in all of North Africa and around the Mediterranean. Much of Africa's Christendom was lost to the sword of Islam.

> When Muhammad, the Prophet of Islam, died in 632 the new religion had already gathered a number of impressive victories on the battlefield. The armies of Islam quickly and easily conquered the Arabian peninsula before moving on to take the homelands of their various neighbors. Marching out of Arabia in 639 they entered non-Arab Egypt; 43 years later they reached the shores of the Atlantic; and in 711 they invaded Spain. In just 70 years they had subdued the whole of North Africa, instituting a new order. This conquest, from the Nile to the Atlantic, was more complete than anything achieved by previous invaders and the changes it wrought proved permanent.[16]

The history of Islam in Africa and the accounts of how the religion was spread by ruthless conquering are not matters up for debate. The only matter of disagreement is the degree of brutality.

It is also a fact that even though Africa was once a center of Christianity, within only a few decades of Islamic jihad, Christianity had virtually disappeared. No matter how the history is whitewashed by scholars, Islam left a bloody trail in the wake of its violent conquest.

The rich history of early Christianity in Africa so thoroughly disappeared that many people today think that Islam is actually a part of African indigenous culture, when in fact Islam destroyed much of African history and culture.

It was estimated in 2002 that Muslims now constitute 45 percent of the population of Africa.

The spread of Christian revival was stopped in Africa by Islam, but it wasn't stopped completely. It continued westward.

DISCUSSION QUESTIONS

1. How do you theologically interpret the Islamic conquest of North Africa?
2. If you had stood with ancient African believers by the ruins of the great Christian institutes after they were destroyed by Islamic armies and they wondered how that could have happened, what would you have said to them?
3. Do you think Christianity can be protected by strong armies, or are we at the core a defenseless religion, whose power is in martyrdom? Why do you think so?

DAY 28

THE AFRICAN MIRROR

———◆———

"When God desires to destroy a thing,
he entrusts its destruction to the thing itself."

—VICTOR HUGO

At first glance, the history of Christianity seems to be marked by significant events that distinguish one age from the next. To the historian, ancient Christianity is a jewel to be found in the pages of a book. To the archaeologist, Christianity is dug up from the ground. To the sociologist, it is merely one religion that emerged from a wide variety of other religions in society.

To the Christian, however, history is a mirror of past faces reflecting our own stories. And it is a history that is unbroken. The persecution of Jesus and the disciples never stopped; it lives on in us—His followers. And those who believe continue to pass their faith on to the next generation. In an odd way, the disciples, traitors, villains, and idiots of the New Testament never really died. Their parts are repeatedly played again and again, just on different stages.

One voice yells, "Hey! Quick! Look over there! Across the sea in China, something is happening in the church that has never happened before." And then before you get a chance to dive into the stories of the Chinese church revival and see what it is all about, you are quickly distracted by another voice that shouts, "Hey! Over there! The church of Africa is experiencing something that is truly unique."

Maybe these are not really new events but are old events happening to new people. Maybe the great biblical philosopher was right when he wrote:

> One generation passeth away, and another generation cometh: but the earth abideth for ever. The sun also ariseth, and the sun goeth down, and hasteth to his place where he arose. The wind goeth toward the south, and turneth about unto the north; it whirleth about continually, and the wind returneth again according to his circuits. All the rivers run into the sea; yet the sea is not full; unto the place from whence the rivers come, thither they return again. All things are full of labour; man cannot utter it: the eye is not satisfied with seeing, nor the ear filled with hearing. The thing that hath been, it is that which shall be; and that which is done is that which shall be done: and there is no new thing under the sun. (Ecclesiastes 1:4–9)

If we are hungry to see a true revival in our lifetime, wouldn't it be of benefit for us to know what prompted it in the past and why it ended? If we are eager to see revival continue, then would there be any advantage to knowing how it had started before and why it stopped?

Learning the history of revival in Africa is not a scholastic endeavor but a personal one that allows us to look into the mirror and see our future. The Christian voices of Africa's ancient Christian revivals are crying out to share the miraculous stories of fire, hope, and healing. They are also sounding the alarm of dangers and pitfalls.

> **If we are hungry to see a true revival in our lifetime, wouldn't it be of benefit for us to know what prompted it in the past and why it ended?**

When I travel the African plains looking for relics of past revivals, surprisingly I do not see the face of a black tribal stranger staring back at me, but instead I see my own reflection. I see the triumphs, tribulations, and trials of my present society.

They learned what I long to know before I am forced to learn it the hard way. They wrote what I long to read before I am sentenced to live it. They spoke the words I long to hear before I am forced to live through the pain of experience.

If education is only a collection of our own experiences, then it is highly unlikely that I will live long enough to have enough knowledge to fill even one book. But if I can sit at the feet of those who have gone before me and learn the lessons they lived, then maybe I can build on their wisdom instead of merely repeating it.

I do not want to learn what has already been learned by someone else just for the sake of learning. I want to learn what has already been learned so that I can move on to learn what has yet to be learned.

I don't want recycled epiphanies and round-robin revelations. I want to peer into the looking glass of the early African church and see what it has to say to me. I want to hear the good, the bad, and the ugly and then build on that to go further, faster, and deeper than ever before.

For me, that African reflection started in the faces of many young SPLA soldiers who were fighting for their independence in Sudan prior to South Sudan becoming a nation of its own. I was traveling in the Nuba Mountains with a group from the UK called Flame International when a local military commander from the Sudan People's Liberation Army (SPLA) asked us to come and speak at a secret base camp of troops that had been fighting the Islamic forces of Omar al-Bashir.

We drove for about two days, crossed into the northern part of Sudan illegally, and slept out in the open night air, until finally we found ourselves in a small forest that wasn't located on any map.

As we drove through the forest, I noticed that we no longer had any real road to follow. Suddenly, our vehicle started to slow down as armed SPLA soldiers appeared out of nowhere from behind the trees.

They led us to a secret base camp. I didn't know what to expect next. Our vehicle parked beside a shaded area while the commander marched hundreds of battle-weary soldiers out into the noonday sun so we could share with them.

As I looked into their eyes, I felt at a loss for words. I had been in the military, but these guys had experienced horrible battle conditions beyond what I had known. They were combat hardened, and some of them had a thousand-yard stare in their eyes.

They were not just exhausted from battle. They were beleaguered by the atrocities that were being inflicted on their people from the north. Sudan was a Muslim nation. Many of the SPLA fighters were Muslim. Why would the Muslims in the north attack the Muslims in the south? Weren't they all brothers in Islam?

The short answer was no. They were not brothers.

The black Africans in Sudan were in fact reliving what their ancestors had been experiencing since the dawn of Islam. When I looked at the freedom fighters of the SPLA, I was looking into the reflection of an age-old conflict where Islam had reared its racist head, revealing the real serpent behind the mask.

As my English colleagues and I ministered under the hot sun of Sudan, it was easy for us to feel sorry for the people in their impoverished war-torn state, but we would be wrong to assume that it had always been this way.

> **Early revival swept through the land of Sudan with such hot flames that the entire nation became one of the strongest lights of Christianity in the entire world.**

The Sudanese people have a long heritage of great accomplishments. Their kings and kingdoms go back thousands of years. There are more great and majestic pyramids in Sudan than in Egypt.

Early revival swept through the land of Sudan with such hot flames that the entire nation became one of the strongest lights of Christianity in the entire world, and its glory lasted for a thousand years.

Muslim jihadists invaded Egypt and began to systematically kill Christians, destroy churches, and drive out the Jewish people. Soon they focused on Sudan to the south, which was a collection of Christian king-doms at that time. The brave Christian Nubian soldiers were able to repel the attack, but eventually they had to agree to a treaty known as the Baqt that forced the Africans to, among other things, maintain a mosque for Muslim visitors and send an annual tribute of 360 slaves.

Slowly, through jihad, slavery, and genocide, the Muslims were able to start the Islamization of Sudan. Not only was the Christian heritage of the Nubian people erased from history, but their language was as well when all were forced to speak the Arabic language of the Koran.

Once the Islamization was complete, Arabization began to take place and has been happening ever since.

The once-great kingdoms of Africa that were built on revival were decimated by the Islamic armies, and the characteristics of the state of those countries before and after could not be more different. As we look into the African mirror, staring back at us are the countless hearts of an entire continent that once had willingly surrendered to the one and true living God. Following the revivals was a golden age of peace, education, and widespread prosperity, but those resources were drained when the African countries were raped. The marauding armies of Islam did not, could not, come in peace. Their teachings were too wanting compared to the truth that the Africans already had. Out of weakness and greed, the Muslims killed. They enslaved others in the same way that they had been enslaved, and pain gave birth to pain.

As I stood in front of the young men in that blazing afternoon sun of Sudan in 2010, I knew that the only thing that could bring them out of the pain and poverty of their current situation was the very thing that had been stolen from them so many years ago: revival.

Are there warm embers buried under the ashes of the previous fire that can be ignited again?

DISCUSSION QUESTIONS

1. If your nation were faced with a military campaign similar to the one that occurred in ancient North Africa when Islam was enforced, what do you think would happen to the church in your country? Why do you think so?
2. Why do you think persecution breeds revival in some countries but the armies of Muhammad were able to wipe out Christianity in others?
3. What force do you see as the biggest threat to the church in your country?

DAY 29

THE LOST TRIBES OF ISRAEL IN AFRICA

———————◆———————

"My favorite writers are all Jews–David, Solomon, Matthew,
Mark–well, you get the picture."

—Zig Ziglar

Little is known about early Christianity in much of Africa because of
Islamization. Eurocentric scholars dismiss or overlook the contributions
of Africans in the early church, not necessarily because of racism or homoge-
nization of the Gospel, but because the records were destroyed when former
Christian African nations were invaded.

How many books are available today about the underground churches
in North Korea? Even today, during the information age, we still have little
knowledge about the real situation there. Communism is to Christianity in
North Korea as Islam is to the continent of Africa.

We will never know what Christian treasures were lost in Africa due to
the invasion of Islamic armies. The churches that were destroyed, the books
that were burned, and the people who were slaughtered or forced into conversion and slavery can never be replaced. Their voices and their mark on
history have been completely erased on this side of history.

What happened in Christian Africa after the invasion of Muslim armies
is not too different from what took place long ago when the ten lost tribes
of ancient Israel were shackled and chained and dragged to the land of the

Neo-Assyrian Empire. Their history was destroyed, their culture was crushed, and their families were divided up and sold at auctions.

It seems, though, that some stories come full circle in Africa, because recent DNA tests have shown that the ten lost tribes of Israel might be partly found in Africa. Genetic tests have revealed that many tribesmen, like the Lemba tribe in southern Africa, have Jewish origins.

The Lemba tribe has seventy to eighty thousand members who live in central Zimbabwe and have customs and practices that are very Judaic in nature. They do not eat foods that are not considered to be kosher, wear yarmulke-like covers on their heads, discourage marriage to non-Lemba tribesmen, celebrate a holy day once a week, use the Star of David as their symbol, and even speak a mixture of Arabic and Hebrew.

According to recent DNA tests, the Lemba tribesmen are directly related to the Jewish priestly line, but they are not looking to be reunited with their Jewish brothers in Israel any time soon. They have stated publicly that they are proud to be Christian by religion, Jewish by culture, and African by location.

> **If early Islamic history has taught us anything, it is that neither Jews nor Christians have ever been safe from Islamic conquest.**

If early Islamic history has taught us anything, it is that neither Jews nor Christians have ever been safe from Islamic conquest. The Africans were no different, but God prepared a way to preserve a remnant from Islamic colonization.

In September 2017, I found myself scaling a thirty-foot rock face on a questionable handmade rope made of cattle skin. I was making my way to a remote Christian monastery called Debre Damo in the vast mountain range of northern Ethiopia.

A monk at the top of the cliff carefully monitored my ascent and steadied the rope for me while women from the village stayed at the bottom and prayed. Women and female animals are not allowed on the mountain. It has been a continuous consecrated training place for male monks and priests for more than 1,400 years.

Ever since the remote monastery was started in the sixth century, it has not been accessible in any other way than scaling the mountainsides by rope. The monastery would prove to be a safe haven from the attacks of Muslims several hundred years later.

The high mountain tops with incredibly steep cliffs found between Ethiopia and Eritrea provided a natural sanctuary for Christians escaping Islamic forces that swept through the rest of the continent. In that place they were able to preserve the ancient writings, practices, and teachings of the Ethiopian Orthodox Church, while others in the remaining parts of Africa are gone forever.

The monastery at Debre Damo was not the only place that provided a safe haven for Christians; just a little south in the mountains of Lalibela are nine-hundred-year-old monolithic churches that have been carved into rock. These churches were built down into the ground so they were not visible from the valleys. They are connected by a series of tunnels so Christians could easily escape with their families to another area if Muslims arrived in a surprise attack.

Saint Lalibela, an Ethiopian king during the twelfth century, visited Jerusalem but knew that it was not possible for other Christians to do so, so with the help of angels, he prepared a secret place in the mountains for Christians from all over Ethiopia to come together where they would be safe.

"We needed these churches," one local told me. "If Christians left Africa to visit the holy city of Jerusalem to be closer to our Lord, they would be killed by the Muslims. If they stayed and attended a visible church in a typical building, they would be killed by the Muslims. If they tried to bring people to worship together in their home, they would be killed by the Muslims, so we looked to the mountains."

The churches still stand strong today, and eleven of them have been identified as UNESCO World Heritage sites.

"Jerusalem is important to us because of our Jewish heritage," one believer told me as we climbed the mountain to see the churches together. "We could not go to Jerusalem, so King Lalibela brought Jerusalem to us."

Some historians claim that the teachings of the lost tribes in Ethiopia and

King Solomon's descendants in Africa are nothing but myth, mainly used to propagate colonialism; however, the more that is learned about the different tribes of Africa, the clearer it is that they are related to the ancient tribes of Israel.

Historians would do well to remember that the connection between the Jewish people and Africa did not begin with King Solomon or the invasion of Israel by the Assyrian army. It started long before that when Abraham and Sarah fled the great famine in Canaan and went to Egypt.

Africa has been the home of many Jews throughout time. From the destruction of the first temple to the boyhood home of Jesus, Africa has offered a refuge to the Jewish people, and in many ways the Africans are now discovering their real heritage.

The Jewish and Christian history of Africa is rich and profound. There are so many rivers of truth to follow in Africa, whether it is the earth-shaking writings and testimonies of the early church fathers or the Jewish heritage of the followers of Jehovah. History runs deep, even if it has been largely forgotten.

> **The Jewish and Christian history of Africa is rich and profound.**

The invasions and attacks over the last 1,500 years seem to have removed many memories of God in Africa, but God has not forgotten His people. It seems that revival springs are not only in African history but are in Africa's present, and in Africa's future.

Africa is currently the scene of Christianity's greatest growth. In the last one hundred years it has become the most populous Christian continent, with more Christians living there today than in North America. The Pew Forum predicts that sub-Saharan Africa will have 1.1 billion Christians by the year 2050.

As Christianity grows in Africa and more and more people realize that their roots are not Islamic, the influence they will have on the rest of the world will increase. If the revivals in Africa continue to grow, their impact on Western nations might be very similar to that of the first-century church.

In the seventh century, Christianity retreated with the advance of Islam, but the spectacular changes that were made around the world by African believers in those first seven hundred years cannot be erased. African Christianity was an agent of change to prepare Europe for its role in the continuing flames of revival.

DISCUSSION QUESTIONS

1. What is your image of the African church today?
2. Do you see any ways in which the church in Africa could once more become a great influence in global Christianity? Do you know examples of how this is already happening?
3. What do you think about the connections between Africa and the Jewish people?
4. Do you think these are spiritually significant for the church today? Why or why not?

PART 4

ROME AND THE END OF THE WORLD

DAY 30

WOMEN RULE

———◆———

"I wonder why it is, that young men are always cautioned
against bad girls. Anyone can handle a bad girl. It's the
good girls men should be warned against."

—DAVID NIVEN

While chasing the history of revival, there was one city I could not
wait to travel to—Rome. Outside of Jerusalem, no other city in
the world exudes more meaning for Christians than the city of Rome. Few
cities have fueled more revivals than this one. An entire book of the New
Testament is dedicated to the citizens of Rome. Paul's ongoing promises to
travel to the city can be found throughout his writings, so it is obvious that,
like me, he could not wait to go there.

Since the vision of the man from Macedonia, the idea of going to Rome
seemed to completely occupy his mind and spirit, and it is easy to see why.
Even today, traveling around Rome as a tourist in the twenty-first century
is not just a surreal experience of historical magnitude, it is a spiritual one:
Vatican City, the Sistine Chapel, the Colosseum, a place of early Christian
torture, the Mamertine Prison, and the vast labyrinth of catacombs that
hosted the early underground church.

Long before American churches experienced revival, Martin Luther's
"Ninety-Five Theses" were nailed to the door of the castle's church in
Wittenberg, crusaders marched off to war to fight off Muslim attacks on
Christian cities, or there was a monastic movement on the Scottish isles,
there was Rome.

It was not just Paul, Peter, and the early Christians who had a fascination with the city of Rome; the entire world has been fascinated with it at one time or another. Almost every language is painted with expressions like "all roads lead to Rome" and "when in Rome do as the Romans." From the legal and social systems that gave life to republics around the world, to the invention of newspapers, to the earliest forms of mass entertainment and competition, and even the first practices of a three-course meal all come from the global influence of the city of Rome.

Perhaps there has never been another city in the world that has had as much influence on the rest of the world as Rome. The city has exercised a spell over the minds of men since the early days of the Caesars. The vast dominion of this city stretched from the raging shores of the Atlantic to the borders of Parthia and from the English countryside to the scorching deserts of Africa. The men and women whom the Romans ruled over were even more diverse than the lands where they lived. They spoke an array of tribal languages and practiced religions that few had ever heard of or seen.

> **Perhaps there has never been another city in the world that has had as much influence on the rest of the world as Rome.**

The fact that the entire New Testament was written and shared in Greek regardless of the mother tongue of the authors is attributed to the incredible influence of the city of Rome. Even the very words *romance* and *romantic* feed the imagination with grand images of the ancient city.

But the great revivals that came to Rome would need to be paid for with blood and sacrifice. The death and suffering that took place in the first years after Christ are well recorded and widely written about. The earliest and most famous of those who recorded what happened in Rome were the apostles Luke, Peter, and of course Paul. The apostle John, the one "whom Jesus loved" (John 13:23), prophesied about the church in Rome in the book of Revelation.

The persecution in Rome is a well-worn theme. At first glance it might seem that there is not much here to learn about revival that has not already been taught, but a closer look reveals that there is always something new that can be learned to fire up our spirit regarding the revival that captured the city of Rome.

The first thing to realize about Rome during the days of the apostles is that over half of the population was slaves. Only a small number of Roman citizens were property owners. The numerous expeditions by the powerful Roman military brought back slaves from all over the known world. Often the captured slaves, from different races, were tradesmen and had extensive knowledge in many different subjects.

Roman slaves were different from most other slaves because they were able to gain their freedom and continue with employment in their trade. In this way, slaves in Rome who heard about Christ could uniquely connect with the idea of spiritual freedom.

When small gatherings came together in homes in Rome to listen to the teachings of the apostle Paul, his words regarding slavery and freedom painted vivid pictures that danced in the listeners' imaginations. To the early church members in Rome, slavery was not just an idea or concept. It was their life.

The ears of all the slaves must have perked up when Paul wrote, "For in Christ Jesus you are all sons of God, through faith. For as many of you as were baptized into Christ have put on Christ. There is neither Jew nor Greek, there is neither slave nor free, there is no male and female, for you are all one in Christ Jesus. And if you are Christ's, then you are Abraham's offspring, heirs according to promise" (Galatians 3:26–29 ESV).

Although the Greek culture of Rome was greatly influenced by logic, reason, and philosophy, many of the slaves were imported from the most mysterious regions of the world where religion was primarily based on spiritual power and experiences. This type of imported citizenry paved the way for a new religion like Christianity.

Whatever the situation in Rome was, there is one thing that is certain: the Christian message took strong root and gave way to massive revival. The revival that took place in Rome was not the kind of tent meetings that the minds of today's Christians might conjure up, but instead it was a series of conversions that took place in homes throughout the city. Christianity spread like wildfire. The number of homes that held weekly meetings was exploding, and the idea of religious clergy was being transformed.

Even though some of the early apostles to bring the Gospel to Rome were men, like Peter and Paul, the people who hosted the meetings, sent out the invitations, and facilitated the early church were women. Women, who were often the managers of their own home, were among the first to revolutionize the city of Rome

> **Women were absolutely key from the very beginning during the birth, ministry, death, and resurrection of Jesus.**

for the Gospel of Jesus Christ. Many of the people Paul mentioned in his letter to the Romans by name were women (Romans 16).

It is impossible to talk about revival in Europe without discussing the role of women in revival. One of the best-kept secrets in history is the prominent role women played in the early church, and because of this, the entire movement was dismissed. A well-known philosopher named Celsus was one of the first authors in history to write an anti-Christian book called *True Word*. He wrote that Christianity only attracts "the silly and the mean and the stupid, with women and children."

But the very people Rome disregarded as silly and "stupid," God used to shame the wise (1 Corinthians 1:27).

Could women be the key to revival in Rome? If so, this would have been the first major religion that spread through women.

It is no surprise that women were used so powerfully in the first revival to hit the most powerful city in the world.

Even though it was a man in Paul's vision that led him to Macedonia, it was a woman who became Paul's first European convert on European soil. This is in direct reflection of what the authors of the New Testament tell us about Jesus. Women were absolutely key from the very beginning during the birth, ministry, death, and resurrection of Jesus.

Against all logic and legal traditions, women alone were the first testimonial witnesses of the resurrection of Jesus. Matthew, Mark, and Luke all record that a significant group of women had witnessed seeing Jesus when all the men were suspiciously absent. Though their testimony could not have been used in the court of law, they were considered to be more than worthy to the first believers in the church.

The church that was built in Rome considered Mary Magdalene an "apostle to the apostles" because of her ministry to the followers of Christ. The women who popped up as leaders among the house churches in Rome included Priscilla, Chloe, Lydia, Apphia, Nympha, and possibly the "elect lady" of the second book of John.

Because women were not viewed as individuals who were capable of much influence, the Romans did not pay particular attention to them and what they were doing in their simple little homes. In their minds, for things to be official and to grow, they need to have official buildings, proclamations, pillars in front of a grand structure, and recognition by an entity that had been elected or selected by a body of robed men.

These women might not have seen themselves or what they were doing as the foundation of a revolution that would one day topple the world's most powerful nation, but that is exactly what they were. They were in fact the matrons who were the center of life for their communities. They were the mothers, daughters, and wives who watched their children go to school, bargained in the marketplace, or cooked the food that gave nutrition for life. They were the silent gears that made the world turn, and what they did provided a light to the millions of women who would follow after them in the generations to come.

The role of women in the first revival in Europe provokes a very interesting question that goes to the heart of the history of revival. The record of their roles, both in the Bible and in history, begs the question of whether women are only an ingredient of early revival or whether they are an essential element.

Whatever the answer might be, what they did changed the city of Rome forever.

DISCUSSION QUESTIONS

1. The Christian women in Rome played an important part in stimulating and facilitating the church's growth. Do you know of other examples in church and mission history where this was the case?
2. What does that tell you about God's view of women's roles?
3. How do you feel about the part women play in your church?
4. Do you think there is a good and biblical balance between what men do and what women do? Why or why not?
5. If you are a woman, how do the stories of your early Christian sisters make you feel?
6. Do you think God could use you in a revival? Why or why not?

DAY 31

THE LONELY REVIVAL

"I was once walking through the forest alone. A tree fell right in front of me, and I didn't hear a thing."

—STEVEN WRIGHT

A battle was brewing for the hearts and minds of the Roman citizenry between good and evil. There was about to be a showdown, the likes of which had never been seen before.

Have you ever felt that everyone around you was against you for one reason or another or felt that nothing you did ever turned out right? Well, welcome to Paul's world. That is exactly what he was going through. Life on the mission field was getting difficult, and it was about to heat up. Paul wrote about how he felt as he was standing trial: "At my first answer no man stood with me, but all men forsook me: I pray God that it may not be laid to their charge. Notwithstanding the Lord stood with me, and strengthened me" (2 Timothy 4:16–17).

If we follow Luke's account of the story, we see that Paul was referring to his first trial before the emperor. The charges against him were treason, heresy, and sacrilege. His defense consisted of an impossible legal strategy of going before the Caesar of Rome and claiming innocence. And Paul was not coming before just any emperor. He would be standing before Nero himself, and he was standing alone.

According to Paul's own handwriting, all of his "friends" forsook him. No one offered support to him. It's hard to blame them, since anyone associated with him could easily meet the same fate. However, it is in those moments that we find out who our real friends are.

In Rome it was customary to allow an accused person to have an advocate to plead on his behalf before the courts. If the advocate was able to display an impassioned argument with eloquence and tears, they could often mitigate the severity of punishment, but when Paul was summoned before Nero, no one came to act as his advocate. No friend was found in the crowd to even attend as a witness.

Intense feelings of loneliness seem to be an element that is not often associated with revival, but so far in the study we have seen it several times, starting with Jesus. It brings to mind when Jesus asked His friends to stay up with Him as He prayed, and they slept instead. Or when Jesus stood before His accusers alone and even Peter, who had promised never to deny Him, actually ended up denying Him three times. His feelings of loneliness and abandonment were further recorded in detail in Matthew 27:46, when He cried out, "Eli, Eli, lama sabachthani? that is to say, My God, my God, why hast thou forsaken me?"

The final emotion we see from Christ was loneliness. It was the same emotion the disciples experienced as they hobbled back to Jerusalem after Jesus left them on the Mount of Olives. It was this isolated and lonely view we get of Stephen as he was stoned to death by an angry mob.

> **The final emotion we see from Christ was loneliness.**

The images that are formed when someone mentions revival are the exact opposite of loneliness. Revivals are associated with crowds of people. When we pray for revival, we pray for the masses to come to Christ. The last thing to enter our mind is loneliness or isolation.

Tragically, against our own desires, as we chase revival we find this element of desolation when the carrier of God's Word and purpose experiences bouts of abandonment. This is what Paul was experiencing in Rome.

When the fires of revival burn hotter, the ring of friends grows smaller, and things were heating up with Nero. Things became so hot, in fact, that the name of Nero is still associated with fire even two thousand years later.

Paul stood trial before Nero, and how striking was the contrast! The most powerful earthly monarch came face-to-face with a man following the true King of kings. One represented the most powerful nation on earth and one represented the Creator of earth. One had wealth, power, might . . . and friends. The other was poor, homeless, and without a single friend to be seen.

Paul stood in a court to be judged by man, and as ruler there was no one who could judge Caesar. Caesar wore a crown made of the finest metals on earth, and Paul was adorned in nothing more than rags.

Caesar lived a life of self-indulgence; Paul led a life of self-denial.

As different as they were, the king and the pauper, they were also very similar. Both were passionate about their beliefs to the point of self-destruction. Both men appeared to have sold their souls to a higher power and were acting out parts in a play that were written before the beginning of time. Both men were extremists and would be remembered in history forever.

In the eyes of many, Nero was a leader who had lost his mind, but to many others so too was Paul.

The two men were so very different. The two men were so very similar.

Without friends, without money, without a home in Rome, the weathered prisoner stood before Nero. He had been imprisoned, beaten, shipwrecked, and abandoned. He was no doubt tired, and this trial was an exercise in futility. In Nero's court, Paul would never be deemed innocent. Nero presumed his guilt long before there was even a trial. Paul could never make an argument strong enough to persuade Nero to allow him to continue sharing about Christ, and Nero could never make a threat cruel enough to dissuade Paul to stop evangelizing. It was a true Mexican standoff. A classic game of chicken where two cars are driving toward one another at full speed and neither one will change lanes to avoid the other.

The history of Nero speaks volumes about his inability to give Christians a fair trial. He had Christians thrown to the dogs to be eaten alive. He nailed them to crosses in an attempt at mockery. At night, when dusk fell in the royal garden and it was hard to see, Nero lit up the evening sky with the burning flesh of Christians strapped to torches.

His passion and hatred for Christians bubbled over with such intensity that Nero was regarded less as a historical emperor and more as an eschato-logical one. Christian Jews began to see the manifestation of ancient proph-esies from Isaiah and Jeremiah embodied in Nero.

To some, he was the anti-Christ himself and would be the one to usher in the apocalypse. The attributes he had in common with the anti-Christ included the fact that the numerical value of his name, Nero, added up to 666, the number of the beast from Revelation (13:18).

When I traveled to Rome I walked among the ancient rubble that scat-tered the ground in an area not far from the Colosseum. I had a tourist map in my hand, but it was a simple map and did not have the place marked that interested me. I made my way alone and away from the crowds as I searched for the Mamertine Prison. I had my two young sons with me when I finally found the prison, which had a staircase that led us down into the dark cham-ber where the original prison was. The stairs had been installed after the time Paul had been there. The area above the prison has gone through many changes over the centuries, but the underground prison remains the same.

Even though two thousand years have gone by, the prison is still the damp, dark, and lonely place Paul would have known. It smelled of mildew and rot. I wanted to get a picture with my two children in the pit, but there was not enough light. We used the flash on the camera, but it made us all squint because of the contrast with the darkness.

Paul would not have had a spiral staircase leading him down into the pit; rather, he would have been dropped down into it from a hole in the upper floor. In that ancient cell, I was able to get a small idea of the solitude and loneliness Paul must have felt in those final hours before he was marched off to his death.

He was in some ways a willing prisoner. No one had forced him to be in Rome; in fact, he had requested it (Acts 25:11–12), and his request was supernaturally confirmed to be God's will by an angel (Acts 27:24). He was fulfilling the very words he wrote to the Galatians, "I am crucified with Christ: nevertheless I live; yet not I, but Christ liveth in me" (2:20).

The isolated, solitary cell did not offer comfort or forgiveness. Today it is marked only by a mantel that carries the symbol of an upside-down cross. It stands in the cell as a motif of defiance to remember the other prisoner who sat in the same cell for the same reason—the apostle Peter. Both men tasted the sour wine of loneliness and abandonment that inevitably comes before the breakthrough of a great revival.

Paul was finally lifted out of the pit through a hole at the top of the cell. According to most historical records, he was led to the execution chamber. He knew what was coming. Only the soldiers were with him. Paul preached a Spirit-filled message without fear. His faith was sealed in blood when his head was separated from his body as punishment for refusing to cease preaching about the love of Christ.

Paul's martyrdom set an example for every Christian who would ever live. His testimony could not be silenced by the efforts of mere mortal men—not even a Caesar.

> **Paul's martyrdom set an example to every Christian who would ever live.**

The legacy of Nero, however, is a pathetic one that almost deserves the deepest of sympathies. Shortly after Paul's execution, at the young age of thirty-two, Nero had to run from his own people. The city of Rome turned on him, and the mobs hunted him down like an animal. The things they wanted to do to him were much worse than anything he had done to the Christians.

Nero served the devil, and now the mob also served the devil. The devil, only loyal to himself, surely delighted in the anger of the mob as they went after his servant Nero. Nero was consumed by terror and fear and desperately prayed for death. In the end he found himself begging his own slave for mercy, who obliged by violently stabbing him in the neck.

The men of Rome destroyed every statue and symbol of Nero in an attempt to erase him from history.

Paul was beheaded, but he is to be resurrected with Christ. Even in death, those who follow Christ will taste life and the revival that follows. And history remembers Paul, not Nero, as the victor.

DISCUSSION QUESTIONS

1. Many people benefit from revival, but some pay a heavy price. Do you
   think the abandonment and lonely struggle Jesus and the apostles experienced was necessary to unlock revival? Why or why not?
2. Where in the world are Christians currently going through this kind of
   struggle?
3. How could we best pray for them?
4. Would you still pray for revival if you would be the one paying the price
   of loneliness and abandonment?

DAY 32

SUFFERING TURNED TO MIRACLES

———◆———

"Miracles are not contrary to nature, but only
contrary to what we know about nature."

—SAINT AUGUSTINE

Maxentius was in Rome and preparing himself for battle. He was
basing his entire military strategy for war with another Roman
leader known as Constantine on the pagan religion of his fathers. His high
priest slaughtered a sheep and began to read the signs of the blood and intes-
tines. He chanted to the ancient gods, asking for help in the coming battle.
Maxentius was anxious to see what the gods thought he should do.

Not content with only one source of guidance, Maxentius sought the
wisdom of the Sibylline prophesies as well. The Sibylline prophesies were
collections of utterances from a group of prophetesses who gave divine revelations in a frenzied state of spiritual possession.

Maxentius was the ruler of Rome, and Rome was now a living hell for
Christians. In fact, a quick search of the term "The Great Persecution" will
only lead you to one time in history: when Maxentius was ruler and during
the reign of his tyrannical predecessor, Emperor Diocletian.

Three years prior, Emperor Diocletian had also prayed to the ancient
Roman gods. Diocletian needed their help because despite the fires of con-
stant persecution, revival had continued to burn throughout the Roman
Empire.

Diocletian sought the guidance of demons disguised as oracles, and the demons gave the only answer they can give: kill the Christians.

This kicked off the worst season of persecution of Christians in the Roman Empire ever. A law went throughout the land demanding that all citizens of the Roman Empire give an offering to the Roman gods. Those who did not would be executed.

Before the Great Persecution started, Diocletian's resolve to wipe out Christianity had been tested in a very personal way. Diocletian had first asked all the members of his royal guard to prove they were not Christians by offering a sacrifice to the Roman gods. To Diocletian's dismay, one of his most loved soldiers refused to make the sacrifice. Diocletian did not want to lose his most trusted member of the royal guard, so he offered him riches, properties, and titles if he would only make a small, insignificant sacrifice to the Roman gods, but the soldier refused.

In the mind of Diocletian, it would be easy for the soldier to just offer the sacrifice without really meaning it and go on serving his God, but the soldier continued to refuse.

Diocletian became infuriated at the gall of the insubordinate soldier and decided to stop trying to protect him and instead was determined to make an example of him for all to see. The soldier knew the ultimate test of his life was coming, so he sold all of his belongings and gave the money to the poor.

Diocletian ordered that the soldier be strapped to a wheel with his body facing outward. Boards with swords facing the soldier were put in place, and as the wheel turned, the swords would filet the skin off of the soldier's body. It was a gruesome display of torture and pain.

As the crowds gathered around, however, something quite amazing happened—when the body of the soldier was removed from the wheel, the sky grew dark and the soldier stood up alive and healed!

Was it a miracle or a malfunction? Maybe the wheel did not work as effectively as it should have. Now the emperor was even more furious. His own soldier had made him look like a fool in front of the crowds.

The crowds were convinced it was a miracle. They thought they were looking at an angel of the Lord.

Diocletian immediately had the soldier beaten with a whip until the blood flowed like water from his body. The blood flowed and flowed, but he did not die. Diocletian's face went white with fear. He was certain the soldier was being helped by some kind of magic, so Diocletian brought in his most powerful priestess, who was a witch practicing black magic. The witch put a toxic potion together that would kill any man.

The soldiers standing guard were ready to force the prisoner to drink it, but they didn't need to. He took it from their hands and drank it willingly, but still he did not die. The witch, knowing the power of her own potion, knew in that moment that the soldier's God was greater than she was. She immediately confessed and accepted Christ as her Savior.

In front of the amazed crowds and royal family, the soldier started to preach about the power of God.

Diocletian ordered soldiers to behead him to prevent him from teaching any more, and on April 23, 303, the soldier received his crown of martyrdom when he willingly laid his neck under the sword.

In the crowds witnessing the events as they unfolded was Diocletian's wife, Empress Alexandra. She could not believe her eyes and wrestled with her heart as she contemplated the eternity of her soul.

She asked the same questions that many in the empire were asking: Why are we killing these Christians? Why are they willing to die for their belief? Why don't they fight back? Love and power were reflected in the life of Diocletian's martyr in a way that was not common in the Roman Empire. Empress Alexandra openly defied her husband and confessed that she too was a follower of Christ. Diocletian went into a fit of rage. He ordered his own wife to be beheaded! Empress Alexandra was baptized in her own blood.

Now it was personal. The Great Persecution began with unprecedented rage from Emperor Diocletian. His goal was to kill all Christians, burn all Christian writings, destroy every church building, and wipe all signs of Christianity off the face of the earth.

He almost succeeded.

What he didn't know was that the story of that soldier would never die.

It would give thousands of Christians—including Rome's own empress—the courage to walk in the footsteps of Jesus, Paul, and Peter.

> ## The story of that soldier thousands of Christians the courage to walk in the footsteps of Jesus, Paul, and Peter.

The soldier's name was George, and his death forever changed history. His flag became the flag of the crusaders, and eventually the flag of the nation of England. It is also the symbol of the flag of the nation that was named after him—Georgia.

The death of Saint George kickstarted another revival and fueled a supernatural vision for a future emperor that would change Christianity forever.

Diocletian tried, but he could not stop revival. The pagan era was soon coming to an end.

DISCUSSION QUESTIONS

1. When you read the story of Saint George, is your first instinct to accept it as history or do you think it is more of a legend? What arguments could be given for both positions?
2. Christians in Rome were put to the test when they were ordered to make a sacrifice to the gods. What sort of test could you be faced with in your culture, something every true Christian would or should refuse to do?
3. Do you think you would pass such a test?

DAY 33

UNITY

———————

"Unity without verity is not better than conspiracy."

—JOHN TRAPP

D iocletian died in the middle of the Great Persecution, and the next emperor, Maxentius, took his place. Maxentius would soon be facing his own challenges. The God of the Christians was about to respond in an awesome way to the nation that was attempting to annihilate His followers. An invading army led by the great warrior Constantine was approaching Rome. At first Maxentius might not have been too worried. Constantine was preparing to attack the fortified city of Rome with an inferior force, and Maxentius was calling out to the same gods that had told his predecessor to kill all the Christians.

When he inquired from the Sibylline prophesies, he was given a clear answer that he would be the victor against the armies of Constantine, but the one true God had other plans, because He was about to speak and alter the course of history.

As Constantine was approaching Rome, he came to the Milvian Bridge. What happened next changed the world forever.

The night before the battle, God gave Constantine a vision of a cross. While looking at the cross—the symbol of Christ and all the saints who had been slaughtered—God spoke to him in a way that shook the army commander to the core. "With this sign you will conquer," God said.

Immediately Constantine commanded his army to make banners with the symbol of the cross with the Greek letters of *Chi Rho*, which were the first two letters signifying the name of Christ. All of the soldiers were commanded to do the same to their shields.

There was mass confusion. Not long before, many of these soldiers had been ordered to kill everyone who was associated with the Christian religion, and now—without being defeated or forced by a Christian conqueror—they were going to follow the banner of the cross into battle?

Constantine, who now called himself the new emperor, was submitting himself to the message of the lowly, defeated Christians. If the cross was such a powerful symbol, why didn't it save the many Christians who had clung to it in their hour of need? It didn't make sense, but the soldiers, who had just hiked across half of Europe and were about to fight a larger, highly trained army, did as they were told and followed the banner of the cross into battle.

Against all odds, they won. The armies of Rome were soundly defeated, and Emperor Maxentius fell into the river and drowned. His body was pulled from the river, and his head was cut off.

To the soldiers who were there that day, the message was clear. The gods of Maxentius were no match for the God of the cross. The God of the Christians conquered the heart of the new emperor and gave him the ability to defeat his enemies in battle. All the gods of Rome could not save Maxentius and his military from destruction.

I traveled to Rome and walked across the Tiber River on the Milvian Bridge where the battle took place. It is not a typical tourist attraction. Not many people have ever heard of it, even though one of the most significant and miraculous events in history took place there.

I was with a pastor from the UK. We marveled at how the bridge had become a gateway to mainstream Christianity for all of Europe. Immediately following the events on that simple little bridge, Christians were given freedom as they had never experienced before. On the banks of the Tiber River, the most powerful nation on earth found itself being led by an emperor who submitted to the King of kings and Lord of lords.

"The events that occurred here sparked one of the largest revivals in European history, and most of the world has never heard of it," I said to Pastor Danny. He responded by nodding his head. It amazed us both how short our memories are.

Christianity exploded overnight. Not only did its revival flames engulf Rome, but it swept throughout every nation and territory occupied by the Roman and also, later, the Byzantine Empire. All of the churches that had been destroyed were rebuilt hundredfold. Christians who had been hunted down were now allowed to travel and preach freely with the protection of the powerful Roman army. The Christian writings that had been ordered to be destroyed were now pulled out of hiding, copied, and sent throughout the empire without angst.

Christianity went from the brink of extinction to the fastest-growing religion in the world. Suddenly everyone from the grassy islands of England to the deserts of the Middle East was being baptized. Churches

> **Christianity went from the brink of extinction to the fastest-growing religion in the world.**

could not be built fast enough to host them all. Clergy members could not be trained fast enough to disciple them all.

Nothing had ever happened to Christians like this before in the history of the world. It was a time of celebration. One Christians writer, Eusebius, wrote about the exuberant jubilation that was on the lips of every Christian: "The whole human race was freed from the oppression of the tyrants. . . . We especially, who had fixed our hopes upon the Christ of God, had gladness unspeakable!"

At the time there was no such thing as a Bible. The writings and letters of the disciples had not been collected into what we now call the New Testament. As modern-day believers, we often assume that the early Christians had the book that we now call the Bible. We also take it for granted that we have a Bible in our own language and that it is readily accessible to us whenever we want it.

That was not the case for early Christians. Only the top leaders of the

Christian church had access to a loose collection of letters written by the apostles, and those writings had been hidden in safe locations and could only be read by those who understood Greek. Because Christian leaders had been on the run for about three hundred years, they had never been able to have a gathering where all of them could come together and discuss in detail what they believed.

With their newfound freedom, 318 Christian leaders throughout the Roman Empire traveled to a small town in Turkey called Nicaea at the invitation of Constantine. It was here that the church was able to come together in unity and make a common declaration about the divinity of Christ. At this meeting they formed the early parts of the Nicene Creed—a uniform declaration about the beliefs of the church, and almost 1,700 years later, the Nicene Creed is still used by churches around the world.

The Nicene Creed was largely an adaptation of what had been established by African theologians a century earlier. Not one word was used in the Nicene Creed that cannot be found in the Bible. They decided when to celebrate the most important celebration of the Christian calendar—Easter—and determined that an annual Easter letter would be sent out from the church in North Africa's Alexandria to all of the churches to encourage them about the resurrection of Jesus Christ.

It was from this annual Easter letter that we see all twenty-seven books of the New Testament listed in the same order that we find them today in our modern Bibles.

The revival fires were now being flamed by unity. The unity that was established was so strong that it has lasted almost two thousand years.

Because of persecution, an unfortunate element in every revival, the church was scattered, leaders were killed, and the holy writings were destroyed. However, we have seen that persecution alone does not bring revival. We find persecution in every revival, but we do not find revival in every persecution. However, unity is one element that seems to be quite consistent in revival.

Of course, not every Christ-ian would agree that Constantine was an actual believer of Jesus Christ. Some Christians believe that Constantine ruined Christianity by making the religion more Roman (pagan) in nature, thus leading Christians astray. When they look at Constantine, they do not see an emperor who paved the way for a huge revival wave in Europe by ending per-secution and bringing unity, but

> **We find persecution in every revival, but we do not find revival in every persecution.**

instead they see a man who led an entire flock into heresy.

Some historians, like some Christians, doubt whether Constantine was ever really a Christian and believe that he merely used the religion of the masses to gain access to power.

As I stood on the Milvian Bridge in the city of Rome, I thought about the view that Constantine was less of a savior for Christianity and more of a manipulator. I contemplated the very real possibility of him faking his con-version only to gain power.

As I pondered the idea of Constantine faking his belief in Christ, I even-tually came to the conclusion that either way, the outcome was miraculous. If I believe Constantine's own words as well as those of the men who were closest to him, then his vision and the words he heard from heaven were a real miracle that changed history.

If I doubt Constantine's own account of his conversion and the accounts of those closest to him, then I have to accept that as a real miracle as well because that would mean that in the face of the most intense persecution in the history of the world, Christians were seen as such a powerful force that Constantine used their God to inspire his army and then gave them freedom and favor in order to gain power. Then, after gaining power, he had to con-tinue to foster the church in a way that brought about such unity Christianity became the largest religion on the face of the earth and has brought untold peace to all mankind.

DISCUSSION QUESTIONS

1. Prior to reading this chapter, what did you know about Constantine and the Christianization of the Roman Empire? What were your thoughts

and/or reservations about this? Has anything you read here given you a new perspective?

2. Do you think the story of the vision of Constantine is probable? Why or why not?

3. Do you feel war under the banner of the cross conflicts with the message of Christ to "love your enemies"?

4. Do you think it is important for Christian leaders to gather together to come agree on a common statement of beliefs?

5. If leaders in your country drew up a statement like that today, what topics do you think it would cover?

6. Do you feel that Christians in your country generally agree on Gospel essentials? Why or why not?

PART 5

EUROPE: A CONTINENT CHANGED

DAY 34

HOMOSEXUALITY

———◆———

"Jesus never said anything about homosexuality."

—Patricia Ireland

C hasing the path of revival in European history is like looking for a car to buy. After following Paul to Rome, I wondered, *Where do I go next?* There are so many places, so many events, and so many amazing people I could follow after the death of Paul. What happened after the first century to the church is exhilarating. Europe was extremely fertile ground. Even though their population is small in comparison to the rest of the world, Europe has been one of the most influential continents on the planet. The stories and testimonies of the saints that fanned revival fires are written in mountains of books with oceans of ink. Where does one begin?

I stood in Vatican City in Rome, pondering what my next move should be. The revival fires that flowed out from Rome traveled in every direction, and I prayed that God would lead me where He wanted me to go. I strolled along the outer walls of the Vatican, headed back to my hotel, and prayed. While in prayer it hit me that Europe's history of revival does not guarantee the future survival of the church. Out of darkness they came and back to darkness they shall return if the faith of their fathers is thrown away.

I wondered how different Europe is today than it was prior to the early Christian revivals. Would the first revivalists be familiar with the Christianity

> **How different Europe is today than it was prior to the early Christian revivals.**

that is now mainstream? Would Paul have known how to deal with the modern struggles that so many European believers wrestle with?

What would Peter have thought about the connection between government and church that exists with the Vatican? Would he have thought it strange that one day the very place where he was martyred would later in history be the seat of the most powerful government in the world that would use his name to rule with a strict form of Christianity, killing those who disagreed? Would he have found it odd that his writings would be burned if they were translated into any language other than Latin, a language that was so far from his mother tongue?

Not far from where I was walking was an advertisement. I could not read the Italian words, but I understood that it was for the upcoming gay pride parade. The idea of a pride festival promoting the homosexual lifestyle has recently divided many believers and the issue of homosexuality is a growing debate among Christians around the world, but things were not much different for Paul.

Before I went on this journey of chasing revival, I thought of homosexuality as a modern-day phenomenon. Of course I knew that it had always existed, but I never thought it was something that was widely accepted the way it is now. But as I walked in Paul's footsteps prior to the outbreak of revival in Europe, I realized I was wrong.

Throughout the Roman Empire, in places like Rome, Assos, and Mitylene, homosexuality was not only practiced, it was institutionalized. Not only were same-sex relationships common and acceptable, but Roman males often proved their power, dominance, and virility through forcing their male slaves to serve their desires. Their conquests were sometimes celebrated through homosexual acts, and young male slaves were the most prized possessions. It was even commonly practiced among the military ranks, as homosexuality was associated with entrance into the military.

Freeborn Roman men were expected to have sex with male partners.

Pederasty, or the erotic relationship between older males and young boys, was so very pervasive that it was considered to be the supreme cultural model for free relationships between citizens.

The early Romans did not need a gay pride parade. It was part of their daily lives.

Nero, the Roman emperor who had Paul executed, took a young boy named Sporus to be his wife. He had Sporus castrated while he was young so that he would continue to look like a young boy. They were married in a public ceremony. Nero often had Sporus dress like a woman and accompany him on official trips. He, like many Romans, was proud of his relationship with a member of the same sex.

Before his marriage to Sporus, he married a man named Pythagoras in a public ceremony where Nero was the bride. Both homosexual relationships and marriages were widely accepted and practiced.

Many young boys like Sporus were castrated and forced to serve the sexual appetites of Roman elites, some in the most grotesque manner, and often when they had served their purpose, they were killed.

The homosexual lifestyle of the Romans was often predatorial, preying on the innocence of small children. Emperor Tiberius, who ruled over Rome when Jesus was crucified, made small children serve him and all of his royal guests. When he tired of violating them, he would send his men out to find new children and kill the abused ones by throwing their bodies over cliffs.

I was completely caught off guard to learn this aspect of Roman and European culture prior to the days of revival. I was totally unaware that homosexuality was in fact more accepted during the days of Paul than it is today, not the other way around. When Paul went to Rome, he was facing sexual practices that were not only instituted at the highest levels of power but were deified.

Zeus, the king of all gods, fell madly in love with Ganymede, the young prince of Troy, and they had a passionate relationship together.

Antinous was a young boy who was later deified for worship by the people of Rome because he was the favorite lover of a Roman emperor.

In Acts 20, we read that Paul traveled to Mitylene, which was the capital of the island of Lesbos. This is the place where the word *lesbian* comes from. Sappho, the Greek icon of hedonistic worship from Lesbos, was the ultimate symbol of female homosexuality. Homosexuality was not just a sensual practice for pleasure or love; during the days of Paul, it was institutionalized as a religion. And while today we often treat the mythology of gods and goddesses as harmless stories, in Paul's time their worship was serious business and their beliefs were deeply held, and homosexuality was a significant part of their worship. Those who dared to offend the gods and goddesses could be beaten, tortured, or even killed. Paul was not just dealing with people who might not agree with him but who could oppose him violently.

Paul could have put himself in less danger and embraced the Roman lifestyle of homosexuality and been thought of more favorably. He could have at least had an easier time ministering in the Roman provinces if he did not write, in a letter to the Romans, "For this cause God gave them up unto vile affections: for even their women did change the natural use into that which is against nature: And likewise also the men, leaving the natural use of the woman, burned in their lust one toward another; men with men working that which is unseemly, and receiving in themselves that recompence of their error which was meet" (Romans 1:26–27).

His words were surely offensive to any Roman.

Why not keep it simple? You know, Jesus loves you and all you have to do is believe in Him to have everlasting life (John 3:16). Why risk insulting people by saying things that would antagonize the locals and their way of life? What good did it do to offend those who practiced this Roman lifestyle?

As I looked at the earliest revivals in Europe, I couldn't help but notice that those who were preaching the Good News did not coddle or cater to the culture; neither did the pioneers peddle a message of cheap grace. On the contrary, because of their countercultural beliefs, new believers were certain to face extreme persecution. The message of love and peace was packaged in a wrapping of persecution.

Paul's message of Christ ran counter to culture, not because Paul hated anyone, but because the hearts of man naturally run counter to the culture of the kingdom. His proclamation was theoretically counterproductive to gaining new converts but was essential for revealing the evil nature of mankind.

Is this possibly one of the characteristics of revival? That man be confronted with his sin?

> **The hearts of man naturally run counter to the culture of the kingdom.**

If Paul would have preached a more seeker-friendly message, would it have been as transforming, and more importantly, would it have led to revival?

DISCUSSION QUESTIONS

1. How does the practice of homosexuality in your country compare to what you read about ancient Rome? What is similar and what is different?
2. Do you think Paul's words in Romans 1 about homosexuality apply to our society as they did to Roman society? Why or why not?
3. Paul's rejection of homosexual practices may have been offensive to the status quo, but what kind of people could have felt this was a liberating message? Why do you think so?
4. How do you think churches should deal with issues of sexuality in the context of evangelism?
5. Should people be in a heterosexual monogamous marriage or be celibate before they can become part of our fellowship, or should we allow new converts time to learn about and accept biblical standards for sexuality?
6. Do you think homosexual sin is worse than heterosexual sin? Do you think sexual sins in general are worse than greed, lying, aggression, abuse, or other common sins? Why or why not? Do you think Paul would agree with you?

DAY 35

A NEW IDENTITY

"I am Patrick, a sinner, most uncultivated and least
of all the faithful and despised in the eyes of many."

—SAINT PATRICK

In 2 Kings 25:1, "Nebuchadnezzar king of Babylon came with all his army against Jerusalem and laid siege to it" (ESV). After the city of Jerusalem was conquered, Zedekiah, king of Judah, ran away but was caught and brought back to be presented to the king of Babylon. "They slaughtered the sons of Zedekiah before his eyes, and put out the eyes of Zedekiah and bound him in chains and took him to Babylon" (v. 7 ESV). The execution of his sons was the last thing he ever saw.

Zedekiah had been warned many times by the prophet Jeremiah to turn Israel back to the Lord, but the king did not listen and had Jeremiah forcefully removed from his presence. After the Babylonians conquered the nation of Judah and dragged the king along as their slave, the prophet Jeremiah left Jerusalem and traveled to Egypt (v. 26).

In sin, Israel lost her identity. But new identities were on the horizon.

Legends about King Zedekiah's children abound. Some believe that not all of Zedekiah's children were killed before he was dragged off to Babylon and that his son, a boy by the name of Mulek, was able to secretly escape death and travel across the ocean to the Americas, where he founded a Jewish tribe known as the Nephites—which became the foundation of the Mormon belief.

Others believe that the prophet Jeremiah secretly took with him his scribe Baruch (Jeremiah 36:4) and Zedekiah's daughter (Jeremiah 41:10), Teia Tephi. Baruch, Jeremiah's scribe, is believed by some to be Zoroaster, the ancient prophet of Zoroastrianism, which became the primary religion of the Persian Empire that eventually defeated Babylon, freed the Jews, and funded the rebuilding of the holy temple of Jerusalem.

And still others hold dear to the legend that Jeremiah and Teia Tephi secretly took with them the ancient Jewish relics of Jerusalem and eventually sailed to the shores of Ireland, where they furnished the first Irish kings with a special stone known as Jacob's Pillow (see Genesis 28:11).

The idea that Jeremiah sailed to Ireland with the king's daughter might sound crazy, but the special stone they carried with them, though few have actually heard about it, is the very stone that all of the monarchs of England— including the current Queen Elizabeth II—sit on at their coronation. If you look closely at the throne of Queen Elizabeth II on the day of her coronation in 1952, you will see a stone underneath, known as Jacob's Pillow or the Sone of Destiny.

The stone itself, though, did not change the identity of the nation of Ireland; instead, that change came from a slave who is connected to another stone: St. Patrick's Rock. The small island nation was completely transformed by a Christian slave who was kidnapped by Irish pirates and was later recognized as one of Europe's most influential missionaries who kick-started the very first Irish revival.

Most people do not know that Saint Patrick, the patron saint of the much-celebrated St. Patrick's Day, was not even Irish. Patricius, now known more affectionately as Saint Patrick, was born in modern-day Great Britain, and many believe that St. Patrick's Rock marks the place where he was born. He was raised in a Christian home before he was captured and taken to Ireland to be a slave. While the rest of Europe was enveloped by the Christian revivals that began in Rome, Ireland was still aggressively pagan.

Several years later Patrick was able to escape from Ireland and go back to his homeland. But then God called him to return to the land of his captors and preach the Gospel to them.

It is a perfect example of giving up your own desires for the will of the Lord; after all, what slave would willingly return to the nation that had enslaved him?

But Patrick gave up his freedom, went back to the dark land of Ireland, and committed himself to the people God called him to for the rest of his life.

He wrote a letter, stating, "Can it be out of the kindness of my heart that I carry out such a labor of mercy on a people who once captured me when they wrecked my father's house and carried off his servants? For by descent I was a freeman, born of a decurion father; yet I have sold this nobility of mine, I am not ashamed, nor do I regret that it might have meant some advantage to others. In short, I am a slave in Christ to this faraway people for the indescribable glory of 'everlasting life which is in Jesus Christ our Lord.'"

These are the words of a man who had not been forced to give up his identity but had willingly emptied himself to become the man God had created him to be.

He became so absolutely Irish that he was said to have written letters to those in England with the opening phrase, "We Irish . . ."

The life and ministry of Saint Patrick was followed by many miracles, but none were greater than the number of people who decided to follow Christ. After more than forty years of ministry in Ireland, Saint Patrick died in financial poverty but spiritual wealth, having planted more than three hundred churches and personally baptizing over 120,000 people! And this was in the fifth century, before TV, radio, and social media.

Saint Patrick is a prime example of someone who could have easily sought the Lord and lived a full life after escaping slavery. He could have roamed the British countryside giving testimony about his days in slavery and the miraculous vision he had had from the Lord that told him when and how to escape from Ireland.

But that was not his calling. Saint Patrick was called to empty himself and live a life of sacrifice among those who looked down upon him. He said, "I speak out too for love of my neighbors who are my only sons; for them I gave up my home country, my parents and even pushing my own life to

> **Saint Patrick was called to empty himself and live a life of sacrifice among those who looked down upon him.**

the brink of death. If I have any worth, it is to live my life for God so as to teach these peoples; even though some of them still look down on me."

In order for revival to happen in Ireland, Patrick had to give up his own identity and take on the image of Christ.

Could this not be another characteristic of revival? Does this idea of releasing our own self-identity to adopt the personality of Christ harken right back to the words of Paul in Romans 6:3–11?

> Know ye not, that so many of us as were baptized into Jesus Christ were baptized into his death? Therefore we are buried with him by baptism into death: that like as Christ was raised up from the dead by the glory of the Father, even so we also should walk in newness of life.
>
> For if we have been planted together in the likeness of his death, we shall be also in the likeness of his resurrection: Knowing this, that our old man is crucified with him, that the body of sin might be destroyed, that henceforth we should not serve sin. For he that is dead is freed from sin. Now if we be dead with Christ, we believe that we shall also live with him: knowing that Christ being raised from the dead dieth no more; death hath no more dominion over him. For in that he died, he died unto sin once: but in that he liveth, he liveth unto God. Likewise reckon ye also yourselves to be dead indeed unto sin, but alive unto God through Jesus Christ our Lord.

This idea seems to go directly against the teachings of the world and even many in the church who encourage us to love ourselves and "be" ourselves. But others teach that in order to be like Christ we must all look and sound the same.

Could it be that we are all misunderstanding God's words in the book of Romans? After all, He is the one who made us so unique. Would He really go to such great lengths to give each of us distinct personalities and gifts, only to make us more like clones when we follow after Him? And what does it really mean to love ourselves?

After thoroughly studying the teachings of Christ and the history of revival in Ireland, I cannot help but conclude that our most basic, unique qualities emerge when we give ourselves over to the purpose for which we were created. Contrary to initial rational thinking, the world's desire to make us more selfish, and thus more unique, actually removes us from our purpose, subtracts from our character, and makes us hollow inside. The void that forms in us is then filled with the world, and when the world in us is compared with the world around us, there is nothing to contrast or make us different, thus making us invisible to each other.

> **Our most basic, unique qualities emerge when we give ourselves over to the purpose for which we were created.**

So the reality is that the world's way of making us unique is counterintuitive.

If the world around us is dark and we too are dark, then how distinguishable is a dark soul in a dark room in a dark world? Everything looks the same to a blind man in a dark room.

How can the darkness of the world be defeated if we share the darkness in us? How can we find fulfillment in ourselves if we were created to serve others? What is more unique in a world of darkness than a glimmering light? What greater identity could Saint Patrick have than as a Brit, living among the Irish, to share about Christ to the pagans?

In the precise moment that Saint Patrick lost his identity, he actually gained it. This concept does not make sense to the rest of the world, but it makes perfect sense to every person who has made a confession of faith to Christ.

This concept also makes sense to married couples. Married couples who have been in a healthy marriage for a considerable amount of time can often be seen as sharing similar characteristics, not because they share a common personality, but because they begin to mimic each other.

In many healthy marriages the husbands and wives are often polar opposites, but their weaknesses and strengths complement their spouse, and in those complementary roles they mimic each other. Research has shown that married couples mimic character traits, even the way they laugh and smile. During the course of their marriage they have learned to unconsciously lean on each other in a way where they psychologically connect without words.

The wife and husband give up their individual identities and create a new one that is mutually shared and reflects the other. They become one—not a carbon copy of one after another, but a representation of what they make up together.

The Bible often refers to our relationship with Christ like a marriage, with the idea that the more time we spend with Him, the more we will mimic His character and His ways. We become more like Him. We lean on Him, rely on Him, and through time and exposure, intuitively begin to mimic His character. In the process we take on a new identity and leave the old one behind.

Is there any better model for us than Jesus Himself? The One who left the glorious throne of heaven and came to earth, taking on the identity of man and living a life of sacrifice so that others might be changed?

He was the King of kings who became a sacrificial lamb. He was the Lord of lords who took on the identity of a carpenter's son. And in His righteousness He took on the sin and pain of the entire world so

> **Is there any better model for us than Jesus Himself?**

that all might be saved. In doing this, His deity was made visible for all to see when He rose from the dead. It was through emptying Himself that He ultimately received the name above every other name.

DISCUSSION QUESTIONS

1. How important is your national identity to you? Would you be willing to lose it if that was required to fulfil your calling?
2. Apart from your nationality, what things define your identity?
3. Have you ever felt any of these things were hindering you from finding your real identity in Christ?
4. Think of the story of the young man who was asked to lay down his identity as a rich person and take up the identity of a follower in Mark 10. Compare this to the story of the fishermen who laid down their nets and followed Jesus in Matthew 4. What did these men gain and lose?
5. What do you think is more difficult: using your talents for God or giving up something you are good at to do something else that God asks of you? Have you ever experienced this dilemma? What happened?

DAY 36

UNITY IN DIVERSITY

———◆———

"Diversity: The art of thinking independently together."

—Malcolm Forbes

When I first began to search for revivals throughout history, I did so with the full faith and conviction that I would find unity within the Body of Christ. It was not long before I discovered the folly of my beliefs.

Do not get me wrong. There was and is absolute unity in the Body of Christ. In fact, it is one of the things I have discovered as an essential characteristic in revival, but the term *unity*, as I have now come to define it, is different from what I had been taught.

Unity among Christians does not mean we are identical copies of each other. We come to the table with unique experiences, individual testimonies, and an array of completely different cultures and backgrounds.

We did not look the same when we were born, and we certainly do not look the same when we are born again. First Corinthians 12:12–14 defines unity in the Body of Christ even more precisely:

> For just as the body is one and has many members, and all the members of the body, though many, are one body, so it is with Christ. For in one Spirit we were all baptized into one body—Jews or Greeks, slaves or free—and all were made to drink of one Spirit. For the body does not consist of one member but of many. (ESV)

185

> **There is unity in the faith and the vision, but there is diversity in the body.**

There is unity in the faith and the vision, but there is diversity in the body.

While chasing the history of revival, I have been shocked at the number of people we now look to as giants of the faith but who were aggressively rejected by the church during their lifetime.

Martin Luther comes to mind. His advocacy for the authority of Scripture and the priesthood of all believers opened the floodgates for one of the greatest revivals in European history. Martin Luther was hated and despised by the leaders of a church he loved dearly. He never intended to break from the church; he only wanted to reform it from within. However, in the end, he broke the hold of a religious monopoly of a few elite members of society and led the masses back to the idea of individual submission before God with no middleman.

Without Martin Luther, it is argued that there might not have been Bible translations made available in the common languages—without which there never would have been a Methodist revival, the Great Awakening, the Azusa Street Revival, etc.

Even secular historians understand this to be a turning point in history. Gutenberg's invention of the printing press for the Bible and Luther's reformation are considered to be among the most important events in the last millennia.

Martin Luther's actions did not go unpunished. He was hated by the Catholic church and was excommunicated.

He was not alone.

Nestorius, who was responsible for much of the ancient Eastern church of Syria and the Middle East, was rejected by the church in the West because his teachings about Mary, the mother of Jesus, did not line up with theirs. Many of his Christian followers were killed by zealous believers who opposed his views.

William Tyndale worked on a Bible translation that would help spread the Gospel throughout the English countryside. At the decree of the church, he was eventually arrested, tied to a stake, strangled to death, and set on fire.

John Wycliffe was persecuted for translating the Bible into the English language so that it could be read by the common Englishman. The church leaders were so angry that even after he died, they dug up his remains, burned them, and threw the ashes into the water.

The splintering off from the church did not stop but multiplied. Today there are more than twenty thousand different Christian denominations, and some are fiercely exclusive in their beliefs, openly persecuting other Christians for not agreeing with their specific theology.

And yet, somehow, God still stirs the hearts of man with the cry of revival.

It is important to remember that we are not evaluating saintly beings that descended down from heaven to our churches in a perfect package, but instead, we are all earthly men and women who are saved from sin by the grace of God.

When Jesus stood on the Mount of Olives and commissioned His disciples to go and disciple all nations, He instructed them with love, truth, and power. He sent them out with one faith in His teachings and Holy Scriptures, but keep in mind that the Scriptures were only those of the Old Testament. His Words and the many teachings He taught had not yet been written down.

> **We are all earthly men and women who are saved from sin by the grace of God.**

We may think that the eleven remaining disciples based their teachings on a single doctrine, but that is not the case. The first apostles, who followed the teachings of Jesus during His life, disagreed among each other about certain aspects of doctrine. The beauty of Scripture is that it does not attempt to hide these disagreements.

This should in no way be interpreted as an endorsement of multiple faiths. It is not. We could no more assume that there should be multiple faiths among the church than that there are multiple gods.

In the Bible we find that there is only one baptism of faith and only one

God. At the fountain of truth that gushes forth from the Triune Godhead, we all find unity for those who believe; however, that does not mean that we do not find differences among the faithful.

The disputes and disagreements of the first apostles were faithfully cemented in the teachings of the New Testament without apology or excuse. During the days of the apostles, there were teachings that they resisted by those who claimed to follow Christ. Shoot, the disciples resisted the teachings of each other! These were more than mere disagreements, but were passionate and heated debates about issues on which, in their minds, the very future of salvation for mankind hinged.

When we see the confrontation between Paul and Peter in Galatians 2, do not think for one moment that this was a holy disagreement. This was as passionate as disagreements get, and it was recorded in its fullness.

When Paul rejected John Mark to travel with him and his good friend and teacher Barnabas on their second mission journey, the Bible says in Acts 15:39 that "the contention was so sharp between them, that they departed asunder one from the other." It is never recorded that the two ever traveled together again.

Their disagreement led to a split in the ministry between the two of them, but weren't they were still unified in Christ? Was the decision not to take John Mark with them relevant to their salvation?

Their split certainly did not end their ministry. Barnabas continued preaching the Gospel in foreign lands until he was eventually martyred in Cyprus. John Mark wrote one of the Gospels, and Paul wrote thirteen letters in the New Testament.

Christians are specifically called to embrace diversity. Our diversity is immediately reflected in our Bible, made up of sixty-six sections written by forty different authors in two completely different languages over a period of several thousand years. In the Bible alone, God is displayed in history, numbers, poetry, and prophesy.

Even the smallest exposure to God in the Bible would lead one to quickly realize how amazing, big, and truly complex God is. It would be ridiculous to believe that one single person or one single group of persons could possibly represent Him or even under-stand Him enough to represent Him. Man trying to understand God is like man trying to teach a ladybug trigonometry.

> **Man trying to understand God is like man trying to teach a ladybug trigonometry.**

Maybe the reason for all of the races, ethnicities, character traits, etc., is that we are all made in the image of God and God's image is too big for one single man or woman to reflect. It would take all men and all women at all times in history—dead, living, and future generations—to even come close to being an accurate reflection of God.

It seems that, even in our arguments among one another, God finds a way to take our struggles and make us stronger, dig deeper, work harder, and learn more about Him than we would have ever learned without the opposition.

DISCUSSION QUESTIONS

1. Do you think Christians should strive for institutional unity, meaning churches should merge and ideally come to the point where there is one all-encompassing church? Or do you think it is fine to have many denom-inations as long as people accept each other as brothers and sisters in Christ? What are your arguments?
2. Are there certain churches you do not consider to be "Christian" even though they self-identify as such? Why is that?
3. Do you believe these churches could still have true believers in them?
4. Have you ever been touched by or found comfort in a Christian tradition that was very different from your own?
5. Choose a denomination or Christian tradition that is very different from yours. Is there any way in which their traditions balance deficiencies or blind spots in yours?
6. Have you ever seen something good come from a church split?
7. Do you believe God can build His church through such tragedies? Why or why not?

DAY 37

MIRACLES

———◆———

"Miracles are not contrary to nature, but only
contrary to what we know about nature."

—Augustine of Hippo

R evival continued to sweep through Europe, but each nation and tongue was unique in their experience. While other religions spread through the sword or forced conversion, the unimaginable was happening during revivals in Europe: the Gospel was spreading through mass conversion. It was not the powerful rulers that prompted the revival, but the power of God in the lives of everyday people.

While chasing revival, I have found few stories that are as miraculous and are as little known in the church as the revival among the Vikings. The Vikings were mainly a band of fearsome pirates made of Danes, Swedes, and Norwegians. They launched raids on northern Europe and killed, raped, and pillaged.

They were a Germanic people who had never been subdued by the Roman Empire and had their own way of living. Take the romanticized picture of Vikings as noble seafaring warriors and throw it out the window. The Vikings were violent and cruel marauders who, more often than not, took great pleasure in the suffering of the people they conquered. Fewer places in the world were as dark and as insufferable as the land of the Vikings.

The Vikings conquered and terrorized most of England, Scotland, and Ireland as well as northern Ger-many, France, and western ports in Russia. The Vikings saw Christians as weak

> **Fewer places in the world were as dark and as insufferable as the land of the Vikings.**

imbeciles. They raided their churches and places of worship with little or no resistance and laughed at their religion of love and forgiveness. The God of the Christians was simply inferior to the Norse war god of Thor.

But something began to happen among the violent Vikings as they occupied Christian lands. The Christians were honest, loving, and merciful. Even though the priests would not fight, it was soon learned that they were not cowards. They bravely refused to abandon their faith in Jesus Christ even under the threat of the cruelest of executions. Though the Christian priests were peaceful, they had hearts of lions and did not fear the Vikings.

Christians believe that their God is all-powerful and all-loving and can heal the sick and work miracles in the lives of those who believe in Him. Vikings soon realized that the healing wisdom of Odin was far inferior to the God of the Christians. Even though the Vikings were the conquerors, God would have the victory.

Around the tenth century, a lowly foreigner by the name of Poppo stood in front of the much-feared leader of the Vikings known as King Harald Bluetooth. Poppo was a believer in the Most High God and did not fear Harald Bluetooth. He didn't see King Harald as a conqueror. He saw him as a lost sinner who was in desperate need of salvation from the Savior who loved him.

Poppo preached to the king but to no avail, until Poppo was challenged to hold a hot iron as he talked to the king. Poppo trusted that God would show Himself in signs and wonders in front of King Bluetooth. At the command, a local blacksmith took a red-hot iron that had been roasting in the fire. Poppo grabbed it with his hands and ministered to the king. When Poppo was finished, he gave the burning-hot iron back to the blacksmith.

Immediately King Bluetooth looked at Poppo's hands and saw that he didn't have a single burn on him. Right then and there, King Bluetooth believed in the true God and became a believer in Jesus Christ.

King Bluetooth led the rest of his Vikings and their families to follow Christ and transformed the entire nation of Denmark. His impact prompted the peaceful Christianization of Scandinavia and put Bluetooth in the hearts of the people forever. We have all heard of this king before even if we don't realize it. The Bluetooth wireless technology that is used all over the world is named after King Bluetooth. The company's logo consists of Norse letters for his name Harald Bluetooth: *H* (✳) and *B* (ᛒ).

Strangely, many modern Christians have a problem with such miracles, but as I continue to chase revival history, I cannot help but see miracles as one of the components of revival that is never absent. Never.

Jesus insisted that the preaching of the simple, naked Gospel be accompanied by signs, wonders, and miracles. Miracles have been recorded throughout revival history.

There is no doubt that amazing stories of miracles can be found sprinkled throughout the history of revival, but lying demons sit perched like wild dogs, ready to snatch the truth from the jaws of our memory. Lies and unbelief come disguised as honest rational reflection to protest the supernatural works of God.

Secular media will not hesitate to flock to witness miracles performed, not to be converted and believe, but instead to be better equipped to hurl flaming arrows of scorn at those who do believe.

So many times as modern-day Christians, we are inclined to be swayed by unbelieving media that makes a mockery of our beliefs than to rejoice at the miraculous power of God. If we believe that God does not change, then it is impossible to accept miracles of the Bible and at the same time deny the manifestation of them in our midst.

Not only is the hypocrisy of accepting the truth of biblical miracles but denying their existence today inconsistent, but it is self-destructive. It makes no sense during the time of battle for souls for Christians to push away the very power they have been given to secure victory.

Be careful criticizing miracles. In the Bible, handkerchiefs and aprons were brought to the sick and the sick were healed; yet Protestants often dismiss and ridicule the custom of preserving the relics of dead saints. As much as we might deny it, God still works in mysterious ways. Who are we to reject it?

It is no doubt easier for us to deny miracles that we do not understand, but do miracles require our understanding? Do miracles that we cannot explain or understand make us feel vulnerable and out of control of our universe? I would assume that any exposure to God and His power would reveal to us in an instant how powerless we really are.

Through observation of natural laws and scientific thought we have learned to better explain the natural world around us, and in that we somehow feel in more control.

Miracles, on the other hand, are defined as the temporary suspension of natural law, and they

> **Do miracles that we cannot explain or understand make us feel vulnerable and out of control of our universe?**

cannot be explained. That means they cannot be controlled. Miracles have a way of making the learned feel unlearned and the powerful feel powerless.

Maybe this is why the Pharisees did not believe in the miracles of Jesus. They wanted and needed to explain how the miracles were happening. They were very learned men. They were the ones the Jews looked to to explain everything about God, but the miracles of Jesus were not explainable—well, they were explainable, but the explanation was not suitable for the Pharisees.

The miracles performed by Jesus were witnessed by thousands of people and still the Pharisees refused to believe them. They begged to see a miracle, and when they witnessed what they asked for, they refused to believe it. They demanded to see a "sign from heaven," and when they were given a sign, they refused to believe it.

So would it be a stretch to believe that it would take nothing short of a divine miracle to bring the barbaric killing Vikings to Christ?

I saw even more of this epic revival history when I traveled to the very western point of Europe, to a small island on the west coast of Scotland called Iona.

I followed in the footsteps of Saint Columba, a man who was followed by both converts and miracles. He made his home on Iona island, a place that legend says is where heaven and earth are only three feet apart.

It was not easy getting to the remote island, but once you arrive by ferry, you are instantly greeted by Martyr's Bay, where sixty-eight monks were slaughtered by the Viking invaders.

Iona was one of the early islands raided by the Vikings. Before the canonization of the Scriptures was solidified, relics were a major part of worship, and pilgrims would bring riches and wealth to the monasteries as an offering so they could see the relics or use them for worship. These monasteries, filled with treasure and offerings, were like ATM machines for the Vikings.

The Vikings would storm into the unprotected churches and find loads of valuable gold and treasure to take back with them to their families in Scandinavia, but they would never be able to steal the miracles that dot the landscape of the island's history.

This island was the epicenter of the most important monastic movement in Britain and Ireland. The Christians, led by Columba, were dedicated to spreading the Word of God. Columba himself was from royal families on both his mother's side and his father's side. But instead of becoming a king himself, he decided to serve the King of kings.

Young kings of that time would have been well trained as deadly warriors, and Columba would train the young monks who followed him to Iona to fight. However, Columba had ambitions much larger than earthly combat. His weapons were spiritual. Saint Columba is responsible for many recorded prophesies and miracles that we could easily write off today as being mere legends. Saint Columba walked on water, raised the dead, and predicted the future with amazing accuracy. Those miracles led to the evangelization of large parts of Europe and eventually Scandinavia.

The small, seemingly insignificant island of Iona on the outer edges of Europe turned out to be the precise location needed to reach into the heart of the continent as well as Scandinavia. It is also as far west as one can stand and peer over the Atlantic toward the "New World."

Revival fires did not stop in Jerusalem, Asia Minor, Africa, and Europe. They spread across the ocean to the Americas.

DISCUSSION QUESTIONS

1. The Vikings found the Christians they attacked vulnerable but fearless. Would that be a good description of the way Christians in your country handle attacks by unbelievers, be they spiritual or physical? Would that be a good description of you?
2. What seems to have conquered the hearts of the Vikings was the combination of three things: the vulnerability of the believers, their courage in spite of their comparative weakness, and the miraculous power of God working through them. Do you think the formula of weakness + courage + miracles is biblical? Can you give examples?
3. Do you think this would still work today in your context? Why?
4. Which of these three do you think might be lacking among believers in your country or in your personal testimony?

PART 6

AMERICA: REVIVAL CROSSES THE SEA

DAY 38

SHIPWRECKED IN A NEW WORLD

"Mistakes are the portals of discovery."

—JAMES JOYCE

Where should we begin exploring revival in America? Should we start with the Great Awakening or should we go back even further—all the way to the pilgrims who escaped persecution?

What if the early Christian revivals in Europe started missions to America five hundred years before historians acknowledge the discovery of America by Christopher Columbus in 1492? What if God had a plan for the New World long before recorded history?

Revival fires are not as randomly combustible as we believe at first sight. Only in ignorance could we possibly conceive that revivals suddenly happen with no rhyme or reason. Of course, like all things, they depend on the whims of God, but the whims of God are only whims to the biblically unlearned. The plans of God were carefully laid out before the foundations of the world. Like a common campfire, revivals are set ablaze by carefully planned kindling that has been lying idle for generations awaiting the perfect moment to burst forth with predestined fire.

The story of the first missionary sent to America starts with the separation of fact from fiction found in the Icelandic Norse sagas. The ancient sagas have always been read as a kind of Scandinavian version of Homer's *Odyssey*, but that all began to change in the late nineteenth century, when many Nordic Americans started to look into the factual nature of the stories.

At the center of the sagas was a Viking by the name of Leif Eriksson, the son of the notorious Erik the Red. He had been baptized by King Olaf of Norway around AD 1000. According to legend, the Norwegian king, a committed Christian and firm believer in the importance of the Great Commission, appointed Leif to leave Norway as a missionary and preach the Light of the Gospel among the Vikings in Greenland.

Leif did as the king commanded and took a priest with him.

Leif, an experienced seafarer, set out by ship to reach the lost, but a mysterious, dark storm swirled about their Viking boats and blew them off course. Leif and his companions ended up in what we now know as North America. After getting back on course and then leading the Greenlanders to Christ, Leif and his crew returned to this Newfoundland, where they built permanent settlements, which included the construction of churches. While the Norwegian presence in North America was short-lived, the fact that the first presence on the continent was Christian is significant.

Leif and the accompanying priest looked for an opportunity to preach and touched land in three different areas of North America: Labrador, Markland, and Vinland. They met indigenous people living in the area, but they were violent and did not take well to the idea of new settlers. Clashes ensued, and Leif's brother eventually died in a skirmish with the Americans.[17]

The story of Leif was never really believed until modern science began to unearth findings of Viking settlements in North America. In 1925, President Calvin Coolidge had seen enough evidence to announced that Leif Eriksson had been the first European to discover America, and in September 1964, Congress approved a public resolution that authorized President Lyndon B. Johnson to declare October 9 as Leif Erikson Day in honor of his Christian missions to America.

Inspired by the power of Christ, Leif's mother came to Christ and built the very first church in Brattahlid, Greenland, and the remains of the churches there are a testimony of the once-thriving Christian community estimated to have been between four thousand to six thousand souls.[18]

While chasing revival and following remote characters like Leif Eriksson who played a pivotal part in the initial seeds sown, we discover another common characteristic: *revival is not planned by man.*

Revival is planned by God. It is not formulaic. It does not contain a list of special ingredients that can be added, baked, and presented. It is inspired, fueled, and ordained by God and God alone.

> **Revival is inspired, fueled, and ordained by God and God alone.**

The common characteristics that we are finding might help us identify revival and prepare our hearts for revival, but they cannot help us orchestrate, plan, or conduct a revival. Man is completely dependent upon God for revival.

It is confusing and demoralizing when we eventually discover how little we know of God's will. How often have young ministers and evangelists set out with zeal and passion, knowing in their hearts exactly what God wanted? Their imaginations are painted with visions of grandeur, their dreams filled with endless victories.

But as the heat of the afternoon sun beats down during the mid-labor of life, young ministers and evangelists find themselves pondering the unthinkable possibility of the most unproductive nature.

The masses never materialized. The unconverted remained entrenched. Much labor resulted in pitiful results. The best-laid plans crumbled, and all of the resources have been spent. That which was planned had failed and given way to glorious opportunities of divinely orchestrated disaster.

Leif Eriksson's boat was blown off course. How often have we heard that story? A shipwreck brought Paul to Crete, according to God's perfect will. Christopher Columbus discovered America when he was looking for a trade route to Asia.

For me personally, being blown off course relates directly to my American heritage. My great-great-great maternal grandfather was a man by the name of Johannes Broyles, born in Dusslingen, Wurttemberg, Germany, on May 1, 1679, and died in Spotsylvania, Virginia, on February 5, 1733.

Johannes and his wife were Waldensians or followers of the teachings of Peter Waldo, who saw their church attacked by the French. Peter Waldo is most famous for his teachings of volunteered poverty, a belief that one can only serve either God or mammon. His followers sold all of their belongings and served the poor.

In 1717, in order to freely practice their faith and share it with others, Johannes and nineteen other German families decided to board a ship and head to America. Their destination was Pennsylvania, but because of a storm they ended up in Virginia, where their entire family was sentenced to eight years of indentured service until they could pay off the fee for their voyage.

Afterward, they set up the Second Germanna Colony in the middle of Native American territory in what is now Fauquier County and began ministering to the Native Americans. All this happened after their ship was blown off course.

The first pilgrims traveled on the *Mayflower* through stormy seas, and strong winds forced them to eventually land on Plymouth Rock, which was not their original destination.

Arguably one of the greatest hymns in American history, "Amazing Grace," was written by John Newton after he begged for his life during a vicious storm that was threatening to sink his ship. Though a captain and slave trader, he would later renounce slavery and become an Anglican priest.

The great eighteenth-century evangelist John Wesley who founded the Methodist Church was on a ship bound for America with both Englishmen and Germans when a massive storm hit, split their sails, and filled the boat with water. The English who did not fear God cried out in fear of the storm, and the German Moravians who feared God only sang praises and did not fear the storm.

On Sunday, January 25, 1736, Wesley wrote,

At seven I went to the Germans. I had long before observed the great seriousness of their behaviour. Of their humility they had given a continual proof, by performing those servile offices for the other passengers, which none of the English would undertake; for which they desired, and would receive no pay, saying, "it was good for their proud hearts," and "their loving Saviour had done more for them." And every day had given them occasion of showing a meekness which no injury could move. If they were pushed, struck, or thrown down, they rose again and went away; but no complaint was found in their mouth. There was now an opportunity of trying whether they were delivered from the Spirit of fear, as well as from that of pride, anger, and revenge. In the midst of the psalm wherewith their service began, the sea broke over, split the main-sail in pieces, covered the ship, and poured in between the decks, as if the great deep had already swallowed us up. A terrible screaming began among the English. The Germans calmly sung on. I asked one of them afterwards, "Was you not afraid?" He answered, "I thank God, no." I asked, "But were not your women and children afraid?" He replied, mildly, "No; our women and children are not afraid to die."

The impact of this event was so profound that John Wesley attributed it directly to his conversion experience.

What is it about boats and raging seas? Even Jesus found Himself in a boat among frightful seamen begging for their lives. Ever since the days of Noah and Jonah, ships have played a significant role. Shipwrecks have been such a transformative method for God to move among His people that it could possibly be one of the missing characteristics of revival.

If revival is what we desperately seek, should we make our way to the nearest port and jump aboard?

I am not sure what it is, but maybe it has to do with the fact that a boat upon the mighty waves of a powerful ocean has a way of making a man come face-to-face with his own ultimate lack of control over anything.

DISCUSSION QUESTIONS

1. Do you find it a discouraging or an encouraging thought that we cannot organize revival, that there is always an element of Divine planning? Why?

2. Have you ever been involved in organizing large evangelistic meetings? If so, how do you deal with the tension between organizing a fantastic event and realizing that only God can touch people's hearts to come and respond?

3. Have you ever experienced a "shipwreck" moment in your life, where God used a difficult event (loss of a job, a disease, or a failure of some sort) to open new doors for the Gospel?

4. Have you experienced a storm in your life that has impacted your spiritual journey in a great way? How has that affected your trust in God's Divine planning?

DAY 39

FROM REFUGEE TO MISSIONARY

———◆———

"I have but one passion–it is He, it is He alone. The world is the field, and the field is the world; and henceforth that country shall be my home where I can be most used in winning souls for Christ."

—Count Ludwig Von Zinzendorf

Maybe a study of American revival begins with refugees. In many ways, all Christians are refugees, homeless and roaming the world like ragged sheepherders from Ur anticipating the day when we will one day go to the land where our forefathers await us.

To feel at home in the world is to forfeit our heavenly passport. Our time on earth is nothing more than a temporary visa for ministry; a "green card" that only allows temporary abode. Like modern-day refugees, we are rejected by those who are of the world as if they too were not foreigners, but they are.

They have adopted the world and the world has adopted them back, but the world they have come to love will never make them citizens. It cannot. It is only a hallway for us to travel through. And the hallway is not as long as we tell ourselves. It is incredibly short, with only two doors to choose from on either end. Though our time in the hallway varies, no one can live in the hallway forever.

We are all refugees.

From the first pilgrims, Anabaptists, and Waldensians (like my family) to the immigrants of the Great Awakening, refugees have long been bringing revival to North and South America.

In American revival history, refugees from a bohemian settlement in Herrnhut, Germany, in the 1700s led to a missionary movement that brought the Gospel to the New World.

In the early 1700s, a refugee colony from Bohemia settled on the estates of Count Nicholas Zinzendorf in Herrnhut, Germany, and experienced an outpouring of the Holy Spirit that would eventually lead to one of the greatest missionary movements of all time.

The seeds that were planted among these refugees were radical and untamed. They became known as the Moravian church, and what they did in America would never be forgotten. They relied on the Word of God and rebelled against the Catholic church by objecting to the practices of indulgences, purgatory, and celibacy for priests and are considered by most to be the world's first Protestant church.

Christian refugees from far and wide came to settle on the Herrnhut estate, and it was not long before intense disagreements about Jesus broke out. Zinzendorf devoted himself to full-time reconciliation among the refugees. He believed that God had called them to be a community of love and unity in order to reach the lost.

The Moravian church started a twenty-four-hour "prayer watch" that continued nonstop for over a hundred years. Revival broke out in their small community, and they began to send missionaries out all over the world, to Greenland, Lapland, South Africa, Egypt, Turkey, and North and South America.

And they inspired many missionaries to preach the Gospel to the rest of the world as well. The famous missionary William Carey read about the Moravian missions in an English magazine *Periodical Accounts* and determined to become a missionary, saying, "See what the Moravians have done! Cannot we follow their example and in obedience to our Heavenly Master go out into the world, and preach the Gospel to the heathen?"

The power of the Holy Spirit swept through the small Moravian church community, and strange and dangerous things began to happen. People gave up everything they owned to share about Jesus with others. Word spread far and wide that Moravian missionaries were ready to be tasked with the most remote and dangerous places on earth.

In the early 1730s, a black servant named Anton served in the court of the king of Denmark. He was allowed to travel to Herrnhut to obtain an audience with Count Zinzendorf and plead for missionaries to be sent to his native St. Thomas (Virgin Islands). His sister Anna was a slave in St. Thomas, and he desperately wanted her to be with him in heaven one day.

> **People gave up everything they owned to share about Jesus with others.**

Two men named Johann Leonhard Dober and David Nitschmann listened to the pleas of the young Anton and were moved by his introduction to his homeland. They decided to travel to the island to minister to his sister, but there was one big problem. Johann and David were not able to minister to the slaves without the slaveholders' permission. Most slaveholders did not want anything to interfere with the workday of their slaves, so in order to reach the slaves on St. Thomas Island, Johann and David would need to be slaves.

Johann and David decided to sell themselves to a slave owner in St. Thomas in order to reach the lost.

Anglican missionaries had already been sent to St. Thomas, but their message seemed hierarchal and put an emphasis on hereditary roles, and so failed to reach the masses. The Moravian missionaries, on the contrary, considered themselves to be equal with the slaves, and their message preached equality before God and encouraged the expression of spiritual emotion.

The response was phenomenal.

Though Johann and David were ready to sell themselves as slaves, they were not allowed to. However, they were eventually given access to the slaves, and they began coming to Christ in the droves. Revival broke out and spread to Jamaica, Barbados, and Antigua. By the end of the century, there were more than eleven thousand people attending Moravian-planted churches.

The small, remote refugee community from Germany engaged in a solid hundred years of round-the-clock prayer and sent out more missionaries than the rest of the Protestant church in any other part of Europe.

Their prayer shook the world and set the stage for revivals in early America.

DISCUSSION QUESTIONS

1. Being a refugee is a vulnerable position. We often think of missionaries as people in positions of influence, like teachers, doctors, or pastors. Do you think it is beneficial to ministry for missionaries to come from a position of powerlessness? Or do you think mission is better served by people in respectable positions who can direct others? Why do you think so?

2. Do you think selling yourself as a slave is a viable ministry strategy? Would your church ever consider a similar thing, for example sending a missionary to work in a sweatshop to reach the workers there? Why or why not?

3. What do you think about the hundred years of unbroken prayer? Have you ever been part of a prayer chain? If so, how was your experience and what was the result?

4. Do you think if we pray long and hard enough, God will cause revival? Why or why not?

DAY 40

THE GREAT AWAKENING

"Denial, Anger, Bargaining, Depression,
Acceptance . . . The five stages of waking up."

—BOGUS CELEBRITY TWITTER ACCOUNT

One could say that there have been hundreds of revivals over the centuries in America, some personal, some affecting entire churches, and some touching the entire nation. But historically speaking there have been only a handful of movements in American history where the Holy Spirit has affected the entire nation simultaneously.

These events are encapsulated in our history books as the "Great Awakenings," a movement based on the call for repentance. The Great Awakening is recorded as starting in the Moravian community in Germany and spreading to England and then on to the US in a westward movement. Because of the scale of revival in the US during the Great Awakening, though, it dominates the landscape of history and is falsely remembered as a uniquely American event. It was in America but actually occurred worldwide.

Secular historians can't deny the universal outpouring of God's Spirit. By all measures, it was an amazing phenomenon that shaped the nation forever, and it came in a most unusual way.

It is easy for Christians who idealize the idea of revival to look back on the Great Awakening as a wonderful moment in history, but the truth is, many

Christians were opposed to it at the time. It was not the Christians in the church who embraced revival but the people in pubs.

The Great Awakening arguably started with one single sermon—"Sinners in the Hands of an Angry God"—delivered by Jonathan Edwards.

Jonathan was a graduate from Yale University at a time when Yale was focused on raising up an army of pastors and missionaries. He was later the president of Princeton University. He could not have possibly known it then, but his simple sermon "Sinners in the Hands of an Angry God," delivered on July 8, 1741, would transform an entire nation.

Edwards opened up the sermon using scripture mixed with imagery and figurative language. He made the argument that "the floods of God's vengeance have been withheld but your guilt in the meantime is constantly increasing."

Nonbelievers, backsliders, and moderate Christians were instantly shamed by the revelation of their own sin. The conviction of the Holy Spirit was strong and spread like wildfire from coast to prairie.

This awesome confrontation with sin can be seen today in the revivals taking place in China. The Chinese, like the American settlers of old, come together in large groups, tears flowing from their eyes, confessing their sins to one another.

I don't know. Maybe revival tarries today because we have yet to come face-to-face with ourselves and confront the evil in our lives. It is not an easy thing to admit we are evil and have evil thoughts. It is not easy to see ourselves as being evil. We like to see ourselves as one of the good guys, but the truth is, as human beings, we are born into evil—that is to say, we are born with the inclination to sin.

Now, it is true that we are wonderfully and fearfully made in the image of God and have been forgiven for our sins—this teaching gets a lot of attention today. That is the easy sermon to deliver. But the Bible also teaches that our hearts, when left unchecked, have an unlimited capacity for evil and death. We humans are able to create ways to make people suffer that no animal can replicate.

Jonathan Edwards brought the evil of man front and center, and thus began the Great Awakening.

Many people do not think of themselves as evil or they think they have not done things as bad as others, but Jesus tells us that the mere thought of an evil act is evil in itself (Matthew 5:28). Tell me a person's thoughts and I can predict their future, not because I am a prophet, but because our thoughts form actions, actions form habits, and habits form character.

You cannot have an honest character if you are in the habit of lying, because you would not be in the habit of lying if your thoughts were full of truth. In order for your actions to produce habits that lie you would need to first be in the habit of thinking those lies.

I would venture to say that most of us deem others to be more evil than we are, when in all likelihood, if we were to pull back the curtain of Oz and take an honest look at ourselves, we are just as bloody evil as the people we detest. The Bible teaches us that the heart of man—our hearts, our thoughts—are a dark and evil place capable of the darkest of sins.

Often in the news we see passionate protestors screaming at the top of their lungs, yelling at people they believe to be more evil than they are. They are convinced that the world is full of good and evil, and they are good and others are evil.

I used to think there was a line on the ground separating good from evil and you had to choose your side, but Jonathan Edwards convinced people that the line is not on the ground but is a line that runs down the middle of the heart of every man and woman.

An honest evaluation of the evil in our own lives will do two things: first, it will heighten self-awareness and next, it will punch us in the face with the reality of how evil our sins are.

This is not easy to accept. Especial today when modern Christian understanding has whitewashed sin.

Being a sinner has been sanitized.

Today if—*if*—we see ourselves as sinners, then we often dismiss our sins as "mistakes." Sin is equated with mistakes. We say nonchalantly, "Well, you know I am a sinner. I make mistakes. God knows I am not perfect."

But making a mistake is not the definition of sin. Sin is evil, not a mistake. When you and I were given a clear choice between good and evil, we willingly and wantonly chose evil. That is the definition of being a sinner.

As hard as it might be to say, sin is evil and has brought the blackest, darkest, most violating behavior to our world and resides in us until it is washed away by the blood of Jesus. Sin is the kind of evil that when we fully recognize it in our own hearts with full disclosure, it haunts us and terrifies us until we cry and weep before the Lord, begging for His forgiveness and come to full repentance.

> **Sin is evil, not a mistake.**

That was the scene of the Great Awakening—people in anguish, crying out in desperation for the forgiveness of God. That is why sinners during the Great Awakening cried out to the Lord and begged for God to come and rip evil from their hearts. The kind of anguish and desperation that Jesus experienced on the cross was the result of our sin and evil, not mistakes. If we are unable to see the evil in our hearts, then it is impossible to bring about repentance that is necessary prior to a phenomenon like the Great Awakening.

DISCUSSION QUESTIONS

1. "Sinners in the Hands of an Angry God" sounds like a pretty severe message. Do you know of similar sermons in the Bible? If so, what were the results of those sermons?
2. Do you think it is a timeless message, or do you think it would not be a good way to reach people in your context? Why do you think so?
3. Do you remember a moment in your life when you realized how depraved you were and how much you needed Jesus? What effect did that have on you?
4. Can you imagine a scene in your church where people would publicly confess their sins through tears? What do you think would keep this from happening?
5. How do you think an event like that would change your church?

DAY 41

A FAN OR A FOLLOWER

---

*"When God closes one door, he opens
another–but it is hell in the hallway."*

—Anonymous

Following revival can easily lead down well-beaten paths worn thin by mobs of believers merely following the person in front of them. The same names of multiple revivalists come up over and over again, but sometimes, on rare occasions, a deeper search will lead down some fascinating alleyways that are full of the most enchanting history.

The Great Awakening helped give birth to a new nation that was different from foreign European governments. The new nation was no longer chained to bloodlines and royal inheritance, but embraced ideals of self-determination and new beginnings. When individuals repented and found renewed faith, they in turn shaped a nation that reflected renewal. It was a nation where the rich could become poor and the poor could be rich. The powerful could be weakened and the weak could be powerful. Race, language, and nationality were no longer the primary factor to determine one's status in society; hard work, dedication, and contribution were.

No one reflected this massive shift in the new national identity following the Great Awakening as did George Lisle.

George was an unlikely character to be used by God in American history, and most people have never heard of him. Every church should know his name, but they do not. George carries the title of the very first American missionary.

George was black and born as a slave on a plantation in the Commonwealth of Virginia immediately following the Great Awakening. Not long after his birth, he was separated from his parents and taken to Savannah, where he would continue working for a British loyalist in Georgia.

In 1773, while sitting in a church that his master attended, he heard Pastor Matthew Moore preach a sermon that made George repent of his sins. He recalled, "I saw my condemnation in my own heart, and I found no way wherein I could escape the damnation of hell, only through the merits of my dying Lord and Savior Jesus Christ."

After giving his heart to Christ, George was immediately burdened with the burning desire to reach other slaves. The leadership at Buckhead Creek Baptist Church recognized that George was especially gifted, so they licensed him to be a minister in the church. His master, Henry Sharpe, saw the passion and power of his preaching and could no longer keep him bound to the duties of a plantation. Henry gave George his freedom to go and preach the Gospel.

Now that George was a free man, he could roam from plantation to plantation to preach the Good News to the slaves. He was on fire. He traveled to South Carolina and started a new church right in the middle of the slave quarters near a place called Silver Bluff, and this is considered to be the first black church in America.

George's wife, Hannah, also became a believer. George was given a barn by a slave owner back in Savannah to use as a church building for the growing number of believers. Soon, he had over seven hundred members and named the church the First African Baptist Church. It was not long before they were planting other churches throughout Georgia.

George was ordained by a white church, planted churches among the black slaves, and in 1802 joined the black and white churches together in a group known as the Savannah Association.

After the death of George's former slave master, Henry Sharpe, Henry's children had him jailed and tried to re-enslave him, but George was able to show his "free papers" and walk away, securing his freedom.

George felt a call to be a missionary and preach the Gospel in nations that had a high number of African slaves. So he set his sights on the island of Jamaica.

When people think of the first American missionaries, they often think of William Carey, who sailed to India in 1793, or Adoniram and Ann Judson, who were sent out to Burma in 1812, but it was actually George Lisle who was the first.

He did not have the money to take his family of four children to Jamaica, but many British troops were fleeing from America to Kingstown, Jamaica, and George was able to find a place on one of the ships for him and his family. In 1782, George was able to connect with Colonel Kirkland, commander of the British troops, and borrowed $700 for passage. In return, George promised to become an indentured servant.

Imagine that! After securing his freedom twice, he gave it up and sold himself back into servanthood in order to take the Gospel to Jamaica!

He immediately went to work preaching among the slaves. Several white Brits were coming to Christ and even joined his church. Some later went out and became missionaries to other nations. Others, like William Knibb and Thomas Burchell, returned to England to campaign for the end of slavery. In 1807, William Wilberforce convinced the British Parliament to abolish slavery.

George personally saw a revival of people and the soul of a nation. By 1814, he had seen more than twenty thousand people come to a personal faith in Jesus Christ and was given the title "Negro Slavery's Prophet of Deliverance." What possessed George, as a former slave, to leave his land of safety and sail with his family to an unknown nation and give up his freedom?

George is easier to understand when you realize that he is a follower of Christ, not a fan. There is a difference.

A fan can lead a solitary life. He can bask in his own freedom and worry himself about the slavery of others; a follower cannot.

Fans have problems that followers do not. Fans can lead lifestyles that are not biblical, justify it, be okay with it, and still claim to be Christian. A follower cannot. A fan can ignore the calling of God on his life to go to a place like Jamaica; a follower cannot.

A follower, like a fan, will sin, but will repent with fear and trembling, knowing full well that one cannot follow Christ and follow sin—it is impossible. A fan of Christ can feel a lot more comfortable with their sin; a follower cannot be comfortable with sin at all.

Following in the footsteps of Christ leads to the daily sacrifice of our own needs and desires. George was not walking in the path of his best interest but in the will of the Father. Walking in the will of the Father leaves no time to walk in the selfish pathway of sin. It is impossible to do both.

> **Following in the footsteps of Christ leads to the daily sacrifice of our own needs and desires.**

First John 1:6 says, "If we say that we fellowship with him, but walk in darkness, we lie." Why would we be lying? Because there is no darkness in Jesus, so if we are following Him, then we are in His light and cannot harbor darkness. We can only harbor darkness when we fall out of fellowship, but not when we are in fellowship with Him, because there is no darkness in Christ—none. "If we walk in the light, as he is in the light, we have fellowship with one another" (v. 7).

While in fellowship with Christ as His followers, we are naturally walking in the light of Christ, and that light exposes sin. Those who follow Christ carry His light. His light illuminates sin. Jesus is the light of the world, right? What does light do? It has "lightyness"; it illuminates. When you are close to the light, your sins are illuminated—exposed—and must be removed, because darkness and light cannot stay in the same space. As a fan of Christ, you are standing in the dark and witnessing the light, not walking in it. Followers walk in it; fans do not.

Jesus said, "Take up your cross and follow Me" (see Matthew 16:24). Paul said, "Follow me as I follow after Christ" (see 1 Corinthians 11:1).

A fan might say, "I believe in Jesus. I read my Bible. I raised my hand to ask Jesus in my heart. Isn't that enough?"

No, that is not enough. Satan believes in Jesus and knows Him intimately in ways that we do not. He has seen the power of God up close, personal, and over thousands of years. He knows the words of the Bible and has quoted it often in order to trick the very elect, but these things do not make him saved. It is good to do those things, but they are not the only signs of a follower.

I raised my hand when I became a believer and even prayed the sinner's prayer, but never in the Bible do we see that Jesus asked anyone to raise their hand or pray a sinner's prayer as a sign of believing in Him. It is nice to do, but there is only one way Christians were identified in the Bible. There was only one litmus test that we know of. Christians were identified as those who were followers of Jesus Christ. Simple.

Conversely, those who denied Jesus and did not believe in Him did not follow Him.

This seems so simple but is profoundly different from what we practice today. Today, fans of Christ are looking to do the bare minimum required to be a Christian. They do not want to follow. Their love of self restricts them from following. They might ask questions like, "Can I live with my girlfriend and be a Christian?" There can be a debate about their salvation, but there is no debate that they are not a follower of Christ. A follower of Christ does not need to ask that question because they are walking in the light that illuminates the sin of cohabitation before marriage.

A follower might ask, "But if I have raised my hand and prayed the prayer on Sunday, can I lose my salvation if I continue the life I have lived before I raised my hand?" No, you can't if you plan to be a follower of Christ. These are questions that come from fans, not followers.

When you are a follower like George Lisle, and not a fan, you are not trying to determine what is the least amount of effort needed to obtain salvation. Followers of Christ do not have to ask that question because they have a relationship. They are walking in the light. Their sins are illuminated and the darkness has to flee. If you want the darkness to stay, then you have to leave the light.

Fans ask questions to defend a philosophy, not to obtain a closer relationship.

The world likes Christians as long as they are fans. They do not like followers. The world is comfortable being around fans. Followers make them uncomfortable because the light they carry chases away the darkness.

Fans compromise and confuse it with love. Followers cannot compromise because they love too deeply. Followers are radical. The world embraces radical hate better than radical love.

George had radical love, the kind of love that led him to sell his freedom so that he could take the Gospel message to Jamaica.

DISCUSSION QUESTIONS

1. In 1 Corinthians 7:22, Paul wrote, "For the one who was a slave when called to faith in the Lord is the Lord's freed person; similarly, the one who was free when called is Christ's slave" (NIV). How does this scripture redefine both slavery and freedom?
2. In what ways are you free? In what ways are you a slave?
3. George Lisle saw freedom as a tool to be used for the Gospel, not as an end in itself. He was willing to sacrifice it. Do you think freedom is essential for happiness? Why or why not?
4. At what point does freedom become an idol?
5. Do you consider yourself to be more of a fan or a follower of Jesus? If you are more of a fan, what holds you back from following Jesus more closely? If you are more of a follower, what makes it worth it?

DAY 42

THE SWORD OF GOLIATH

"And David said, There is none like that; give it me."

—1 Samuel 21:9

There is a small story in the Bible that brings excitement to anyone who discovers it. It follows one of the most notable events in the Bible about David and Goliath.

Everyone knows the story about David fighting Goliath. Goliath was a massive giant, intimidating the armies of Israel, and David was a humble, inexperienced shepherd boy whom God used to defeat the giant, but the story does not stop there.

The Philistines were supposed to serve the Israelites and be their slaves if David beat Goliath (1 Samuel 17:9), but they did not. In fact, they continued to terrorize the Jewish people. A few chapters later, we see that David was once again forced to fight the Philistines and once again his men were too scared to do so (1 Samuel 23:1–5), but at the command of the Lord, David fought them and was victorious.

The fact that he was victorious in the battle with the Philistines might have something to do with the sword he was using. What did he have in his hands to fight the Philistines?

Before David went to battle, we are told that he was in a place called Nob. He was without a sword or a spear, so he asked the priest if there was anything nearby that he could use as a weapon, and the priest responded, "The sword of Goliath the Philistine, whom thou slewest in the vale of Elah, behold, it is here wrapped in a cloth behind the ephod: if thou wilt take that, take it; for there is no other save that here. And David said, There is none like that; give it me" (1 Samuel 21:9).

The very sword that was swung by the enemy Goliath to kill David was now in David's possession to be used to protect him.

Sometimes, while researching the history of revival, I have found that the very thing the enemy tries to use against the church to destroy it becomes the very thing God uses to bring about His glory!

> **The very thing the enemy tries to use against the church to destroy it becomes the very thing God uses to bring about His glory!**

In the darkest hour, during your most seemingly humiliating defeat, you may suddenly find yourself saying the words of David: "Bring me Goliath's sword; there is none like it."

During the summer of 1900, one of the deadliest events in history took place. A group of men in China who belonged to a secret society known in English as the Boxers came together with a plan to attack foreigners in China. They saw the foreigners who were living in China as occupiers and found their presence detestable.

They prepared for a war that would come to be known as the Boxer Rebellion, but they didn't train like a regular army would. Instead, they had a different plan. They believed they could conduct rituals, chant dark prayers, and ask demons to possess their bodies. Their secret society allowed their hair to grow long, they wore special black clothing, and they followed ancient rituals of black magic.

When demons took possession of these men, they immediately felt supernatural strength. The Boxers believed that the evil spirits that possessed them would make them impervious to bullets or being sliced by a sword.

The Boxers had some valid reasons for hating the presence of foreigners in their land. Foreign nations like England were strategically encouraging and promoting an addiction to drugs in China in order to debilitate the people and take the resources they wanted. If the Boxers wanted to fight the foreign armies and force them out of their land, there would have been a lot of sympathetic support for their efforts at home and abroad.

In fact, the foreign missionaries in China were also resisting the activities by the imperialists. They campaigned against them at home, provided the world's first drug rehab centers, and conducted the world's first research on the impact of drugs.

We take it for granted today that drugs are bad, but actually it was not a proven fact in the late 1800s. It was the missionaries who provided scientific proof that the impact of opium was harmful to the human body. It was the missionaries who started the very first clinics and hospitals in China. They started the first schools for women and trained female doctors.

Thousands of Chinese came to Christ because of the good work of the Christian missionaries, and the enemy got scared.

The Boxers began their attacks and went about killing foreigners, but not the foreigners responsible for the drug trade. They specifically targeted Christian missionaries. Hundreds of missionaries were dragged from their homes. Their wives were stripped naked and marched through the streets, raped, and killed. Their children were forced to crawl on their bellies at the feet of the Boxers, and their tiny heads were smashed in by the crowds.

Nuns were dragged out of orphanages they had started, stripped, beaten, and brutally murdered. Their corpses were displayed on posts like trophies.

It was not just the foreign missionaries who were maimed and killed. The Boxers hunted Christian Chinese converts. About thirty thousand men, women, and children were slaughtered in some of the most horrific ways. The Boxers killed and killed until the demons that possessed them were drunk from the rivers of Christian blood that ran through the streets.

The Boxer Rebellion is remembered as the largest foreign missionary slaughter in recorded history.

That was the summer of 1900. As news went out to America and Europe, churches and families wept over the deaths of the missionary families. There were no bodies to be returned for a proper burial.

A few months later, on the evening of December 31, 1900, in a small corner of the United States, in Topeka, Kansas, a revival began that would emerge in places all over the world.

A man by the name of Pastor Parham, who had been kicked out of his church, held a New Year's prayer service in an old upper room. As they began to pray throughout the night, a woman by the name of Agnes Ozman started praying in a language that no one understood and she could not stop.

They continued to pray, and for three days Agnes Ozman could not pray in English. She could not speak in English. She could not even write in English. People came from far and wide to witness the phenomenon, and it was discovered that Agnes was praying in Chinese, a language she had never heard or been exposed to.

Revival broke out in 1901 in Topeka, Kansas, and it looked a lot like the revival on the day of Pentecost in Acts 2.

The following year, in 1902, revival broke out in Wales. A few years later, in 1906, revival broke out in Azusa Street in California. The following year, in 1907, revival broke out in Scandinavia. It was a mighty wave of revival, and it was sweeping through the world.

The immediate result of the revival was missions.

The immediate result of the revival was missions. Missionaries were sent out, and most of them only had one place on their mind: China. More missionaries were sent to China in the wake of the Boxer Rebellion than any other time in Chinese history. In fact, it led to what many refer to as the golden age of Chinese missions.

The Boxers swung Goliath's sword, but it didn't destroy the church in China. In fact, it had the opposite effect. It started a revival that went around the world and sparked one of the largest Chinese missionary movements in recorded history.

DISCUSSION QUESTIONS

1. Demon possession is no longer widely accepted as a real thing. Would it be possible to explain the Boxer Rebellion without this element? Why or why not?

2. Are there other events in history that are difficult to rationally explain apart from a direct influence of evil powers?

3. With hindsight we can see that even this unspeakable evil was used by God to accomplish His will. But during and right after the rebellion, that must have been nearly impossible for the missionaries and their families to believe. Have you ever experienced grave injustice to the point where it was hard to trust God? Have you ever seen God take the sword that was used against you and bring about something good?

4. Why do you think God gave the church in Kansas a miracle, the woman speaking Chinese, instead of just a regular "burden for China"? How does this miracle fit a pattern of miracles in other revivals?

DAY 43

AMERICA AND THE BIBLE

———◆———

"If our Founding Fathers wanted us to care about the rest of the world, they wouldn't have declared their independence from it."

—Stephen Colbert

As I travel in America today, I can't help but wonder what happened to the great revivals. Where did they go? Has the Spirit of the Lord become the victor in America or is He now being ignored?

Has Christianity in America grown into a club where believers feel empowered but are toothless and harmless? American Christians take great pride in being Christian, but could that be their weakness? Is there a certain egotism that comes with knowing that Christianity has been entrenched in America for so long that it is now taken for granted, creating an atmosphere of complacency?

> **Is there a certain egotism that comes with knowing that Christianity has been entrenched in America for so long.**

Have they traded the idea of being victorious Christians for a self-centered existence?

When Christians are told that the main purpose of *their* faith is to focus on *their* life, *their* finances, *their* ministry, and *their* health, then all of the knowledge and power of the Gospel is squandered in a quarantined environment while the lost world goes to hell.

The Mesoamericans are said to have played a ball game that was extremely intensive and brutal. Some say the winners would be awarded as a sacrifice to the gods, meaning that winning would be certain death. Being brutally sacrificed does not sound like much of a trophy for the winning team.

Are American Christians playing a losing game when they cling to royal robes of revival but abandon the cross of sacrifice? Is it possible to stop the digression and return to the sacrificial Gospel that focuses out instead of in?

When Jesus prayed that we would be in the world but not be "of the world" (John 17:14–17), what did that actually mean and how can we manifest it in our lives?

There is one group in America that has effectively removed themselves from mainstream society. They experienced amazing revivals long before America was even a nation. They are collectively known as the Anabaptists, and there is no other group in America quite like them.

Their presence in the United States predates the founding of the nation by about two centuries, and even though their expression of faith looks much different from mainstream American Christianity, they have greatly shaped the laws of the nation in a way that benefits all believers.

When we think of revival, we usually do not think of Anabaptists, which include the Amish and Mennonites. They seem to represent the exact opposite of revival fire. They are ultraconservative and are made up of small communities of people that have chosen to be separated from the world, but their history of revival fires run deeper than many know.

Outside of the Anabaptist communities very little is known about their revival renaissance, but the impact God had on their people was transformative and, in turn, the impact they have had on America is irreplaceable.

The idea of one being baptized as a result of an individual decision seems very normal today in America, but it was a very radical idea when championed by the Anabaptists in the 1520s. The idea of separation of church and state might seem to be very natural today in America, but it was an idea that led to many Anabaptists being hunted down and slaughtered. Having the right to freedom of speech and freedom of religion are ideas that are ingrained in the minds of Americans, but the seeds sprang forth, not from the colonialists, but from the Anabaptists, who have a long tradition of expressing strong suspicion of empires, power politics, and church-state relationships.

The revival experienced by Anabaptists made them useless to the world. They abandoned everything that did not bring them closer to God and have attempted to stop time from progressing from the point of their conversion. Much of what they believed is closely shared with the Waldensians, Bohemian Reformation, and the Moravian movement that brought revival to the US.

Anabaptists believe that there are two worlds: one that belongs to God and one that belongs to Caesar. Christians must decide which world they want to belong to. Anabaptists have clung so tightly to the idea of a Jesus who loves man unconditionally that they cannot be convinced that He would ever want His disciples to harm another human being. They do not believe in participating in any act that would harm anyone, especially war.

Anabaptists are radically anti-violent and detest fighting, even in the case of self-defense. They have suffered greatly for their faith. During WWI, four Anabaptists (David, Joseph, and Michael Hofer and Jacob Wipf) from South Dakota were drafted into the military but could not overcome their strong feelings of faith that prevented them from putting on the uniform. The deep lessons that their ancestors learned during the revival of their radical reformation could not be tossed aside, even during desperate times of war.

Conrad Grebel perfectly summed it up when he wrote, "True Christian believers are sheep among wolves, sheep for the slaughter. . . . Neither do they use worldly sword or war, since all killing has ceased with them."[19]

The four men were shipped out from their hometown in South Dakota with a group of drafted young men. They looked suspiciously different from the others. Their plain black clothes, black broad-rim hats, and long beards stood out in direct contrast to all of the clean-shaven men in military uniform.

They were further viewed with suspicion because they spoke German, the language of the enemy.

They were rejected by their fellow Americans, who beat them, held them down, and forcefully shaved off their beards. After being beaten and shaved, they were tried by military court-martial.

The camp authorities charged the Hutterites with disobeying orders, thus violating two of the Articles of War. In the trial, officers recounted their efforts to persuade the men to line up and fill out the requisite forms. Jacob Wipf was the first defendant to take the stand.

Jacob answered the questions the best that he could as an uneducated farmer whose mother tongue was German.

The military prosecutor began to question Jacob:

Q: Are you willing to take part in any noncombatant branch of the service of the army?

A: No; we can't.

Q: What are your reasons?

A: Well, it is all for war. The only thing we can do is work on a farm for the poor and needy ones of the United States.

Q: What do you mean by poor and needy ones?

A: Well, those that can't help themselves.

Q: Would you include soldiers who are crippled for life?

A: Yes. They are poor and needy ones. . . .

Q: If you were in the service, such as the Medical Corps, where you would attend the wounded soldiers, would your conscience and the teachings of the church permit that?

A: We can't do that, because a soldier, he will go and fight, and that is helping the war, and we can't do that.

Q: And if there were wounded soldiers about, you couldn't help them? You couldn't help them because you would be afraid they might recover and go back to the war; is that it?

A: Well, it would be helping the war.

Q: Would you be willing to be placed on a farm by the government and grow wheat for soldiers?

A: No.

The prosecutor then wanted to know if the commitment to nonviolence extended to the home.

Q: Does your religion believe in fighting of any kind?

A: No.

Q: You would not fight with your fists?

A: Well, we ain't no angels. Little boys will scrap sometimes, and we are punished; but our religion don't allow it.

Q: To put the case like this: If a man was attacking or assaulting your sister, would you fight?

A: No.

Q: Would you kill him?

A: No.

Q: What would you do?

A: Well, in a way, if I could get her away, I might hold him. If I was man enough, I would do that. If I couldn't, I would have to let go. We can't kill. That is strictly against our religion.[20]

All four men were found guilty of disobeying orders during a time of war. They were immediately sent to one of the most notorious prisons in the US that was reserved for the most violent criminals: Alcatraz. They were among 142 other Anabaptists who were imprisoned for refusing to go against their belief in God and participate in the war effort.

Upon arrival they were beaten, starved, and thrown into solitary confinement cells. They were left in the cold with no clothes and cuffed to the cell so high that only their toes could touch the floor. They weren't given access to toilets, warm clothing, or food.

Like a scene from a Communist gulag, the guards took great delight in beating them. The four men of God took refuge in the Words of the Lord, often quoting scripture to keep hope alive.

After the war was over, celebration filled almost every street in America. The four men from South Dakota were shipped to a military prison known as Ft. Leavenworth. Ft. Leavenworth was the last place Michael and Joseph would ever see. They had been beaten so badly that their bodies could no longer take it. They both died shortly after arrival.

When their families came to pick up the bodies, they were shocked to discover that, to further humiliate them, the officials had dressed them in full military uniform as a final insult to their beliefs.

The question must be asked, what would possess a nation founded on Christian principles to treat Christians with such disdain and vile hate? How far from redemptive revival fires does one stray before casting away the renewal of mind and heart that is filled with empathy and love for his fellow man?

After evaluating revival in America, it is clear that few things give more hope than revival and few things reveal more flaws. The flaws of a nation are only exposed through the magnifying lens of revival. A sinful nation without revival is not reflective because they have no measure in which to compare their destitution.

A nation that has never experienced revival does not question events like what happened to the four men from South Dakota. Men and women who have never tasted the sweet waters of revival readily drink from the fountains of pain and misery without question. The kingdom of man knows nothing else. How can a man who has never tasted chocolate ever miss it or desire it?

The equal distribution of suffering is the natural outlet of institutions established by man. Pain received translates to pain given. Hurt people hurt people.

But a redemptive people ought to know better. A nation transformed by revival should be haunted with the vivid images of those they wronged until effort is made to make it right.

The consequence of revival is that higher standards of responsibility exists. Christians cannot rejoice as victors while people in their midst suffer at the hands of injustice. They should celebrate their salvation with the ever-present, sober knowledge that many more are dying while awaiting the Good News. They ought not to become too intoxicated with their own inflated status that they fail to observe that they are surrounded by a sea of those who are drowning because they are lost.

> **The consequence of revival is that higher standards of responsibility exists.**

DISCUSSION QUESTIONS

1. In what ways do you think America's revival history has impacted the United States and the rest of the world?
2. Do you agree that countries that have known revival have a higher social conscience? If so, can you give examples?
3. Mennonites and Amish have chosen to form close-knit communities. Do you think a degree of isolation from society can preserve elements of revival within that group? If so, do you think these isolated groups can still impact society in a positive way? Can you give examples?

PART 7

CHINA: REVIVAL IN THE MIDDLE KINGDOM

DAY 44

THE WORLD'S LARGEST REVIVAL

"The Chinese culture belongs not only to the
Chinese but also to the whole world."

—HU JINTAO

From the Americas, the winds of revival continued their westward march.

In recent history, because of the missionary efforts of the Western church, many in China have mistaken Christianity to be a Western religion. It is not.

China is as far from Western culture as can be imagined, and any exposure to the religions in China would lead one to falsely believe that China has never experienced a revival.

Because China is a Communist country, many think that it is and always has been atheist, but a simple stroll through a few older mountain villages would quickly prove your assumption wrong. Even with the brutal enforcement of Communism, many colorful villages of China are still heavily sprinkled with images of Buddhism, Animism, Taoism, and Confucianism that lead the lives of many people.

> **Many in China have mistaken Christianity to be a Western religion. It is not.**

In China there are altars built to Buddha and for ancestral worship, but these ancient beliefs are not as old as the Chinese culture. Taoism and Confucianism can be traced all the way back to the third and fourth centuries BC, which is an impressively long history for any nation, but it is still not as old as the ancient Chinese culture.

Chinese history stretches back almost to the beginning of time and is more than two thousand years older than the oldest traces of Taoism, Confucianism, or Buddhism. So the question is, what religion did the ancient Chinese practice before the arrival of these other religions that are found in China today?

The answer might be surprising.

Today China is experiencing the world's largest Christian revival numerically. At first glance, it might seem to be a new phenomenon, but if you pull back the veil on Chinese history, you will find a garden that God planted in the hearts of the Chinese generations ago.

Their revival is rooted in the country's foundations. Although it would be impossible to give a comprehensive account of China's long and rich history prior to the arrival of other religions, it is possible to give a brief account of the One Supreme God of China who was worshipped in ancient history.

One dreary fall day in Beijing, a very well-known underground house church pastor took me on a tour of the most popular tourist attraction known as the Temple of Heaven. The pastor's name is Zhang Rongliang, and he is no stranger to the modern-day revival in China. His church is currently estimated to have about 10 million believers.

The Temple of Heaven houses the largest altar in the world. Pastor Zhang pointed out that the purpose of the temple was to offer sacrificial worship to Shangdi (the God of Heaven) for a good harvest.

Shangdi is the name that Christians in China currently use for the God of the Christian Bible. The very word *Shangdi* is thought to be the Chinese pronunciation of the Jewish word *Shaddai,* which is one of the Hebrew names for God.

Is it possible that Shangdi of the famous ancient Temple of Heaven in Beijing is the same Shangdi the Chinese Christians pray to today? The Shangdi of ancient China was the creator of all things and was alone in

His rule. It was a monotheistic faith that existed thousands of years before Confucianism, Buddhism, Taoism, or Communism.

As I walked around the Temple of Heaven with Pastor Zhang, he pointed out several noteworthy things.

First, there is not even one picture of Shangdi. Of all the gods in China, Shangdi is the only one you will not find a picture of. This seems to be directly in line with Exodus 20:4: "Thou shalt not make unto thee any graven image, or any likeness of any thing that is in heaven above, or that is in the earth beneath, or that is in the water under the earth."

Also, throughout the temple, there are clear reflections of the Trinity. The roof of the temple and the steps leading up to the temple are both divided into three parts. Even the entire area is divided into three parts, with the sacrificial alter on one side, the temple on the other, and a bridge in the middle. There were common courts, outer courts, and inner courts. The ancient sacrifices that were performed by the emperor took place after he had fasted for three days.

Pastor Zhang stood together with me at the Temple of Heaven and shared openly that the current revival being experienced in China is not a new movement, but rather a return to the nation's most ancient spiritual roots.

If we look at the timeline of Chinese history and compare it to the timelines found in the Bible, then it is not a stretch to believe that the founder of China, Huang Di, heard the stories of Adam from some of Noah's direct descendants.

Adam lived 900 years. Methuselah, 969 years. It was only eight generations from creation to the Flood. That means that Methuselah was alive during the lifetime of Adam and during the life of Noah.

And that means that Noah would have known the stories of Adam directly from the generation of Methuselah and would have been able to share them with his three sons. And this means that the Yellow Emperor (Huang Di) could have very well heard the stories of the Jehovah directly from the sons and grandsons of Noah.

The oldest existing Chinese records date from the Shang Dynasty (1600–1046 BC). These first archeologically verifiable records of Chinese history, known as oracle bones, were written on tortoise shells and cow bones. They mention Shangdi as the One Supreme God who ruled over all other spirits and had control over the weather, the harvests, and the outcome of battles. The Chinese characters on the oracle bones are interesting in themselves because they contain references to pre-Flood biblical history and theological concepts.

> **Chinese is one of the oldest continuous languages on earth, and has clear traces of the stories of the Bible.**

Chinese is one of the oldest continuous languages on earth, and the writing they use has clear traces of the stories of the Bible.

Here is just a sample of Chinese characters that have biblical connections:

Genesis 2:17 says, "Of the tree of the knowledge of good and evil you shall not eat" (ESV). God forbad them to eat. To forbid in Chinese is 襟. This Chinese character is made up of several smaller characters. God (礻) put them in the garden with two trees (林) and then gave them revelation 示 (*shi*) that they should not eat of the fruit.

Genesis 3:1 says that the serpent was more cunning than all others who came to tempt the woman. *Mo* is the word for tempter (魔). In this character there is a garden (田) and then there is movement in the garden. There was one man (儿). There is a secret told to the man in the garden (厶). This character means devil (鬼). A tempter is the devil (鬼) that comes under the secret cover of two trees (林).

Genesis 4 records the first murder. The word for brother in Chinese is *xiong* (兄). The word for murderer sounds the same as brother—*xiong*. The only difference between the two is the way that it is written—兇. In Genesis, Cain, who killed his brother, had a mark on his head, just as the story is told in the Chinese characters.

The ancient character for boat combines the pictographs for eight (八) and mouth (口) (referring to people), and ship or vessel (舟). Together they make the word for boat (船). According to the Bible, there were exactly eight persons on board Noah's ark.

Pastor Zhang continued to teach about the ancient God of Shangdi at the Temple of Heaven so boldly that I thought we might get arrested, so I asked him to follow me to a quiet area of the park, where we continued our conversation. Pastor Zhang believes that these elements in Chinese history are being re-revealed to the people of China to show them that the God of heaven is not a Western invention but is the original God the Chinese worshipped!

DISCUSSION QUESTIONS

1. Can you find evidence in the Bible that the worship of the one true God was not limited to Abraham and his offspring?
2. Do you think it is possible that traces of knowledge of the true God remain outside of Christianity in people groups that have not heard the Gospel? Why or why not? Have you heard of any examples of this?
3. If you were not a Christian, do you think it would be easier for you to accept the Gospel if you knew your ancestors had served the same God in the distant past? Why or why not?
4. Do you think it is good to go back in a nation's history to find foundation stones that can be used to build the proclamation of the Gospel on?
5. Are there such foundation stones in the history of your culture?

DAY 45

CHINA'S FORGOTTEN BELIEVER

---

*"Calamity has its roots in prosperity,
prosperity has its roots in calamity."*

—CHINESE PROVERB

Along a narrow, windy mountain road in a small rural village outside of the ancient capital city of Xi'an stand towering sandstone Persian pillars. They are completely out of place. They do not fit in with the environment at all.

Up the mountain, overlooking the Persian pillars, is a multilevel Buddhist temple that is cared for by a few lonely monks.

After driving around for several hours looking for this remote temple, I finally arrived and met with the monks as they were tending to their small temple garden.

Next to the garden was a stone tablet that looked a lot like a tall grave stone. Engraved on the stone was the history of the temple. The stone was the reason I had flown all the way to Xi'an. The history was written in both Chinese and Persian and plainly explained that the temple was not a Buddhist temple, but is actually the oldest church in all of China.

The church was built almost 1,400 years ago by the first missionaries who came to China from the area that is now Iran. These missionaries climbed over the mountains carrying nothing more than a basket, a walking stick, and the Word of God in their heart.

Few people would guess that the oldest church in China is that old, and even fewer would guess that it was built from missionaries from Iran! Chasing revival history has lead me down some roads that have completely shaken my understanding of world history.

History really is His-story!

These missionaries came with a simple message of salvation for the Chinese. Unlike the Roman Catholic Church, which burdened unreached nationals with the obligation of learning their language and adopting their culture, the Nestorian missionaries from Iran were adaptive and assumed the culture and learned the language of those they were trying to reach.

They planted the seeds of the Gospel in the Middle Kingdom, and those seeds took root at the highest levels. Not even the emperor was immune to the seeds of the Gospel that these first missionaries had sown. China has had more than three hundred emperors who have ruled throughout their history, but few of them are as well-known as Kangxi. Emperor Kangxi was the longest-ruling emperor (1661 to 1722); he took the thrown when he was only seven years old and lead China for sixty-one years.

Kangxi proved to be an amazing ruler in both war and peace, and during his reign, China prospered greatly and that period is considered to be China's golden age.

Kangxi ruled during the Qing Dynasty and is where we get the word *China*, because the Persians referred to China as "Sheen" or "Sheena," which became the popular name along the ancient Silk Road.

What most people do not know is that Kangxi was actually a believer in Jesus Christ. He was the first leader of the Qing Dynasty to be born in the Forbidden City of China and the first emperor we know of who recorded giving his heart to God.

Look at this poem he wrote called the "Treasure of Life":

> The treasure of heaven is comprised of Sun, Moon and Stars;
> The treasure of earth consists of crops, gold and silver.
> The treasure of a kingdom is to have righteous officials;
> The treasure of a family is to have descendants with piety.

Yet, Gold, silver and jade are not as precious as one's life.

Hundred years of age is nothing compared to eternity.

Coming and going in life is like a dream.

The best food and clothing don't mean a thing.

It's no exception for someone born in a royal family.

The most important thing in the world is life.

Something that white jade, gold and silver can't buy.

Even plain porridge can be satisfying;

No cloth is fit to wear for a thousand years.

The heaven's gate was closed due to the first man's sin;

The path to salvation is through the Son only.

I would like to accept God, the Son and the Holy Spirit;

And receive from thee my free gift of eternity.

—Written by the hand of KANGXI of Qing Dynasty

After reading a few of Kangxi's amazing writings, most historians will reluctantly concede that Kangxi appreciated Christianity, but they stop short of saying he was a Christian. Unfortunately for those who would try to hide this, Kangxi's vivid poetry describes his own confession and then he even signed it!

Kangxi trusted in Christ, and the Chinese culture flourished under his rule. He ordered the compilation of Chinese words to make the first language dictionary. He compiled Tang poetry so that it would not disappear. The term *china* in reference to blue and white porcelain dishes comes from this period. He learned to play a musical instrument from the West and imported Western technology that greatly benefited the Chinese people. He worked with Christians like Karel Slavíček to make the first precise map of China. He invented the first Chinese calendar.

Kangxi was the King Solomon of China and was perhaps the wisest emperor in the history of the Middle Kingdom. Kangxi was keenly aware of where his blessings came from and made efforts to share the Gospel with others. He was the first emperor to send Chinese Christians from the royal court to Europe to be trained as clergy members with the plan that they would later return to China and teach the Chinese about Jesus.

Kangxi issued the Edict of Tolerance, which recognized Christianity and made it illegal in China to attack churches or Chinese Christians, which ushered in a brief time of Christian missions and evangelism.

It was an amazing time in China that the next emperor would frantically try to erase. Before his death, Kangxi wrote a poem that would one day echo in the hearts of the Chinese people.

THE POEM ON TRUTH

Everything as seen by the eye is His creation.

He who has no beginning and no end, is three persons in one.

The heaven's gate was closed to the first man's sin and reopens through the Son.

Rid of all false religions, we should become real disciples admired by everyone.

DISCUSSION QUESTIONS

1. How do you think missionaries should approach local cultures and customs? Is learning the native language important or not?
2. What do you think about the strategy of sending your smartest people as missionaries to assist foreign governments?
3. In our day, would the conversion of a president or king make a big difference to the nation? Why or why not?
4. China was known as an accomplished civilization. Do you think the level of scientific development of a nation or people group should make a difference in what kind of missionaries we send? Why?

DAY 46

FROM BANDIT TO BELIEVER

———◆———

"If you want happiness for an hour, take a nap. If you want happiness for a day, go fishing. If you want happiness for a month, get married. If you want happiness for a year, inherit a fortune. If you want happiness for a lifetime, help someone else."

—Chinese Proverb

When China flickers in our modern-day imagination, it is void of any Christian foundation. That is by design. The enemy has gone to great pains to hide the country's true identity. The prince has been dressed in the rags of a beggar and raised in the squalor of a stable, but the royal bloodline has not been diluted.

From the mountaintops of China's highest peaks, the enemy has been shouting, "China belongs to Buddha, China belongs to Confucius, China belongs to Communism." China is far too large for the snake to swallow. The serpent has bitten off more than he can chew and is choking. The true identity of China is surfacing from an uncontrollable gag reflex.

Trails of rich heritage long buried deep are now bubbling up to the surface in the final days, and the religion that China has deemed a foreign devil is now embraced as heritage. The restrictive web of lies is coming unraveled with renewed revelations, and it is exciting.

> The religion that China has deemed a foreign devil is now embraced as heritage.

Today's revival in China might have aspects that are

mysterious to outsiders, but they are nothing more than logically chained events that do not pose a surprise to the divine Conductor.

"Oh, look, there is a new revival over there in China," they say, but they are so very wrong. It is not new! It is far from new. In fact, there are few things on this earth that are older. The ingredients were put in the oven generations ago, and now the time has finally arrived for the dish to be served.

The fresh aroma of revival fills the air, and hungry guests await at the table. They have been waiting for a long time.

The first missionaries from Iran mixed with the omnipotent Shangdi at the Temple of Heaven, sprinkled with a pinch of Boxer Rebellion, and left to marinate in the leadership of Emperor Kangxi have created a savory revival like none other.

Today, one could easily assume the revival being experienced in the coastal city of Wenzhou is new, but upon investigation one can see that it is the result of careful preparation spanning the centuries.

It is common knowledge among the politburo that there are a large number of Christians in Wenzhou. It was one of the first places in the country where the government had to openly admit defeat to its aggressive resistance of proselytizing. The number of Christians in Wenzhou was just too high, and after thirty years of persecution, authorities came to the conclusion that the persistent faith couldn't be stamped out. At one point the Chinese government was reported by the *New York Times* as saying that 10 percent of all Christians in China were in Wenzhou alone.

Unregistered churches in Wenzhou built meeting places throughout the city with large red crosses prominently displayed on the steeples. The government attempted to destroy all these buildings in 2016 and 2017 and even bulldozed many to the ground, but it hasn't stopped the growth. Today there is said to be one church in Wenzhou for every square kilometer.

Wenzhou is only one city. There are many other cities throughout China that share a similar story to Wenzhou. If the Chinese were forced to look at their reflection in the mirror of time, I should think they would be incredibly embarrassed at the number of testimonies they keep hidden in their cupboard. It appears they have forgotten more than they have learned.

One of these stories concerns the very first president and founding father of the Republic of China, who was a man after God's own heart. President Sun Yat-sen overthrew the Qing Dynasty and paved the way for Chinese independence. He is uniquely loved by both the Chinese and the Taiwanese. There have been few leaders like him in the twentieth century.

In the late 1800s, as a young man Sun joined a group of likeminded men in Hong Kong, and they later became known as the Four Bandits. Together they attended the Hong Kong College of Medicine for Chinese, a school that would later become the University of Hong Kong.

Sun became a radical Christian believer and quit medical school so he could bring reform to China. Other scholars, like Chan Siu-bak, joined his band of bandits. Chan came from a family of Christian scholars and knew the importance of building a society on the foundations of Christian principles. In 1895, Chan and Sun started the Revive China Society. Together they formed a radical group of reformers that was ready to change China forever.

Sun believed his endeavors were similar to the salvation mission of the Christian church, and he believed God had called him to bring China back to Him. These beliefs drove his aspirations to make China a free society.

In 1912, Sun became the first president in the history of China. That was a huge change from four to five thousand years of China being ruled by an emperor. Like the most famous emperor in China, Kangxi, Sun publicly sought the will of Christ. He did not just merely refer to himself as a Christian, but boldly proclaimed, "As for my religion, I worship Jesus!" Not many Western leaders in charge of traditional Christian countries would make such a bold claim today.

Sun once said, "I am a Christian; God sent me to fight evil for my people. Jesus was a revolutionist; so am I," but was he really a revolutionary? President Sun saw himself as ushering in something new and different for China, but in actuality, he was bringing back something old. He and his band of Christian bandits attempted to bring China back to the roots of their heritage. Perhaps that makes him more of a reformer and less of a revolutionary.

Sun was among the earliest to awaken that which was long thought to be dead and gone. Now the seeds of old have sprouted. Slumbering in the bitter winter cold, the ancient seeds were only dormant for a spell. Spring has arrived and ushered in the pleasing song of resurrection.

The old bones are coming to life. The valley of the dead was only hibernating.

Awaken and pulled from the pages of history are the wisdom of our fathers and the heart of worship that is enshrined in our relics. Purposefully imposed ignorance paves the path of slaves, but radical bandits buck the lies, stir the masses, and point to the icons of freedom that are brandished in the unbroken chain of time. Those who wake the sleeping are not always well received. Sacrifice is needed. As President Sun Yat-sen said, "When we undertake a task, we should not falter from first to last until the task is accomplished; if we fail, we should not begrudge our lives as a sacrifice—this is what we mean by loyalty. The ancient teaching of loyalty meant sometimes death."

> **The old bones are coming to life. The valley of the dead was only hibernating.**

DISCUSSION QUESTIONS

1. Do you think believers should ever overthrow a government? Why or why not?

2. Sun wanted to found China on three principles: nationalism, democracy, and welfare. Do you think these are good principles to build a Christian country upon? Why or why not?

3. Do you think Christians in your country have an awareness of their nation's spiritual roots? If so, are those roots appreciated and preserved, or do Christians tend to believe their faith has to be reinvented for every generation?

4. How do you think Christians should view their Christian history?

DAY 47

A PRESSURE COOKER FOR REVIVAL

———◆———

"It does not matter how slowly you go so long as you do not stop."

—CONFUCIUS

I t is impossible to talk about the recent revival of China without exposing the conditions that gave birth to it. It is arguable that the current revival China is experiencing would not be possible without the persecution brought on by the Communist Party.

The environment of persecution that paved the way for revival in China is being repeated today in other countries around the world. History is repeating itself. If we know what we are looking for, we can recognize and understand the markers along the way.

Communism in China has a face and a name that will live forever in infamy: Mao Zedong. His face is printed on the Chinese currency, his portrait hangs above the gates of the Forbidden City, and his body is immortalized in a preserved tomb in Tiananmen Square.

He is loved by the Chinese people even though he killed more people than Hitler. After suffering from generations of humiliating occupation of European nations and the rape and pillaging by the Japanese Imperial Army, Mao brought a sense of power and pride to the Chinese. He showed them what they could be. He defied all the odds, appealed to the underdog spirit of the Chinese people, and championed the ideas of Marxism.

Mao did not trust government leaders when he came to power. They had been his enemy for many years prior to 1949. He trusted the people who helped get him into power. He trusted the university students who zealously attacked anyone who dared to disagree with their enlightened ideology. He trusted the union workers who staged riots and fought those in power. He trusted the farmer who struck fear in the heart of the land owner.

It was not the institutions of pre-WWII China that adopted Communism; it was the common people. The common people who made up of the fabric of China rallied around Mao Zedong.

Soon after Mao came to power in 1949, the common people were empowered to enforce the new laws of Red China. The new laws were rational. They were scientific. They were equal. They were productive. They were modern.

Mao Zedong's new Red China had no use for old ideas and mystical beliefs. They were dangerous. Traditions were anti-progressive. Christians represented everything Communists hated so they became enemy number one. Anyone who believed in Jesus or owned Christian books was targeted by Mao's new citizen army.

Christians represented everything Communists hated so they became enemy number one.

Pastor Zhang Rongliang remembered those days vividly when he wrote about his Christian grandfather in the book about his life *I Stand with Christ.*

He was brought out by local officials and forced to walk down our hometown street with a board hanging around his neck on which was written in huge letters, "Follower of Jesus." . . . He was marked as an antirevolutionary and humiliated by the Communist Party. As a young man, I watched this happen; how painful it was for me to see him marched through the streets while being taunted and abused by vicious townspeople.

Grandfather Sun was forced to wear a tall hat, made out of newspaper, that resembled a Western dunce cap. He looked like a helpless lamb among wolves.

Pastor Zhang's grandfather was not tortured and killed by government officials. He was humiliated, marched through the streets, tortured, and then lynched by everyday people who were swept up in the emotion of the moment.

Mao's followers wore red bands on their arms to mark them like the "Brownshirts" of Hitler.

Mao had learned from the Russian mind masters. They were the best. They truly understood the game of propaganda. Mao learned how to divide and conquer. He was taught how to use victimhood to appeal to the masses. Mao had been trained by the Russians on how to make everything about "us" and "them"—the victims and the oppressors. The system worked like this: identify as a victim, rally the victims, pit the victims against the oppressors, lead the victims, overthrow the oppressors, and take power.

It was a pretty ingenious strategy.

Mao ran secret printing presses and held secret meetings to prepare for protests that were intended to lead to violence. Violent reactions were pure gold for Mao's propaganda. They pushed authorities until there was a violent reaction and then they promoted the reaction as proof of oppression. This solidified Mao's base of support for a Communist revolution.

Anyone who disagreed with Mao was immediately labeled an antirevolutionary, on the side of the oppressor. Even a poor person with no influence who might have looked at the senseless violence perpetrated upon innocent people and questioned it was immediately defined as an enemy.

As Mao grew in power, questioning him or his actions became extremely dangerous. Fear gripped those who were not convinced by the rhetoric and propaganda, and they followed with fiendish passion just to keep from becoming a target.

Mao worked the system like a master conductor. The masses fell at the feet of Mao Zedong, and they burned with passion against all who opposed their dream of a new society. When the emotions of the mob had been stoked to a boiling point, they were let loose on society.

The Christians suffered greatly, something Satan had planned all along.

In the absence of religion, the followers of Mao found themselves in a spiritual vacuum. It was a void that needed filling. Like the Jewish people in Exodus 32 sitting in the desert without Moses after they fled from Egypt, they decided to make gods for themselves.

The Chinese people needed a new god, and Mao was more than willing to fill that void. He became the god of China.

His words were written down and distributed all over China in what became known as "The Little Red Book." Everywhere the Chinese went, they were required to carry this book in their hand. Men and women were required to memorize entire passages from the book and quote them on demand.

Field workers, factory workers, and professors would all break during the day from their arduous tasks and read from the "Little Red Book" together. Second only to the Holy Bible, Mao's "Little Red Book" is the next most printed book in history. It also holds the world record for being the most printed book in the history of man for having 720 million copies printed in less than four years between 1963 and 1967.

A picture of Mao Zedong, like the one at the entrance to the Forbidden City in Beijing, was required to be hung in every home. No matter how poor a family was, all were required to keep a picture of Mao in an expensive picture frame that was to be cleaned every day.

A personality cult was born that continues to this very day. For example, it is very easy to find a cab in China today with the image of Mao hanging on the rear-view mirror, which they think will bring good luck or protection.

Looking back on the insanity of the days that lead to the death of more than 70 million people, it can be hard to understand what Mao could have said that

The very same tactics are being used today, and the results, though smaller, are similar.

was so convincing to the masses. However, the very same tactics are being used today, and the results, though smaller, are similar.

As I was writing this Bible study, I witnessed groups rise up in the same manner as Communism in China. They are easy to spot if you understand the rise of Mao Zedong.

Of course these modern groups do not carry Mao's "Little Red Book" or wear the red armband of Communism, but they have many of the same characteristics, use the same tactics, and express the same goals.

Because of the absolute failure of Communism in every country and on almost every continent on the planet where it has been tried, advocates of traditional Marxism have been forced to repackage it.

Instead of the tired old categories of rich and poor or bourgeoisie versus proletariat, instead people have been divided according to race, ethnicity, gender, religion, sexual orientation, etc, people are either victims or oppressors.

If you think what happened in China cannot happen again, there might be a few movements you should look into that have recently gained a lot of popularity.

While I was traveling around America following the roots of revival, I saw protests in Berkley, California, led by a group known as Antifa, which is short for the German phrase *Antifaschistische Aktion*, "anti-fascist network." Their roots go back to the paramilitary arm of the German Communist Party supported by the Soviet Union, the same as Mao Zedong. Like I said, their movement is not new; only the wrapping of Communist atheism is different.

Using the same tactics as Mao Zedong's student-led Red Army, members of Antifa start fires, break windows, destroy property, and physically attack anyone who gets in their way. They justify their violence as righteous anger against anything they categorize as pro-Nazi or pro-racist behavior. They label their opponents Nazi, racist, homophobic, sexist, bigoted, chauvinist, intolerant, hateful, privileged, etc.

Just like during the days of Mao Zedong, it doesn't matter whether the label is correct. You are guilty till proven innocent.

Assaulting people who merely disagree would create a disconnect with the masses, so like Mao Zedong, Antifa quickly finds an evil label to apply to their opponents and establishes themselves as victims of an oppressor. As a victim, they have an innate "right" to physical resistance, arguing that any law they break or person they harm is merely a pillar of the established social hierarchy that institutes oppression.

It is this ideology that then grows into persecution of Christians and Christian-Judaic values.

For example, another group closely related to Antifa is Black Lives Matter, which makes no attempt to hide their Communist roots and even goes one step further than the idea of economic collectivism employed by Mao Zedong. Black Lives Matter, a group started by atheist lesbians, believes that the traditional family is irrelevant and fathers have no purpose, and that a collective state that embraces their beliefs of deep-seated racism and sexism should be responsible for raising children.

On their website[21] they have clearly written, "We disrupt the Western-prescribed nuclear family structure requirement by supporting each other as extended families and 'villages' that collectively care for one another, especially our children, to the degree that mothers, parents, and children are comfortable."

Black Lives Matter vigorously attacks the biblical foundations of a nuclear family and reconstructs it in a way that excludes men so that the enemy can have control over the children. Jesus warned us about this when He said, "How can one enter into a strong man's house, and spoil his goods, except he first bind the strong man? and then he will spoil his house" (Matthew 12:29).

The same spirit of godlessness that entered into China through Mao Zedong to destroy the Christian faith is the same spirit that is roaming the earth today.

An easy way to identify the motives and tactics of groups that reflect Mao Zedong's Red Army is by looking at the way people quickly capitulate, not out of empathy, but out of fear and hate. Fear and hate are never the by-products of something good.

And fear and hate lead to the persecution of Christians. That

> **What Satan meant for evil, God used for good (Genesis 50:20).**

is the entire purpose of the enemy, who is behind this blindness that divides.

But what Satan meant for evil, God used for good (Genesis 50:20).

Romans 8:28 is a promise that helps give hope during the darkest hour. During the days of Mao there were a few brave men who were not afraid to be labeled as antirevolutionaries and stand against the angry mobs. They were not ashamed of the name of Jesus Christ. The Chinese faced the deadly persecution, but their bold stand led to one of largest revivals on earth!

Mao Zedong made every effort to destroy Christianity and kill Christians, but he failed spectacularly. When Mao was alive, many people believed that Christianity had died, but when the curtain lifted in the 1980s, the world saw that it was Mao Zedong who was dead and Jesus was still alive.

DISCUSSION QUESTIONS

1. A professor in theology once said, "Communism is Christianity without God." In what ways do Communist and Christian ideas overlap?

2. In spite of similarities with Christianity, why do you think Marxism/Communism always leads to the persecution of Christians?

3. Why do you think labeling people can be such an effective and dangerous strategy?

4. What kinds of groups are often labeled by Christians or in the church? Why do we sometimes choose to label groups instead of engaging with them?

5. Are you afraid of being labeled as homophobic, transphobic, Islamophobic, intolerant, bigoted, hateful, or whatever labels are being put on Christians nowadays? How does it make you feel?

6. Do you ever refrain from speaking out for fear of getting an unfair label? How do you think Christians should respond to this injustice?

DAY 48

REVIVAL IN THE COUNTRYSIDE

———◆———

"City people. They may know how to street fight but they
don't know how to wade through manure."

—MELINA MARCHETTA

In the eastern part of China lies a little farming community in the rural
part of Anhui Province called Lixin County. Throughout history, Anhui
has been an extremely poor region, and Lixin County has always been one
of the poorest areas of Anhui. Nothing significant has ever really happened
there. People live and people die in the small Chinese hamlet, and there has
been little else.

Anhui Province was particularly dark during the reign of Mao Zedong,
who burst onto the world stage before a cheering crowd of supporters in
Tiananmen Square on October 1, 1949.

Mao Zedong's rise to power was carried on the backs of zealous university students and union workers who demanded equality and embraced the
ideas of wealth distribution. In their minds they were right, and they quickly
silenced anyone who did not agree with them.

Radical followers of Mao Zedong found solidarity in their ideology of
equality, strapped red bands on their arm, and marched through the streets
to show their power. Nothing could stop them. They had enthusiasm on
their side.

The villagers in Lixin County did not know enough to disagree.

Anyone in Anhui who represented the top 1 percent—land owners, entrepreneurs, doctors, lawyers, etc.—was rounded up and publicly humiliated. There was no longer any room for dialogue. The followers of Mao Zedong were on a mission to create a brand-new society that would rid them of the binding chains of the traditional class system. In their minds, the wealthy only exploited the poor. And they believed the wealthy used religion to manipulate the simple minds of the uneducated poor masses through the power of superstition. Therefore religion, specifically Christianity, needed to be eradicated. Religion was a disease. It was the "opiate of the masses." The first order of business was to kick out all the missionaries.

Throughout the 1950s and 1960s, China saw many pastors and Christian leaders sent to gulags and reeducation camps. At the very same time as Christians were being systematically imprisoned, persecuted, and killed, China was also experiencing the worst man-made famine in their recorded history. Millions of people died during that time. Before it was all said and done, an estimated 70 million people lost their lives. Oddly, this paved the way for the largest Christian revival that Anhui Province had ever seen.

Somehow the winds of persecution carried the scattered seed of Christianity into the small, rural village of Lixin, where it landed in the hands of a farmer boy named Enguan.

> **Somehow the winds of persecution carried the scattered seed of Christianity into the small, rural village of Lixin, where it landed in the hands of a farmer boy named Enguan.**

Enguan, like everyone else, was doing everything he could possibly do to stay alive. Friends and relatives were dying from starvation. The situation was even more dire in Enguan's family because his mother was insane. She would go into fits of rage, foam at the mouth, and was physically out of control.

There weren't any hospitals around at that time that would be able to help, and doctors were in short supply. Before the rise of Mao Zedong, many of the doctors in China were either missionaries or had been trained by missionaries. When Christian missionaries were kicked out of China, many resources for medicine dried up.

According to Communist ideology, medical care should be available for everyone, not just those who could afford it. So Chinese doctors were stripped of their practice and forced to go and serve the peasants for free in the countryside. This created a class of medical practitioners called "barefoot" doctors. This worked for only a short time. Without ongoing medical training or money for medicine and supplies, the barefoot doctors became little more than a joke. They were not really able to help people and would definitely be of no help to Enguan's mother.

However, in the absence of medicine and doctors, Enguan's family was forced to look for other solutions to help them. There were rumors of a man named Jesus who was able to help sick people get better. Enguan had never heard of this man before, and because of his name, he was certain that Jesus was not from Anhui Province.

There were older ladies from a nearby village who knew about Jesus and knew about His power to heal the sick. The ladies had listened to the words of the old Christian missionaries and tried to repeat from memory their words. Soon the ladies were known by others in surrounding villages as individuals who might be able to help the sick by praying to a man named Jesus.

One day the ladies came and prayed for Enguan's mother. Enguan listened intently to how they prayed. He did not know if they would be able to come back to his village again so he carefully tried to memorize every word they said in their prayer in hopes that he would be able to repeat them.

Soon after the visit of the Christian women, he knelt down and began praying for his mother. Suddenly she was healed. Enguan was completely surprised. He did not know how or why it happened, but it was evident that there was power in the name of Jesus.

Locals heard about the healing of Enguan's mother and they rejoiced. A small light of hope began to flicker in the dark world of Lixin County. Maybe they too could call on the name of Jesus to heal them.

At that time there were no established churches or a body of believers in Lixin County, so Enguan held small, intimate meetings in his home. He knew very little about Jesus or Christianity, but he knew there was power in the name.

He didn't have a Bible, but he dearly wanted to know more and teach what he knew to those who wanted to learn. Enguan did not know it then, but this was the very beginning of the Lixin revival.

Others in the county who had been experiencing mental problems came knocking on the door of Enguan. They wanted to know more about this Jesus who could heal the sick and deliver the mentally insane, but not everyone could travel to Enguan's village, and before long Enguan was getting requests to travel around and meet with different villagers who wanted to know more about Jesus.

When Enguan prayed for people, it was not a complicated prayer. It was not even a well-informed prayer, but it was a prayer in the power of the name of Jesus. When he prayed for people who were disturbed mentally, according to eyewitnesses who were there, they were immediately set free from their troubles.

Soon, people who were sick and were not able to obtain medical attention in any other way were being healed when Enguan prayed for them. After they were healed, they would immediately become followers of Jesus. Soon, entire families were getting saved and becoming Christians.

As the church grew, the need for Bibles grew too. No one had ever seen a Bible or even knew anyone who had seen a Bible. The church members had nothing more than the prayers of Enguan and a few fragments of songs taught by foreign missionaries years before. They cherished those fragmented songs and simple prayers.

In the 1980s, a man was seriously ill and about to die. One day his wife decided to become a Christian and get baptized. She thought that if she got baptized Jesus would see her and bless the water surrounding her even though she had no biblical reference for the act of baptism. She was baptized and immediately collected the water around her in a bottle. She brought the bottle of water back to her sick husband and asked him to drink it. She believed that the water she had been baptized in had healing properties because it was holy water.

In her simple understanding of the power of Jesus, she asked her husband to drink the water. He did as she asked and was healed of his disease.

The village rejoiced.

So many people were coming to Christ that homes were no longer able to hold the crowds where Enguan taught. It was getting dangerous. Everywhere Enguan went, the crowds would follow.

Enguan had never anticipated so many people joining the fellowship and looking to him for leadership. He didn't set up an advertising campaign to get people to come. He didn't build a website or start a social media group to spread the word. He never built a building and put "Enguan Ministries" in bright lights outside the door.

On the contrary, Enguan tried to keep a low profile, knowing it was only a matter of time before the police would be after him. He didn't want all of the attention, but he got it anyway.

The revival spread throughout the entire county of Lixin and then to the entire province of Anhui. Tens became hundreds and hundreds became thousands. Eventually, churches were being planted all over China. All those who believed during the initial movement in Lixin County simply referred to themselves as the Lixin County Church or the Lixin Church.

The government quickly understood that there was something happening and that they needed to get a handle on it. They started to monitor Lixin Church members. Phones were tapped and leaders were followed. Filtering software was put in place and were triggered at the mention of "Lixin."

But the movement in Lixin grew into a nationwide revival that lead to a network that is today known simply as *Mongfu*—the Chinese word that means "Blessing."

DISCUSSION QUESTIONS

1. How does this story fit or not fit in your understanding of how God works?

2. How much understanding do you think people need to have of Christian faith to be a Christian?

3. Do you think it is important for Christians to have a "memory bank" of prayers, songs, and Bible passages in case we ever get cut off from resources?

4. What is in your memory bank? Is there anything you would want to add?

5. In the light of this story, do you think teaching people to pray for healing should be a part of discipleship?

DAY 49

REVIVAL TURNS TO MISSIONS

"Here is the test to find whether your mission on
Earth is finished: if you're alive, it isn't."

—RICHARD BACH

As much as Mao Zedong attempted to destroy Christianity, I often wonder if he now knows in the afterlife what a failure he was. What would he would say if he could see what good that came out of his persecution for the church in China?

With all of the passionate hate he showed toward Christians, and all the years that he devoted to inflicting death and pain upon the church, I am sure he would not be happy that what he did paved the way for the largest revival in the world.

Despite all his dark desires to destroy the church in China, Mao actually implemented many practical things that greatly assisted the spread of the Gospel. Just like the Sanhedrin that hated Jesus and plotted his death unwittingly played into the hands of the crucifixion that was necessary for the salvation of all mankind, so too did Mao play into God's hands to ignite the rapid spread of Christianity.

> **Despite all his dark desires to destroy the church in China, Mao actually greatly assisted the spread of the Gospel.**

In his bloodthirsty efforts to consolidate his power, he united a diverse nation that included the radical Muslims in western Xinjiang, militant Buddhists in southern Tibet, and prideful Mongols to the north. These areas of China are as different from one another in language, customs, and culture as the Middle East is from Europe.

Very few people on earth could have brought these different ethnic groups together under one roof that would be represented with a single flag, but Mao Zedong did it. Today, one can travel from the former Manchurian Empire on the edges of the river bank of Korea all the way to the border of Pakistan and never need a passport.

This ease of travel inside of modern China has been a huge blessing when compared to the difficulty of travel through the ancient fiefdoms of old. The millions of Christians who have traveled relatively unrestricted for years and planted churches in the most rural areas owe a huge thanks to Mao Zedong.

Before Mao, the majority of people in the geographical area that we call China today did not speak Mandarin Chinese. There were thousands of different languages used. It would have been almost impossible to get God's Word into the hands of so many people in China without the unification of language. Mao made it mandatory for everyone in China to use one single language: Mandarin Chinese.

Printing the Bible and making it available to millions of people would have been a hundred times more difficult if it were not for Mao Zedong. After coming to power, he swiftly moved to simplify the Chinese characters to make reading and writing easier and faster to learn for those who lived in poor areas who might not get more than a primary education.

China is riddled with harsh terrain and some of the world's most unforgiving mountain ranges. Going from one side to the other was extremely difficult before the implementation of a national railway system and highway structure. Mao connected the entire nation through a series of roads and railways, and made it possible for evangelists and pastors to travel from church to church quickly and comfortably.

Ironically, Mao's pragmatic approach to making his country more mobile, literate, and competitive would defeat his other goal of destroying

Christianity in China. Even his intense persecution of Christians served to extend the kingdom of God. Just like the first-century church in the book of Acts was forced out of Jerusalem during persecution, when Mao began persecuting Christians, preachers and evangelists were forced to travel far and wide. This resulted in many remote areas hearing the Gospel that might not have been reached otherwise.

It is safe to say that few people in the history of China did more for facilitating revival in China than Chairman Mao.

What Mao could not have predicted, of course, is that in his attempt to destroy the church, he would actually fuel a revival that would lead to one of the most significant changes in world missions in the last several hundred years.

Out of that revival came the vision to raise up at least 100,000 missionaries and send them out to every tribe, nation, and tongue between the Great Wall of China and the Western Wall of Jerusalem. If this happens, this will be the largest coordinated mission movement in the history of man.

Back to Jerusalem is the name of the vision of the Chinese church to leave China, follow the old trade routes of the Silk Road, and take the Gospel to the most dangerous areas and unreached people groups in the world today.

When people first hear the term *Back to Jerusalem* used in China, they naturally assume that it has something to do with a messianic vision to return to the city of Jerusalem, but that assumption would be wrong. The term *Back to Jerusalem* has more to do with the "land between the walls" or the nations between Jerusalem and China. This is where we can see a continuum of the western movement of revival.

Understanding the history of revival gives us hope for its future.

In the early 1920s, a group from Shandong Province known as the Jesus Family had a vision to take the Gospel message to the Buddhist, Hindu, and Muslim peoples living between China and Jerusalem.

Shandong was a province that was greatly impacted by the missionaries who were sent from the Azusa Street revivals. The Jesus Family planned to travel along the ancient Silk Road and plant churches and fellowships in all the of countries, cities, towns, and ethnic groups in the land between the walls.

At the same time, other Christian fellowships were also receiving the same vision. A group known as the Back to Jerusalem Evangelistic Band from Henan Province independently developed their own vision to do the same thing.

Yet another group known as the Northwest Spiritual Group (*Xibei Ninggon Tuan Dui*) had the same vision. It is important to note that these three groups had similar visions but did not necessarily see their vision or efforts as a collective one.

Contrary to our grand visions of what these first Back to Jerusalem pioneers must have been like, they were actually simple, uneducated Christians. They did not hold theology degrees, they did not write books, they did not outline an elaborate strategy of world domination or have a room full of strategic maps, and they did not have language training or cultural exposure.

Unlike the comparatively wealthy missionaries sent out from Western churches, these first Chinese groups did not have any mission support. They set out on the ancient Silk Road and trusted in the Lord to provide all of their needs. They were not a static mission group that sent people out. They were a mobile mission group that went out in obedience to the Great Commission given by Jesus Christ.

The fact that they were so unimaginably unqualified really points to the lack of influence that this vision had from the Western church. This first group of Back to Jerusalem visionaries did not know what they were supposed to fear and prepare for. They took the Word of God at face value (Luke 9:3).

They hungered to see supernatural revival. They did not have a time schedule or a planned route. They simply followed the leading of the Holy Spirit with the intangible goal of seeing people set free from sin. The suffering they experienced along the way was considered to be a part of the journey.

By the end of WWII and the Japanese occupation, the first Back to Jerusalem visionaries had arrived in the far reaches of Xinjiang Province. The customs and language of the local people were strange. The missionaries did not understand anything but continued to pray for revival.

Almost all of them were eventually arrested for being antirevolutionaries.

Many of them died in jail, and the rest were confined to lives of poverty in western China.

By every measurable standard, the first missionaries who carried the Back to Jerusalem vision were complete and absolute failures. Their efforts seemed to be a complete waste.

One night in the late '90s, while I was traveling in Guizhou Province in a small town known as Liupanshui, I could not find a hotel to spend the night in. During those early years, foreigners could not stay in hotels that were not registered for foreigners.

I was working together with the government on a humanitarian project and ended up having to reside at the local hospital. On the first night I found myself surrounded by many staff members and government officials who wanted to chat late into the evening. At some point I felt the Lord urging me to share about the Back to Jerusalem vision.

It was an awkward moment, because I was not working with Christians and I was not doing overt mission work, but as I shared, an elderly woman who was listening became very emotional. She eventually stood up and said, "You do not know me, but my grandfather was Pastor Jing. He was the founder of the Jesus Family."

I was completely shocked. To this day, I do not know how I ended up in the same room as this woman.

"I remember clearly when the government persecuted my family for being Christians. My father and grandfather were thrown in prison. My mother and I were persecuted. My mother could not get a job because she was the wife of what society labeled an antirevolutionary. We were poor and hungry," she continued. "I was angry. I did not choose to be a Christian; my parents did and I was punished for it.

"But I made a promise to myself during those days that I would never do anything that would be against the government.

"But here you are tonight. You are from a different nation, a different generation, and speak a different language, and that speaks volumes to me. The government killed my grandfather. They killed my father, but they could not kill the vision!"

The Jesus Family, an indigenous Chinese Christian movement in Shandong Province, like the disciples in the book of Acts, sold all of their belongings and lived in communes together. They started a Pentecostal movement that grew into thousands of followers. Pastor Jing Dianying, the founder of Jesus Family, supported the Communist movement and was promised to be given more freedom under Communist rule, but as soon as Mao came to power, the real face of Communism emerged and Pastor Jing was put in prison, where he eventually died.

> **The Back to Jerusalem vision of those early dedicated saints seemed to die before it began, but their efforts were not in vain.**

The Back to Jerusalem vision of those early dedicated saints seemed to die before it began, but their efforts were not in vain. The next generation had a fiery furnace in front of them that would test them and prepare them for the final frontier of missions.

DISCUSSION QUESTIONS

1. Mao's reforms and the unification of China assisted the spread of the Gospel. How do you think President Xi's policies now facilitate the Back to Jerusalem mission movement?

2. Can you give examples in your own country of when either neutral or downright evil policies of leaders have led to the spread of the Gospel, in history or more recently?

3. In what ways do you think the Chinese believers are more suitable than Westerners to spread the Gospel in these closed nations between the walls? Can you also think of disadvantages?

4. In what way could they use the support of the Western church?

PART 8

———

THE LAND BETWEEN THE WALLS

DAY 50

THE FINAL FRONTIER

"If God closes a door AND a window, consider the fact
that it might be time to build a whold new house."

—MANDY HALE

This section is where we seemingly come to the end of the road for the history of revival and arrive at the dark time and place that has yet to be transformed by revival between China and Jerusalem. Many of the dark areas between Chin and Jerusalem have actually experienced periods of revival, but the history of revival in the East has been erased by the conquering of non-Christian empires, whereas the history of revival in the West firmly established societies that continue to shape world history.

As we noted earlier, in Acts 16:6, the apostle Paul and his team were forbidden by the Holy Spirit to go and preach the Gospel to Asia. Two thousand years later, we can see that the message has gone all the way around the world in a westerly direction, and the very place that Paul was once refused entry into is now seeing the world's largest revival.

The revivals in China are forcing missiologists in the West to rethink several hundred years of mission strategy. The Western methods of sharing the Gospel are not working for the "land between the walls," the nations between China and Jerusalem. Instead, the Back to Jerusalem vision of the Chinese underground house church is giving new hope for completing the Great Commission in the final frontier of missions.

One reason that Back to Jerusalem is creating so much excitement is because the revivals in China have taken place during periods of intense persecution, as has been the case during other times in history, and the movements have been largely underground and illegal.

The number of new believers in the underground house churches has been growing exponentially for the last three decades. The army of young people ready to give their life on the mission field is extraordinary.

> **The Back to Jerusalem vision of the Chinese underground house church is giving new hope for completing the Great Commission in the final frontier of missions.**

Many experts in the West continue to view the Back to Jerusalem vision with extreme skepticism, seeing their lack of education in formal missions training as a major liability. At the beginning of the twenty-first century, when Brother Yun, also known as the Heavenly Man, began sharing about the Chinese vision to take the Gospel into the land between the walls, he was met with resistance. Several ministry leaders who had worked in missions their entire lives did not believe that such a vision would ever take form. They believed that the uneducated Chinese missionaries would eventually suffer the same fate as the early pioneers did—stuck in China.

Several made claims that the Back to Jerusalem vision was primarily a sensational vision, not a practical one, and that it was being promoted by organizations that wished to make financial gain from the emotional enthusiasm the vision stirred.

One of the original pioneers who attempted to take the Gospel westward and spread revival throughout the Muslim world all the way back to Jerusalem was Simon Zhao. Simon spent more than thirty-one years in prison. He had also written many songs about the Back to Jerusalem vision.

When he was released from prison, he found himself in the midst of a spiritual revival in China that was being led by leaders of what would soon be known as the Sinim Fellowship. One of the leaders of the Sinim Fellowship was evangelist Brother Yun.

Simon heard Brother Yun singing one of the Back to Jerusalem songs during an underground service one day and was livid that Brother Yun had unwittingly changed the words. The songs and poems that Simon wrote reflected the suffering and tears of serving the Lord all the way back to Jerusalem. He corrected Brother Yun and shared with him the vision of taking the Gospel message to the ends of the earth.

Brother Yun has been one of the major voices of the Back to Jerusalem vision since that spiritual encounter with Simon and has trumpeted the final words of Jesus to take the Gospel message into the harshest, most unreached places on earth.

Mark Ma, one of the foundational pioneers of the Back to Jerusalem vision, desperately wanted to see the Muslim nations between China and Jerusalem experience revival. He and his small team of partners all suffered while preaching along the Silk Road.

Grace Ho was one of the women who traveled with Mark Ma to complete the Great Commission before the rise of Communism in 1949.

I sat down with her in Kashgar in the early 2000s and listened to her stories. We were able to spend several days with her recording her testimonies of failure and triumph. She told us stories of her husband, Mecca Zhao, who was also one of the founding fathers of the Chinese pioneer movement.

What they attempted to do back then can be looked on by many as a failure, but their simple actions of dedication inspired an entire generation of believers. No one would have thought of doing mission work outside of China in those early days. Everything was geared toward survival. If the poverty in

> **Somehow out of the ashes came something priceless.**

China did not kill a believer, the persecution was certain to, but somehow out of the ashes came something priceless.

Even though there have been many doubters and naysayers, the vision never died.

Today, several years later, the Back to Jerusalem vision of the Chinese house church is no longer a whimsical pipe dream but a reality. Missionaries are at this very moment leaving China for some of the most dangerous countries on earth, and they are not going as renowned preachers and evangelists. They are going as businessmen, workers, and students, ready to work for little pay, live in the worst areas, and abandon everything for the sake of the Gospel.

The Back to Jerusalem vision to preach the Gospel to all the world is happening deliberately and systematically, but perhaps not with a methodology that appears normal to the Western observer. Many churches in the West have been programmed to expect missions movements to be built around denominations or personalities, and to include headquarters, control mechanisms, a centralized authority, and often a fair amount of media-driven hype. Yet none of these characteristics would accurately depict what is taking place with missionaries from China today.

Like the early Back to Jerusalem pioneers, Chinese missionaries are working in closed countries with very little (if any) funding and very little control from a centralized authority.

You see, Back to Jerusalem is not the name of an organization per se, but a vision. It is the call of God to evangelize the most unreached people groups in the world and, as such, *cannot* be owned by any denomination, organization, church, or personality. It is shared by charismatic and conservative Christians alike.

Back to Jerusalem comes from very humble beginnings and was ignited by God. It is sustained at His pleasure and cannot be contained by any geographical borders. It is the Chinese version of the Great Commission, or as some would say, "It is the Great Commission with kung pao flavor."

Much like the mission of the first-century church, Back to Jerusalem is a concept that exists outside the Western drama of separation of church and state. The Chinese underground house church has never promoted a dichotomy between their secular and spiritual life. Concepts that separate Christ from any part of the life of the Christian experience have not yet been adopted by Chinese Christians. For the Chinese believer, church is a body of believers that assembles in homes, caves, or even prison cells, and it intertwines with everyday life—it is not separated.

Because of their history of intense persecution, the Chinese church was not born inside the institutional walls of man that are often maintained by harsh, rigid guidelines invented in the minds of feeble men. The liberty of the Lord has proven to be without limits, and no building is able to contain Him, and, more importantly, no country's borders are able to keep Him out.

The Chinese missionaries who are leaving China are not going as marked soldiers wearing traditional uniforms prepared for conventional warfare with the enemy in the Middle East, Africa, and Southeast Asia. They are not walking in the footsteps of Western missionaries wearing priestly garments and carrying missionary visas in their passports.

They are the new warriors, prepared for guerrilla warfare. They strike fear in the heart of the enemy because their mission efforts exist in all things pertaining to the life of man: business, relationships, politics . . . everything.

They do not have the dichotomy of life and religion, and everyone is a potential target for the Gospel message. They are camouflaged by business or student visas and operate in the most secular aspects of everyday life. They could be everyone and anyone.

There are so many Chinese working in the nations between China and Jerusalem that there is no way to ferret the Christians out. The Chinese are used to working in illegal environments, and they are not familiar with sharing the Gospel message within a legal framework. They can't be intimidated with the threat of prison or even death. They are the worse kind of Christian—the kind that can't be convinced to exhibit rational behavior.

The Chinese missionaries do not play by the gentlemanly rules that have been adhered to for generations. They do not wait for ordination or proper training. They do not advertise their intentions or seek public recognition for their efforts. They are not interested in fund-raising efforts that would compromise their locations and activities. They are not operating under the authority of a centralized command. If you cut off one head, another will sprout up and continue.

Back to Jerusalem missionaries are responding to the primal instincts of the Great Commission that was given to the first disciples. Coming directly from the flames of persecution, the comforts and riches of this world has not yet lured them into a numb state of apathy.

They believe that the completion of the Great Commission will usher in the Second Coming of Christ as stated in Matthew 24:14: "And this gospel of the kingdom will be preached in the whole world as a testimony to all nations, and then the end will come" (NIV).

The remaining nations between China and Jerusalem are under the power of Islam, atheism, Buddhism, and Hinduism. These are the hardest places to reach, and they are also the most neglected by current mission groups around the world. The Chinese believe that this final mission field has yet to be claimed by any body of believers. Pastor Mark Ma, one of the early pioneers of the Back to Jerusalem vision, wrote, "The Gospel will be proclaimed back to Jerusalem with triumphal hymns. As we look upon from Mount Zion, we praise the Second Coming of Christ."

Perhaps the greatest revival is yet to come. The nations that are putting up the most resistance against the Good News of Jesus Christ could be the very ones that produce the greatest fruit of all time.

Imagine the dams of revival being held back by large, reinforced walls that were never constructed to withstand the kind of force that is building up today. Those walls may prove to be ill-prepared for the onslaught of missionaries and hungry citizens who continue to grow in numbers unimagined only a decade ago.

The final frontier of missions is still in front of us.

I believe that the final frontier of missions is still in front of us. The greatest testimonies are yet to be heard. The greatest move of God has yet to take place. The last inheritance has yet to be claimed. The final songs of the martyrs have yet to be sung. The clock is ticking, and the enemy's time is running out. There is plenty of room for one more cross to be erected in the unreached areas of the world.

The winds of revival are blowing, and they are blowing westward of

China. There are many nations in between China and Jerusalem. We will only look at a few of them that are ripe for revival.

DISCUSSION QUESTIONS

1. Why do you think it has been hard for the Western mission movement to get a foothold in the land between the walls?
2. Do you expect a revival in the Muslim world in the next decades? Why or why not? Are you praying for that?
3. How do you feel about a mission movement that is completely decentralized and has no headquarters? Is that something that scares you or excites you? Can you explain why?
4. Do you think material prosperity makes it difficult for Westerners to be involved in mission work, or is it a blessing God uses to further missions? Explain your reasons.

DAY 51

WHY REVIVAL IS NEEDED IN THE LAND BETWEEN THE WALLS

"The blues–the sound of a sinner on revival day."

—William Christopher Handy

Looking at the land between the walls, one thing is certain: they need Christian revival. If I have learned anything from following the history of revival, it is this: all things equal, countries founded on Christian principles or that have experienced Christian revival are the best countries to live in. Revival is the best thing that can ever happen to a people group. Revival changes the future of a country for the better.

People are blessed by revival, and the impact can be felt for several generations. Revival brings a blessing to everyone, even those who did not participate in the revival. A revival even blesses those who persecuted Christians and tried to prevent the revival!

> **Revival brings a blessing to everyone, even those who did not participate in the revival.**

During my travels, there was an immutable truth I kept seeing: the standard of living in nations where revival took root and changed the society is the highest in the world. It is better to be an atheist in a country that promotes Christian principles than for an atheist to live in an atheist country. It is better to be a

Buddhist in a country that has experienced Christian revival. It is better to be a Muslim in a nation of Christian foundations than for a Muslim to be a Muslim in the Muslim country. This fact is indisputable, but out of cowardice or ignorance, it is not often voiced.

Nations where Christian revival fires burned hot have the most religious freedoms in the world. In contrast, countries run by atheist or Islamic governments like Vietnam, North Korea, Iran, or Saudi Arabia have the lowest.

There are defenders of atheism and Islam, of course, who would vehemently dispute such a claim, but ironically, many of them do their defending from the comfort of nations that have a Christian background with a radical history of revival.

To give an example, I observed the refugee crisis of 2015 and 2016. The majority of the refugees came from central Africa, Iraq, Syria, Pakistan, and Iran, which were the areas I traveled in extensively while observing the land between the walls.

I sat with them, ate with them, and spent many weeks talking with them about an array of subjects. We talked about their heritage, trials, dreams, and aspirations. Without fail, regardless of their background, nationality, origin of their crisis, or language, they were all unified in their desire to immigrate to nations that had a history of Christian revival.

It made me ask the question: Wouldn't refugees from Iraq and Syria be better served to immigrate to a nation like Saudi Arabia? Saudi Arabia speaks the Arabic language, has similar food, endorses the same religion, and could provide safety for a family fleeing from war. If the refugees were looking for economic reprieve, wouldn't Dubai or Abu Dhabi be the perfect destination?

While writing this study, a troubling image of a three-year-old little Syrian boy lying facedown on a sandy beach in Turkey went around the world. On September 2, 2015, Aylan Kurdi was traveling with his family to secretly sneak into Europe with the hopes of making it to Canada.

The international response was swift and clear. The Western world should feel ashamed of itself for not immediately welcoming refugees needing safety and care. Much blame for the crisis was also placed at the feet of Western nations. They helped create an unsafe Middle East and Africa and therefore should accept the consequences by taking care of the refugees.

However, what was lost in the emotional media blitz following the death of three-year-old Aylan Kurdi was that his family had already arrived in Turkey. His father had a job working in Turkey. They had been able to save up $5,860 USD to pay an illegal smuggling group to get them to Europe.

During the same year, I was traveling in the Turkish costal area of Bodrum where Aylan Kurdi took his last breath. I was looking for the ancient city of Troas, where Paul received the Macedonian vision. By accident, I arrived in a remote wooded area full of brand-new life jackets. At first I was confused. Why would so many life vests be scattered about in the forests?

Then I understood that we had stumbled upon the hideout of a human smuggling ring for refugees who were willing to risk their lives to make it out of the Islamic world into the world of freedom.

All of the arguments of Islam being a free and peaceful religion died right there. The people who knew Islam the best risked their lives—by the millions—to escape it. In Greece alone, refugees were pouring in at a rate of one thousand per day from the Middle East and Northern Africa. Not even Turkey, arguably one of the most secular Muslim countries in the world, would satisfy the father of Aylan Kurdi. He paid an amount equal to an annual wage to put his family with sixteen people on a rubber boat made for eight and attempted to cross a dangerous ocean just for a chance to taste freedom in a land transformed by revival.

Aylan's father's gamble did not pay off. Aylan, along with his older brother and mother, died that night trying to make their way from Turkey to Europe.

Take all of the arguments about Islam being equal to Christianity and throw them straight into the trash can, because all the arguments in the world cannot explain why Muslims risk their lives and die every single day trying to escape Islam just for a chance to get into a country founded on Judeo-Christian principles.

At least 270 million people were slaughtered during the conquest of Islam, the majority of them being African. The entire region between China and Jerusalem has experienced a significant sustained level of suffering since the conquest of Islam. People are suffering and dying every day and are willing to do anything to make it out. Helping them escape to a Christian country might help a fraction of a percent, but it will not fix the problem.

This is why the final frontier of missions is so very important. If there is a true desire among Christians to help those in the poorest and most dangerous places on earth, then our focus must be to see a Christian revival in the region between the Great Wall of China and the Western Wall of Jerusalem. History has shown us that there is no alternative.

If our desire is to see the return of Jesus Christ, then we must complete the Great Commission between China and Jerusalem.

> **If our desire is to see the return of Jesus Christ, then we must complete the Great Commission between China and Jerusalem.**

More than 3 billion people live in nations that are forcefully kept ignorant about the name of Jesus Christ. They are slaves to their evil empires, and their souls perish. Forget all of the apologists for the equality of other world religions. They are peddling ideas that do not line up with reality. It is clear that the people in these regions crave freedom that Christian nations have. Christian nations must wake up from their stupor. Christian nations have enough people and resources to bring the message of Life to every person living in the land between the walls.

It is estimated that Christians in North America spend more per year on costumes for their pets during Halloween than they do on mission efforts in the land between the walls. An estimated 96 percent of mission funds go toward those working in areas that are considered to be reached. According to the World Christian Encyclopedia, of all money designated for missions, not for tithing or domestic purposes, but all the money specifically given for missions in the United States, only 5.4 percent is used for foreign missions. The rest is for domestic missions.

Of that 5.4 percent for foreign missions, only 1 percent is used to take the Gospel to unreached people who don't have access to the Gospel. Of that

1 percent, less than that is used for the area with the greatest need between China and Jerusalem.

Two-thirds of the world's population live in the area between China and Jerusalem. Nine-tenths of the unreached people groups live in this region as well, but roughly speaking, Christians in Americans only spend one penny of every hundred dollars given to missions in this region of the world.

The final frontier of missions remains unreached because the Great Commission has not been a priority for Christians, but the good news is that China is waking up and her Christians are helping to complete the task of Acts 1:8 and Matthew 28:18–19.

Not only is China waking up, but they are being assisted by the very government that persecutes them.

The top phrase in Chinese state-run media in 2016 was "One Belt, One Road." "One Belt, One Road" is a massive Chinese initiative that is changing the entire world. This extremely ambitious initiative is China's way of targeting about 65 percent of the world's population, reaping about one-third of the world's GDP and controlling one-fourth of all the world's goods and services.

There has never been an initiative like it.

The name "One Belt, One Road" comes from the imperial transportation system that linked ancient China with Central Asia and the Arab world. The Silk Road was named after China's number one export: silk.

The "One Belt, One Road" initiative would comprise of building massive roads, bridges, gas pipelines, ports, railways, and power plants and all of the hotels, restaurants, and services needed along the routes that would connect more than sixty countries. It would be the largest land-bridge initiative ever conducted in the region between China and Jerusalem.

China plans to move along the ancient Silk Road to economically engage the nations between China and Jerusalem in ways that have never been done before in modern times. This massive plan conceived in Beijing is already in motion. Over $21 trillion in possible deals would need to be committed to build transportation, business, and services that are needed.

This initiative provides an amazing platform for Chinese Christian missionaries in some of the most closed nations on earth. At a time when

American or European missionaries are not readily accepted in Iran, Kazakhstan, or Uzbekistan, the Chinese government is opening the door wide open for Chinese missionaries to have free access to the entire country through the "One Belt, One Road" initiative.

Before, the idea of sending 100,000 missionaries to the countries between China and Jerusalem seemed like an unlikely dream. How could that ever happen?

One Christian organization that positions itself as an expert on Christianity in China casted many doubts on the idea of Back to Jerusalem. On their website they wrote, "Many are concerned about the suggestion that BTJ workers will be sent with no regard to local government policy and restrictions, particularly in the Middle East. The talk of a large number of workers being put in prison and sacrificing their lives is frightening to all of us. Such a plan is certainly not strategic and can hardly achieve the goal of taking the gospel all the way to Jerusalem. . . . The BTJ Movement has been compared to a chain with many rings linked together. The problem is that all of the rings are incomplete, and many of them are missing altogether. . . . There is no structure within China for sending out cross-cultural workers. . . . Given the current state of affairs, it is unrealistic to expect large numbers of workers to be sent outside of China in the near future."

The Chinese Back to Jerusalem missionaries did not wait for a visible plan to be presented to them before they answered the call of sending out at least 100,000 missionaries. Of course, as is our human nature, we questioned the ability of the Chinese to do this. We pointed out the many challenges that made such a vision impossible, but our doubts did not stop the Chinese from preparing. They have not allowed experts to get in the way of telling them what God could and could not do.

Now, with zero help from the Western church, the Chinese have the widest open door in history into the most unreached area on earth and, of all things, that massive open door was provided by a Communist nation that persecutes Christians!

Now the only question is, of the nations between China and Jerusalem, which one will experience the next massive revival first?

DISCUSSION QUESTIONS

1. Do you think sending missionaries is the best way to help Muslim nations flourish? Do you see this as a realistic approach to the trouble in the Middle East, for example? Why or why not?

2. Do you think there is enough revival power left in Western nations to transform the lives of the millions of Muslims who come to these lands as refugees and immigrants, or do you think the Muslims will "take over" and impose or even force their values? Why do you think so? Can you support your ideas about this with examples?

3. How do you feel about the great economic and political vision of China? How do you think it will affect mission in the long term? In what ways does it compare to how colonialism influenced the Western mission movement?

DAY 52

THE LARGEST MUSLIM REVIVAL
IN THE WORLD

"If at first you don't succeed, ... then skydiving definitely isn't for you."

—STEVEN WRIGHT

I n the winter of 2014, I found myself standing at a place that is often referred to as Revolution Square in Tehran, Iran's capital city. I was waiting on a ride from an Iranian underground house church coordinator. Smoke was rising into the cold evening air from the hundreds of different food venders at every corner.

In the distance, I could hear the faint sound of the call to prayer, but it didn't seem that anyone was paying attention. No one stopped. No one prayed. Traffic congestion was bumper to bumper around the boarded-up circle of the city square. Old box-shaped cars that looked like throwbacks to Soviet-era style vehicles that had been assembled in Iran filled the streets in Tehran.

It was a Thursday evening, which is considered to be the beginning of the weekend for Iranians, so there was a festive bustle in the air. Though the people did not seem to pay much attention to the call to prayer, the reminders that Islam is the main religion in Iran are never far away. The Iranian flag can be seen in some form or fashion in most shops in Tehran. It is still the same red, white, and green flag that was adopted in 1980, with red representing martyrdom and green representing the color of Islam. Centered in the middle of the flag is the white band with a shape that might look like a tulip to most people who are not familiar with Arabic writing, but is actually the stylized representation of the word *Allah* and the phrase "*La ilaha illa Allah*"—"none is worthy of worship but Allah." Along the inner edges of the green and red bands is the phrase "*Allah Akbar*" or "God is Great," which are usually the last ringing words of Islamic fighters. The phrase is written twenty-two times.

The city of Tehran has many faces. One side of Tehran is modern, progressive, and inclusive, and other side is dark, religious, and intolerant. The face of intolerance is ever present in the large posters of the Supreme Leader Ruhollah Khomeini that are plastered all over the city and that represent the evil of Iran.

What is not found on the posters and written on the walls of the ancient city of Tehran is that Iran might very well be experiencing the world's largest Muslim revival.

> **Iran might very well be experiencing the world's largest Muslim revival.**

Most people do not know this because Iran is considered to be a closed country and does not allow any open sharing of the Gospel message. The open distribution of Bibles or Christian materials is banned. Conversion can result in death. Christian missionaries or mission organizations are not allowed to operate openly. Iranian children cannot be proselytized. At the writing of this book, no legal church is open that could serve the needs of the Iranian people.

But these laws are not stopping the Gospel message from spreading.

A radical spiritual change is sweeping through Iran today, and it is one that is not being reported in international news. A battle is raging inside between the young Iranians and the Islamic leaders. Most of the young people in Iran that make up 70 percent of the population are looking for answers that they are not finding in Islam.

These young people between the ages of fourteen and twenty-eight have been living at home and listening to their parents; however, many of them are growing more independent in their thoughts. They have been born into and live in a country that has been smothered in Sharia law. Many have seen their family and friends suffer for things they cannot understand, and they are fed up with the current situation.

There is a momentum today in Iran that we like to call ABI—Anything but Islam. The young people are hungry for truth and justice, and they are not finding either in Islam. The injustice that has been imposed on women in Iran is not sitting well with many of the younger people. The impossible counterproductive laws as they pertain to the Internet are growing less acceptable by the day. So each person in Iran is traveling their own road to ABI.

Iran has the perfect storm for the largest Christian revival of any Muslim nation on earth, and some would argue that they are already experiencing the beginnings of it. Currently there is a huge vacuum of Christian leadership, workers, and materials, but many Iranians are coming to Christ, not because of hearing it from a missionary or TV broadcast, but because of a dream or a vision.

"How many Christians would you say are in Tehran?" I asked my friend from the underground house church in Iran.

"I don't know," he replied back in his broken English.

"Well, how many fellowships would you say exist here in Tehran?" I tried again.

"I am not really sure."

"Okay. How do we know if there are Bibles needed here?"

"The Bibles are needed. So many believers need Bibles here," came back the response.

"Great, so how many Bibles should we arrange then?"

"A lot."

His response was one of the most honest I had come across. At least he admitted that he did not know the numbers in Iran. Many Iranian "experts" who are not living in Iran throw around all kinds of numbers with no real way to prove or disprove them.

Iran is trying desperately to stop the growth of Christianity. They have one of the largest numbers of executions in the world, carried out according to Islamic law, but this does not seem to be helping them curb the growth of illegal Christianity.

For many people who only think of Islam whenever they think of Iran, Christianity might seem like a foreign invasion, but Christianity is not as foreign to Iran as one might think. The God of Abraham, Isaac, and Jacob is not new to Iran, but the religion of Islam is.

When looking at the current revival that is sprouting up in Iran, it is important to keep in mind that the Bible is not a Western book; it was written entirely in the Middle East. In fact, one book of the Bible carries an Iranian name—Esther—and it takes place from beginning to end in Iran.

Iran, or the Persian Empire, comes up again and again in the later part of the Old Testament because much of that time, the Middle East was ruled by Persia.

It would not be a stretch to say that one can better understand Iranian history by reading the Bible, and one can better understand the Bible by studying Iranian history.

Christianity is not new to Iran, and neither are the concepts. Christianity has been in Iran since the beginning. Elamites (Persians), Medes, and Parthians were present on the day of Pentecost in the book of Acts (2:9) and brought Christianity to Iran long before Islam set foot on Persian soil.

> **Christianity has been in Iran since the beginning.**

Famous biblical figures believed to be buried in Iran include Esther, Daniel, Cyrus the Great, Darius the Great, and the disciple Thaddeus.

The bones of the prophet Daniel are believed to be buried in Iran, not far from the old capital city of Susa.

Many people believe that the magi of the Nativity came from Iran and that they took the message of the birth of Christ back to Iran. That would mean the magi were the first Christian missionaries to Iran. This also means that the Iranians would have been the first foreigners to worship Jesus the Christ!

Modern-day Iran is first mentioned in the Bible as Elam, after one of the sons of Shem, who was the son of Noah. Later, Iran is referred to collectively as Persia. Just to see what God has done in Iran already, it might make a big difference to say Iran whenever you see the word *Persia* in the Bible.

Of all of the empires that have ever ruled over the earth, few did more for the Jews than the Iranians. The Iranians rescued the Jews from slavery in Babylon and allowed the people to return to their homeland. Not only did the Iranian king set the Jews free, but he allowed roughly forty-two thousand Jews to return to their homeland carrying silver and gold. The Iranian king himself gave gold and silver to the Jews to take back with them on their journey (Ezra 1:7–11). This sparked the revival of rebuilding the temple that had been destroyed and desecrated by the Babylonians.

God gave the founder and king of Iran, King Cyrus, a huge task that has really been unparalleled by any other Gentile in history. Cyrus was anointed (Isaiah 45:1) to deliver the Jews and rebuild the city of Jerusalem. More promises are recorded for the Gentile king Cyrus of Iran than most of the kings who served Israel!

On October 29, 540 BC, crowds filled the ancient city of Babylon, anxious to see the man who had just disposed of their king and conquered their land. The famous city of Babylon, which was one of the most powerful city centers in the known world, fell into the hands of King Cyrus with very little resistance. Those who lined the streets that day waited to hear from their new master to see what their fate would be. Every battle that had ever been fought in the known world at that time naturally followed with the enslavement of women and children, the execution of men, and untamed looting and destruction.

Instead, the Iranian king Cyrus showed something that had never been seen before by a conquering king: mercy and justice. He abolished slavery and liberated the captives of those he conquered.

King Cyrus is considered to be the author of the very first human rights charter, known as the Cyrus Cylinder. Under the calling of God, King Cyrus formulated and proclaimed racial, linguistic, and religious equality for all. Slaves were set free, and laborers were paid wages. Like the justice of Yahweh as recorded in the Old Testament, Cyrus promoted respect for humanity and justice for the oppressed. This earned him the overwhelming support of his subjects.

The cylinder has been translated into all six official UN languages, and a replica is kept at the United Nations headquarters in New York City.

According to the Bible, Cyrus's son, King Darius, followed in the footsteps of his father when he wrote clearly in Daniel 6:26, "I make a decree, That in every dominion of my kingdom men tremble and fear before the God of Daniel: for he is the living God, and steadfast for ever, and his kingdom that which shall not be destroyed, and his dominion shall be even unto the end."

This decree was spread throughout the Persian Empire and everyone heard it. Even today, with satellite TV, radio, email, Internet, social media, etc., a decree of this nature would find it hard to be heard by as many people as it did then, because at that time there were fewer mediums to compete with.

The Persian Empire stretched from Egypt and the borders of Greece, through the Middle East, to Pakistan, India, Central Asia, and to the borders of China. This territory includes modern-day Egypt, Jordan, Iraq, Kuwait, Oman, UAE, Iran, Lebanon, Turkey, Armenia, Azerbaijan, Turkmenistan, Uzbekistan, Tajikistan, Afghanistan, Kazakhstan, India, and even the birthplace of Islam—Saudi Arabia. This is the area of the land between the walls of China and Jerusalem.

The first missionaries to China were from Iran. The Daqin Temple, which is the oldest church in all of China—1,400 years old—was built by Iranian missionaries who brought the Gospel to China for the first time in recorded history.

Just a quick view of the Bible shows us that Christianity is not foreign to Iran, but Islam is. Islam has enslaved the Iranian people. They did not have a choice whether or not they wanted to be Muslim. The enemy has even tried to wipe out their history by changing the name of their country to Iran, a name that was given to them during the days of Hitler, who claimed that the Iranians were a part of the Arian race. The Iranian people have been forced into their current situation, but their time of revival is coming. It is promised in the Bible.

For all of the hardships that the Iranians have endured and will endure throughout time, it has been promised in Jeremiah 49:39: "But in the latter days I will restore the fortunes of Elam, declares the LORD" (ESV).

Let the revival fire burn through the land of Elam!

DISCUSSION QUESTIONS

1. Do you know any people from Iran? If so, do you recognize the hunger for truth that this chapter describes?

2. If you know any Iranian believers, do you know how they came to know Christ?

3. If large numbers of Iranians turn to Jesus, what do you think that could mean for the balance of power in the Middle East and those countries' relationship with Israel?

4. Do you think an oppressive regime ultimately makes people more receptive to the Gospel? Can you give examples for or against?

DAY 53

THE DOOR TO BABYLON IS OPEN

"Why struggle to open a door between us when the whole wall is an illusion?"

—RUMI

There are few places on earth where Christianity is as old as it is in Iraq, and even fewer places are mentioned in the Bible as many times as Iraq. According to the Bible, the geographical location of Iraq is central to the story of the creation of man and the end times. The question is, will revival come to the land of Babylon prior to the end?

Our understanding of what the Bible teaches about Iraq can be diluted with all of the news of bombings, kidnappings, and war over oil. The idea of a revival in Iraq seems ridiculous. The long, rich culture and heritage of Iraq has easily been forgotten as militaries from all over the world come and go as they please and leave destruction and devastation in their wake.

War after war has been the main staple for the Iraqi diet for so long that the world cannot remember a time when there was ever anything promising about the future of Iraq. Just the mention of someone traveling to Iraq can quickly conjure up images of kidnappings and crossfire. If a family member learns that someone they love is traveling to Iraq, they immediately try to talk them out of it.

It hasn't always been that way. It may not be easy to believe this, but Iraq is arguably the first place that revival ever took hold outside of Jerusalem. It happened immediately after the ascension of Jesus. In fact, the early disciples carried the very cloth that Jesus was buried in and used it to see a great miracle that has been almost completely forgotten. I learned about it when I traveled to Iraq in 2014, shortly after the invasion of ISIS.

Iraq is arguably the first place that revival ever took hold outside of Jerusalem.

"If you want to know how Christianity first came to Iraq, then you should talk to the priest," Jacob said. Jacob was a member of one of the few Christian families who lived in the Yazidi area of the Sinjar Mountains when ISIS invaded in 2014.

Jacob took me to the home of the elderly Christian priest who had to flee from the Sinjar Mountains when ISIS attacked his home village. "He knows everything about Christianity in Iraq," Jacob said. "I am sure he can tell you the whole story."

When we entered the home of the priest, he was sitting on a wraparound sofa that doubled as a bed at night. More than one refugee family from the Sinjar Mountains was living with him. The priest was frail, but excited to have visitors. He was happy, but it was apparent that running from ISIS and living as a refugee for the last several months had taken a toll on the ninety-one-year-old man. He sat nervously twirling his brown wooden prayer beads and adjusting his dirty white prayer cap as he tried to remember how the Gospel message first came to his people.

"Adda the teacher was the first to bring the Gospel message to Iraq," the priest said with confidence, but then he looked down at the ground with sadness because he was not able to remember much more than that.

"He would like to share more about the history of Christianity in Iraq, but he had to leave all of his books behind in Sinjar when we fled from ISIS," one of the family members sitting in the same room explained. "He has all of the history of Christianity in Iraq written in piles and piles of books that he has studied his entire life, but sadly, they were all lost in the attack."

The old priest's memory may have been vague, but he remembered one thing—the teacher Adda brought the Gospel to Iraq. I later learned that

Adda is another name for Addai or Thaddeus or Judas the brother of James, as he was referred to in the gospel of Luke, who was one of the twelve apostles of Jesus and the author of the book of Jude.

According to church records, Thaddeus served as the leader of the church in northern Iraq from the years AD 66 to 87. Both *Assyrian* and *Chaldean* are terms that are used synonymously for Christians in Iraq and have been in Iraq since the early days of the first church. They are among the few Christians in the world who can trace the roots of their beliefs back to the apostles Thomas, Bartholomew, and Jude.

The Chaldean Christians have been believers since the first century AD and turned northern Iraq into a center for Christianity and Syriac literature.

Peter specifically gave his blessings to the church in Iraq when he wrote, "She who is in Babylon, chosen together with you, sends you her greetings, and so does my son Mark" (1 Peter 5:13 NIV).

Adda the Teacher, as he was known to the Iraqi priest I met, is known by many other names such as Thaddeus, Jude, and Addai because no one wanted to confuse his name with Judas of Iscariot, who betrayed Jesus. Even Matthew and Mark dropped the name Judas and used the name Thaddeus instead when listing the twelve apostles.

The apostle Jude wrote the book of Jude, the next to last book of the Bible. Notice how the English translation of the book of Jude isn't called the book of Judas so as not to confuse the reader.

Jude might have shared a name with the most notorious traitor in history, but what he did in Iraq brought about the same kind of revival that we thirst for today. The miracle that started the revival took place in the ancient Iraqi city of Edessa, not far from the modern city of Erbil on the Tigris River. It was here that Jude would do something that would change the future of Iraq for generations to come.

The king of Edessa was an Arab called Abgar the Black, also known as Abgar of Edessa. According to tradition, King Abgar was deathly ill with a disease that had no known cure. He had heard about the healing power of a Jewish teacher named Jesus and desired for Jesus to come and see him. Jesus was not able to come, but after His resurrection, Jude eventually made his way to the throne room of King Abgar, carrying with him a cloth with the image of Jesus on it.

After receiving the cloth, King Abgar was healed and became a believer in Jesus Christ and declared his kingdom a Christian kingdom. This event is actually recorded on the back of the $100,000 bill that is currently used in Armenia today.

If true, this would mean Jude was responsible for Edessa becoming the first Christian country in the world, long before those in Armenia or Ethiopia accepted Christ. History is clear that this relic played a major part in ancient Christianity in northern Iraq, but it might go even further than that. Astoundingly, it could be that this is the same cloth that is referred to today as the Shroud of Turin, or the burial cloth of Jesus, which is the most studied relic in history.

A revival in Iraq would not be something that would need to be started from scratch. A revival in Iraq would actually be built on a historical foundation that goes back to the very beginning of Christian history and even to the beginning of biblical history.

Revival has taken place in Iraq before. To learn about the revival in Iraq, you don't need to enroll into a Middle Eastern evening class at a community college or read a complicated thesis paper from an expert. You merely need to wipe the dust off your Bible.

The Bible reveals Iraq's history. The Bible goes into great detail about Iraq and explains the history, the land, the people, and the culture in ways that Wikipedia can only scratch the surface. One of the main challenges, however, is that the name Iraq is never actually mentioned in the sixty-six books of the Bible. The names that are synonymous with this region that can be found in the Bible are Ur, Babylon, Chaldea, Nineveh Assyria, Mesopotamia. Though several of these items may be debatable among some theologians, the following is a list of events that took place in the Bible in Iraq.

- The garden of Eden was in Iraq (Genesis 2:10–14).

- God created the first man and woman in Iraq (Genesis 2:7–8).

- Satan is mentioned in the Bible as having appeared in Iraq (Genesis 3:1–6).

- The first sin took place in Iraq (Genesis 3:6).

- The first birth took place in Iraq (Genesis 3:24; 4:1).

- The first crime took place in Iraq (Genesis 4:8).

- Cain tried to run from God and escaped to the land of Nod in Iraq (Genesis 4:16).

- The first boat was arguably constructed in Iraq (Genesis 6:14).

- The first boat arguably landed in Iraq after the Flood (problem with translation of Mt. Ararat).

- The world's first sacrifices before and after the Flood were made in Iraq.

- The world's first wine was arguably made in Iraq (Genesis 9:20–21).

- After the Flood, Nimrod started the world's first city in Iraq (Genesis 10:9–10).

- Nimrod became the world's first dictator in Iraq, ruling many cities under his control (Genesis 10:10–12).

- One of the cities that was started by Nimrod was Uruk, an ancient translation for the word *Iraq* (Genesis 10:10).

- The confusion of the world's languages (or arguably the start of every language in the world today) took place at the Tower of Babel in Iraq (Genesis 11:5–11).

- Abraham came from Ur—in Iraq—making him an Iraqi by birth (Genesis 11:31).

- The world's first empire was in Iraq (Daniel 1:1–2).

- The Israelites were first taken into slavery by a kingdom that included modern-day Iraq (2 Kings 17:6).

- The kingdom of Judah was taken into slavery to Babylon (Iraq) (Daniel 1:1–7).

- Isaac's bride came from Iraq (Genesis 24:10).

- Daniel was thrown in the lions' den (most likely) in Iraq (Daniel 6).

- Shadrach, Meshach, and Abednego were thrown in the furnace in Iraq (Daniel 3).

- Belshazzar, king of Babylon, saw the "writing on the wall" in Iraq (Daniel 5).

- Nebuchadnezzar was a king in Iraq (2 Kings 24).

- Ezekiel preached in Iraq (Ezekiel 1:1–2).

- The book of Nahum was a prophecy against Iraq (Nahum 1:8).

In addition to those past events, when it comes to the last days of missions, Iraq is one of the main places thought of as the subject of warnings from the book of Revelation (14:8; 16:19; 17:5; 18:2, 10, 21).

When following in the footsteps of revival, it is impossible not to look at Iraq. The world's first great Old Testament revival was recorded in Iraq when the entire kingdom of Nineveh repented (Jonah 3).

Today there are Back to Jerusalem missionaries from China working and serving in Iraq. They believe that the Spirit of the Lord is going to break the chains of bondage in Iraq. They are praying for a revival that is greater than the days of Jonah or King Abgar the Black.

The spirit of Islam is working very hard to keep end-time revival at bay, but the days have been counted and time will soon be up. God's Spirit is moving again, and revival is on the horizon in Iraq.

DISCUSSION QUESTIONS

1. Do you think all the references in the Bible to locations that are part of modern-day Iraq have spiritual significance for the country today? Why or why not?
2. The king of Edessa was said to have been healed by a special cloth, which became an important relic. How do you feel about the use of relics? Is it a way to stimulate healthy devotion, or do you think it is a form of idolatry?

3. The majority of the original Christian community has fled Iraq in recent years. Do you think Western countries should support their return and help protect them?

4. Do you think the presence of an ancient Christian community in Iraq is important for the spiritual future of that country? Why do you think so?

DAY 54

REVIVAL IN THE HERMIT KINGDOM

———◆———

"There is no word 'impossible' in the Korean language."

—KIM JONG IL

I have traveled to North Korea many times over the more than fifteen years I have been working there. Each time seems as strange as the next. There are many things I am not able to share about my travels inside North Korea because it would jeopardize the lives of many of the dear people I work with.

When looking at the land between the walls, I had a desire to say something about each nation between China and Jerusalem, but instead, I found myself gravitating toward three nations: Iraq, Iran, and North Korea.

North Korea is indeed a land of mystery, but it is not as much of a mystery as many of us assume. There are many things we know about North Korea.

The problem with North Korea is not that we do not know what is going on. The problem is that we know exactly what is going on but do not want to do anything about it.

Today, North Korea is one of the darkest nations in the world. The government actively blocks the spreading of the Good News. Any material with Christian writing or teaching is destroyed. Any Christian who is discovered is jailed or killed. Any sign of active Christianity in North Korea has been practically erased from the nation.

However, there is a story of revival in North Korea that cannot be hidden.

Many experts and missionary hopefuls have searched for signs of Christian life in North Korea. They look for religious books being sold or written. They look for buildings with crosses on top. They look for believers walking around with gold crosses hanging around their necks. They are searching for clergy members in traditional clothing that signify their importance in theolog-ical hierarchy. The experts have searched high and low as best they can, and many of them have come to the conclusion that the church in North Korea is dead.

There is a story of revival in North Korea that cannot be hidden.

But I can tell you from experience that the church in North Korea is far from dead! It is alive, thriving, and indeed growing! Though the winter may be harsh, though the ground may be frozen, though the wind may blow, the Korean church is like a beautiful winter lily that dares to grow even in the worst conditions.

If you are looking for the same signs of Christian life as you will find in the West, then you will come up emptyhanded. You can look inside the doors of all three official state churches in Pyongyang, but you will not find anything there.

The revival you will find in North Korea is both behind and ahead. If you look back far enough in Korean history, you will find an amazingly rich his-tory of revival, and if you look ahead, I am certain you will find many signs of a coming revival to be excited about.

The question, of course, is all about timing.

Believe it or not, the part of Korea now known as North Korea was once recognized as one of the most thriving places for Christianity in all of Asia. It was once called the "Jerusalem of the East." Missionaries from all over Asia sent their children to boarding schools in Pyongyang because of the strong missionary influence there.

The Pyongyang Foreign School (PYFS) was founded in 1900 as a high school for children of missionaries serving in China, Korea, and Japan. By the 1930s, there were four main missionary schools in Pyongyang. At that time there were also more than eight hundred Christian schools for Korean children, and together they taught an estimated forty-one thousand children of various grades.

In the 1930s, virtually all Western foreigners in Pyongyang were either missionaries or educators with a mission focus. PYFS operated for forty years and provided an education for many children whose parents were serving on the Asian mission field.

The mission community had built hospitals, boys and girls dormitories, training centers, Soongsil University, vocational centers, and even a Presbyterian theological seminary. All of these buildings stood as tangible testimonies to God's faithfulness and the dedication of the missionaries who toiled to make a difference in the lives of Koreans.

In addition to the more famous PYFS, there were also well-known establishments in Pyongyang founded by Catholics, who were often referred to as "Maryknollers." They had their establishments across town and away from the Protestants. There were also German Benedictines in Wonsan, Irish Columbans in the Cholla provinces, and French MEP missionaries who were down south in Seoul. There are even records of Seventh-Day Adventist activities in Korea with a hospital in Sunan where there is now an airport.

One of the reasons that Pyongyang was considered to be the Jerusalem of the East is no doubt partly due to the number of missionaries who flocked to the city, but also because of the number of new believers that sprouted up as a result. Revivals were breaking out everywhere in Korea and Manchuria. So many new believers were coming to Christ in such a short time in the early 1900s that mission boards sent even more missionaries. The mission activities were fueled by the growing number of indigenous converts, and the sudden surge of new converts fueled more missionaries to respond. It was cyclical.

It was reported during the 1930s that as many as one out of every five Koreans in Pyongyang was a Christian! This figure is considered to be a conservative estimate, and some reports claim there were more.

This was a substantial increase in less than fifty years of mission work and would be considered to be a revival by any standard. One of the more famous students at Pyongyang's PYFS that benefited from the great education that was provided on the coattails of this revival was Ruth Bell Graham, the future wife of well-known evangelist Billy Graham.

There were so many missionaries in Pyongyang during those days that postcards depicting everyday activities would actually show missionaries handing out tracks in the middle of the city.

When the Communists came to take over the nation and imposed the uncompromisable teachings of atheism, many of the Christians from Pyongyang fled to the south. That is one of the main reasons why South Korea is so populated with Christians today.

The largest Christian churches today are found in South Korea. There are more than seven thousand churches in the capital city of Seoul alone. While America might have a few megachurches with ten thousand people, the world's largest mega-church in South Korea boasts a congregation of about 800,000.

> ## The largest Christian churches today are found in South Korea.

The South Koreans have been very serious about prayer. More than 2.7 million people gathered for prayer in Yoido Plaza in Seoul in one day, and that event is considered to be the largest face-to-face meeting of humans in history.

It might seem that the revival fires that burned hot a century ago in North Korea are gone forever, but there is reason to believe that they are coming again. North Korea has a serious geographical problem—it is sandwiched between the country with the one of largest revivals in the world (China) and the country with the largest church in the world (South Korea). They have a rich history that goes back to their founder (Kim Il Sung's parents were house church pastors, and Kim even played the organ during worship service).

Back to Jerusalem missionaries from China are currently living and working in North Korea. So far we have delivered over 100,000 Bibles, and there is still a demand for more. The Chinese believers can closely relate to the challenges of the North Korean people because they too have been severely persecuted for their faith and have operated their church services primarily underground.

The Chinese missionaries are bringing hope and light to the North Koreans during the darkest hour. Nothing else is helping. North Korea is just as closed today as it has ever been and remains the number one human rights abuser against Christians. The situation is not going to get better in North Korea on its own. It is going to take a praying church to tear down the barriers.

Politicians don't have a clue how to fix the situation. They are at a loss for an effective strategy. North Korea is one of the poorest countries in the world with the fewest resources, yet it seems that the leadership has completely out-foxed every high-priced consultant in the world. Billions of dollars have been spent to find ways to bring down the regime, obtain military intelligence, or get the regime to open up dialog in a meaningful way, but it has all been to no avail.

The preacher's words in Ecclesiastes couldn't be truer for international dealings with North Korea: "Vanity of vanities; all is vanity" (1:2). Every effort done without the Holy Spirit has been and will continue to be futile in that land.

The only way to reach North Koreans or see a lasting change in that country is through a Spirit-led revival. The only way North Korea will have any chance of improvement is through the Gospel of Jesus Christ being preached effectively within its borders.

BTJ missionaries are planting churches, baptizing new believers, teaching them scriptures, and distributing Bibles. The borders between China and North Korea are becoming more and more vulnerable to the attacks of zealous missionaries. Every time the government closes one door, the Lord opens up ten more. People are going in; Bibles are going in; projectors and training materials are going in; video players and even miniature audio players with the Word of God are penetrating those fortified borders with the message of the eternal Gospel.

The walls are coming down around North Korea because underground house churches are slowly starting to rise. The government's rule is absolute, and punishments are severe because they are genuinely afraid of what is to come. The enemy knows that his time is limited, but he won't go down without a fight. The unconquerable Light of the World is sending in truth-bearers to set the captives free, and no darkness can overcome them.

Let the word be pronounced from border to border: "Revival is coming to North Korea!"

DISCUSSION QUESTIONS

1. North Korea went from a quickly Christianizing nation to an atheist dictatorship within a few short years. Politically this is not difficult to explain. How would you explain it spiritually?
2. Can you think of any reason why the church in North Korea has been repressed like no other church today?
3. What do you think the Body of Christ should prepare for concerning North Korea?
4. South Korea is free and prosperous, and churches are thriving. If you were a believer in North Korea, how do you think you would wish your fellow Christians in other countries would pray for you?

DAY 55

LESSONS FROM LEBANON

———◆———

"Islam is not a race. . . . Islam is simply a set of beliefs, and it is not 'Islamophobic' to say Islam is incompatible with liberal democracy."

—AYAAN HIRSI ALI

I was ten years old when my home exploded around me, burying me under the rubble and leaving me to drink my blood to survive, as the perpetrators shouted, 'Allah Akbar!' My only crime was that I was a Christian living in a Christian town," Brigitte Gabriel remembers as she shared her personal testimony. "At 10 years old, I learned the meaning of the word 'infidel.'

"I had a crash course in survival. Not in the Girl Scouts, but in a bomb shelter where I lived for seven years in pitch darkness, freezing cold, drinking stale water and eating grass to live. At the age of 13, dressed in my burial clothes going to bed at night, waiting to be slaughtered. By the age of 20, I had buried most of my friends—killed by Muslims."

Lebanon should not be a part of the land between the walls. At the fall of the Ottoman Empire at the end of WWI, the French carved out a refuge for Christians from the Muslim aggressors in Syria. Under Christian control, Lebanon quickly became known as the Paris of the Middle East.

Along with Israel, this was a beacon of peace and prosperity in the Middle East. They had the best economy, the best universities, the best hospitals, the most just laws. Tourism, agriculture, democracy, and education flourished in the 1950s and '60s.

Muslims in nearby nations looked at Lebanon as a bastion of hope. They looked to escape from their nations and move to Lebanon. It became common knowledge among the nations in the Middle East that one could flee to Lebanon and have a better life there. They could start over and have a wide array of opportunities.

People could find jobs. Children could go to great schools in a safe environment free from war. Families could create a future of unlimited possibilities. Their prosperity was reminiscent of Lebanon in the Bible.

Lebanon is mentioned at least sixty-five times in the Old Testament. It was the coastal land to the north of Israel and supplied King Solomon with the cedar forests. It was the land that sent thirty thousand men to cut and carry precious timber to be used in the Holy Temple in Jerusalem. Later, as a Christian nation, it began to quickly make ties to the newly formed nation of Israel.

In the 1960s it was clear—Christians, Jews, and Muslims alike found equality in Lebanon, and Israel had a new friend. Refugees from war-torn Muslim nations poured in looking for shelter from their hell-on-earth experiences. Ironically, when the Palestinians were being persecuted in Jordan, it was not another Muslim nation that took them it. It was the Christians in Lebanon.

Think of all the outcry today from nations around the world regarding the sad plight of the Palestinian people. Where were those voices in the 1960s and 1970s? No other Muslim nation raised their hand to help. Ironically, it was the nation of Lebanon that did.

Lebanon took the refugees from surrounding war-torn Muslim nations with open arms and the refugees found peace, but the enemy could not allow that to happen for long. Why? Perhaps for the same reason the enemy cannot allow Israel to stand for too long in the Middle East.

The side-by-side contrast is too much. The difference between a Christian nation sitting right beside a nation enslaved by Islam would be too easy for the world to compare. It would be too easy for the world to see.

The freedom of the Lord is never more apparent than when viewing it from the prison cell of Satan.

The freedom of the Arab Christians in Lebanon would be a voice to the Arabs in the Middle East, prompting revival. Arabs who only identify with Islam could see that the freedom of the Lord could set them free.

> **The freedom of the Lord is never more apparent than when viewing it from the prison cell of Satan.**

The voice of their Father in heaven could call out to them and make Himself known.

God deeply desires to be praised in every tongue, and He wants to hear His name worshiped in the Semitic language of Arabic. Those who became Christians in Lebanon did so as the result of early revival. They survived the harshest winters of jihad and Islamic rule. They pushed through the Ottoman Empire and WWI. They saw the end of WWII and the founding of the land of Israel. Like the Jews, the Christian Arabs were only given a micro-sliver of their ancient homeland to dwell in peace and harmony.

Implementing the Christian-Judaic principles of the Bible, they built a society that shined out to the rest of the world. They were Arabic, and they were Christian.

But a new revival in the Middle East would have to wait. It would not come through the Arab Christians in Lebanon. Things began to change. As the number of Muslims increased, so too did the level of unrest. The once beautiful nation of Lebanon that had carved out a peaceful haven in the Middle East became unbalanced. The Muslims saw the land of Lebanon as their inheritance. The infidels who did not accept Allah as their god would need to submit to Islamic rule.

The Muslims would not bring peace. How could they? They cannot give what they do not have. Lebanese and Palestinian Muslims, led by the father of terrorism, Yasser Arafat, set out to take over the Christian land of Lebanon, annihilate Israel, and establish a caliphate. Jihad was declared, which marked the beginning of violence and atrocities against the Christians and the Jews.

As I look at the history of revival, I want nothing more than to give stories of victory and jubilation. Don't most Bible studies do that? Don't most Bible studies leave the reader with a sense of justice, peace, and closure? When I first started following the history of revival, I was certain that I would find endless examples of great men who conquered evil.

I have.

However, there are many things that go beyond my ability to explain. I see the Christian Arabs of Lebanon and their willingness to take in the refugees and provide shelter to them. At least on the surface it looks like they have suffered for doing the thing Christians are supposed to do. I can try to explain it, but my feeble mind is unable to provide an answer that is worthy of the truth of the Lord.

Why did God allow some revivals to flourish and others to whither?

Instead, I find myself learning more from the writings in the Bible that have never really spoken to me before. When God makes perfect sense, I gravitate to scriptures that inspire and feed my feeling of understanding, but in looking at the land of Lebanon, I find myself frustrated. When observing the lands between the walls of China and Jerusalem, I am left dumbfounded.

Why did God allow some revivals to flourish and others to whither? Why did He allow His enemies to have power over His people?

Did He not hear the call of His people when they cried out to Him? It is in these times that I turn to the irrefutable frustrations of David when he wrote in Psalms 83:1–4:

> O God, do not keep silence;
>> do not hold your peace or be still, O God!
> For behold, your enemies make an uproar;
>> those who hate you have raised their heads.
> They lay crafty plans against your people;
>> they consult together against your treasured ones.

They say, "Come, let us wipe them out as a nation;

let the name of Israel be remembered no more!" (ESV)

It makes sense to me that God would withhold His blessings from those who hate Him or deny His name. I can understand that there are parts of the world where He seems to be silent because His name is unknown and so people aren't calling out to Him.

But where was God when the Christians in Lebanon needed Him? Would the Lebanese have benefited more if they had put their trust in guns and border control than in prayer? I wish I could end this section of the Bible study with the common words of comfort that we all hear during times of pain and loss. Words like, "God has a plan that we do not understand," "All things will be revealed in the end," or "All things turn out for good for those who love the Lord."

I cling to those cliché phrases when I am on the sunny side of pain, but when I am punched in the face with the memories of a ten-year-old little Brigitte Gabriel, who had to live in a bomb shelter for seven years and crawl through a war zone to find grass to eat, I am not so cocky and confident with my cute Sunday school answers.

With everything in my body, I want to say that revival will bring the Spirit of the Lord, wipe away all pain, build the most perfect societies, and God's Word will never be wiped away. I want to write that Lebanon built a Christian society that gave a light to the Middle East. Revival among the Christian Arabs took hold and burned like a fire across the desert. The spirit of Islam rose up in anger and tried to destroy it but was not able to.

While following the history of revival, I have died a thousand theological deaths. My ideas and concepts about God have been built up, destroyed, built up again, and destroyed again. I have found no solace in my own understanding. My confidence in my own explanation has melted. I have written and rewritten sections in this Bible study over a hundred times in the five years it has taken to piece this together.

As I look at the nation of Lebanon, I can't help but see the parallel in all of our lives. Just in case I get cocky in my superior understanding, I am pulled right back down to the humbleness of the true Gospel message. Just because we do the right thing and show that following God's Word can bring prosperity to our lives, we are not removed from the pain of sin and general suckiness of being in a fallen world.

Many great men and countless great nations have proceeded us in their attempts to live rightly before God. Just like them, we must face the struggle to overcome sin and evil. It is a daily battle. Evil does not rest. It constantly dwells even in the hearts of good men, but it will not last forever. Evil is not eternal.

Lebanon was carved out by France to give the Christians a place among the Muslim nations. It was a good and worthy endeavor, but the sanctuary of peace built by the hands of man will not last forever.

Unfortunately, our victories in Christ continue to come through suffering. I wish they didn't. For once, I wish victory would come through increasing strength, escalation of understanding, accrual of territory, and expansion of dominance over evil.

But I am learning that revival is not for human comfort. It is not for the establishment of worldly kingdoms. It is not to prove that we are right and the enemy is wrong. It is not to bring a utopia on earth. It does not erase the fall of man.

> **Unfortunately, our victories in Christ continue to come through suffering.**

Revival builds up the Body of Christ, prepares us for suffering, and brings about the return of Jesus. But between now and the return of Christ, there is always the counter-productive aspect of hell.

DISCUSSION QUESTIONS

1. When Lebanon let in many Muslim refugees, and as a result was undermined as a Christian nation, do you think they were doing the right thing to help these people?

2. What do you think Western nations should do in the light of what happened in Lebanon regarding refugees from Muslim nations?
3. Do you think having a "Christian nation" is desirable or even possible?
4. If Christianity is the main religion in a country, should that be something to defend, with violence if necessary? Why do you think so?

PART 9

BACK TO JERUSALEM

DAY 56

WATER FROM THE DRAGON WELL

———◆———

"And I went out by night by the gate of the valley,
even before the dragon well."

—NEHEMIAH IN NEHEMIAH 2:13

Chasing revival has led me around the globe, and I have arrived right back where I started—in Jerusalem. It has been a full circle. The land between the walls of China and Jerusalem has shifted my hope for the future to the revivals pumping up in the East.

Of the things I have learned, there is one thing that stands out the most, and that is the underground movement of revival under persecution. And that has led me to an obscure scripture in the book of Nehemiah.

The book of Nehemiah records one evening when Nehemiah went out from the walls of Jerusalem through the Dung Gate: "And I went out by night by the gate of the valley, even before the dragon well, and to the dung port, and viewed the walls of Jerusalem, which were broken down, and the gates thereof were consumed with fire" (2:13).

The Dung Gate referred to in the book of Jeremiah was so named because it was the main access point for those who took all of the garbage out from the city. Today this is actually the southeastern point of the old city and is the gate that leads into the place of the ancient city where the temple once stood. Because of the proximity to the Western Wall in Jerusalem, the ancient site of the holiest of holies, the Dung Gate is now one of the cleanest gates in all of Jerusalem.

Nehemiah 2:13 tells us that the Dung Gate was once located by the water source called the Dragon Well. This scripture jumps out at me because of my exposure to China, the land of the dragon.

Even though the Dragon Well can no longer be located today, many believe that it must be the same as the Gihon Spring that fed the pool of Siloam, which connected through Hezekiah's Tunnel. This is the only water source for Jerusalem. Without this water source, Jerusalem never would have been inhabitable.

Water springs are important because access to water is the essential for the building of any major city. They are the source of life in desert communities, and without them the people will die of dehydration.

The Gihon Spring is in the valley between the Temple Mount and the Mount of Olives. The walls of Jerusalem do not defend the water spring because the water spring is in the valley. If the walls of Jerusalem would have extended to include the water source, the walls would have had to descend down into the valley and would have been vulnerable to attack from the elevated points in the east.

This was a major problem. If Jerusalem ever came under attack, the enemy could close off the water source outside of the city walls and wait for the people to die of thirst. Hezekiah's Tunnel was built for this purpose. The Gihon Spring was hidden underground and then channeled into the city of Jerusalem so that the city could keep getting water even when the city was under siege.

Today the city of Jerusalem is under siege spiritually. Every nation around the nation of Israel wants her destroyed and wiped off the planet.

The city of Jerusalem was physically attacked over and over again until the Muslim armies finally took control of it. Jerusalem has been controlled by Muslim conquests off and on for more than one thousand years.

After the Islamic armies took over the holy city of Jerusalem, they noticed that the Christians and the Jews had the same prophecy: they both believed that the coming Messiah would return through the Eastern Gate of Jerusalem.

The commander of the Islamic armies was nervous about these prophecies so he immediately set about closing up the gate in an attempt to prevent the Christian and Jewish prophecies from being fulfilled. When I traveled to Jerusalem to see this for myself, I saw that the Eastern Gate is still closed. A wall has been built in its place.

The closing of the gate happened according to prophecy. The prophet Ezekiel wrote,

> Then he brought me back the way of the gate of the outward sanctuary which looketh toward the east; and it was shut. Then said the LORD unto me; This gate shall be shut, it shall not be opened, and no man shall enter in by it; because the LORD, the God of Israel, hath entered in by it, therefore it shall be shut. It is for the prince; the prince, he shall sit in it to eat bread before the LORD; he shall enter by the way of the porch of that gate, and shall go out by the way of the same. (Ezekiel 44:1–3)

As I walked near the Eastern Gate, I was not permitted to get too close because not only was the Eastern Gate sealed up by the Muslims, but an Islamic graveyard has been constructed at the foot of the gate.

The Muslims knew that the Jews believed that a person is made unclean by touching a dead body (Numbers 19:11), so if a person is made unclean, surely a Messiah would be made unclean. So they put the graveyard directly in front of the holiest of gates to desecrate the area, make it off-limits to visitors and to prevent the return of the Messiah.

As I gazed westward at the Eastern Gate from a distance, it suddenly occurred to me: the Muslims did not just seal up the Eastern Gate to prevent the return of the Messiah; they built a graveyard on one side and a temple on the other. They did not just try to block the Eastern Gate; they have taken over the entire eastern front to try to prevent the return of the Messiah!

From the Eastern Gate to the Ningxia Province of China, Muslims have sealed off the way to Jerusalem and have tried to block the way for the return of the Messiah.

This region between the Eastern Gate and China's Xinjiang Province is the corridor for the House of Islam. To the north and east are seats of atheism. To the south is the house of Buddha and Hinduism, but the primary window between Jerusalem and China belongs to the house of Islam.

It is in this area where we see the most resistance. If the Chinese face west, toward the Eastern Gate, they will find the most violent and unrelenting areas with the most resistance against the Gospel. Perhaps this is by design.

Has this been the case all along? Does the enemy know that Jesus is returning to the Eastern Gate from the western area of the Mount of Olives just as He promised? Will Jesus complete the westward moving circle and enter into the Eastern Gate just as He promised?

> **Will Jesus complete the westward moving circle and enter into the Eastern Gate just as He promised?**

"For as lightning cometh out of the east, and shinest even unto the west; so shall the coming of the Son of man be" (Matthew 24:27).

The Islamic armies are putting up a fight. They are trying to delay the return of Christ for as long as they can by enslaving as many people in darkness as can be enslaved. Satan has spent generations entrenching himself on the eastern front of Jerusalem, trying to prevent any penetration of the Gospel message. The core has been Islam, insulated by Buddhism, Hinduism, Animism, and most recently atheism. The entire eastern front from Jerusalem to China has largely remained a spiritual wasteland.

However, could there be a secret weapon in the last days?

Could Nehemiah have given us a hint about the battle that is yet to come that will spur the revival of the last days? Could there still be water in the Dragon Well outside of the walled city of Jerusalem?

What if the source of Life is still flowing from the Dragon Well to provide Living Water to God's people during the final attack?

Remember the very first conquest of the city of Jerusalem by King David? How did David's army take the city? They did not come over the walls or through the city's walls, but under them! Perhaps this is the same today.

When the tunnels of Hezekiah were built, the purpose was to bring water from the spring outside of the walls to God's people inside. When the attackers stood outside of the walled city, they were completely unaware that they were standing on the source of life for God's people. The water flowed freely right under their feet.

Today, perhaps the streams of Living Water are flowing freely under the feet of the enemy. Likewise, the underground house church is operating under the feet of the enemy and making their way all the way back to Jerusalem.

The underground church is flowing through the land of Muhammad like water through Hezekiah's Tunnel, and they are bringing the glory of the Lord. This image paints a picture similar to what is described in Ezekiel: "Then he led me to the gate, the gate facing east. And behold, the glory of the God of Israel was coming from the east. And the sound of his coming was like the sound of many waters, and the earth shone with his glory" (43:1–2 ESV).

> **Perhaps the streams of Living Water are flowing freely under the feet of the enemy.**

China and the lands between the walls are east of Jerusalem.

Today, the land east of Jerusalem sits in darkness, and its inhabitants are blind. The Eastern Gate has been sealed. Muslims have built the iconic Dome of the Rock on top of the ancient Jewish temple and block any study of the area for fear of the truth being revealed. The land east of Jerusalem is closed to those carrying out the Great Commission and has been locked up for generations. It remains the last frontier for westward movement of the Gospel, but it was prophesied through Zechariah 14:3–4:

> Then shall the LORD go forth, and fight against those nations, as when he fought in the day of battle. And his feet shall stand in that day upon the mount of Olives, which is before Jerusalem on the east, and the mount of Olives shall cleave in the midst thereof toward the east and toward the west, and there shall be a very great valley.

The people who live in this area between China and Jerusalem are blind from the darkness imposed by Islam, but the Word of the Lord that is marching westward from the east brings life and truth.

The Living Water that is carried in the vessels of the underground Chinese church can make the blind see. The Dragon Well can once again bring living water.

DISCUSSION QUESTIONS

1. The prophesies about the coming Messiah discuss Him entering through the Eastern Gate. Do you think that will literally happen? If so, do you think any Muslim resistance can delay Him?
2. What do you think will happen to the closed gate and the Dome on the Rock when the Messiah returns?
3. Do you think the current city of Jerusalem will still have significance, or do you think it will be replaced by the New Jerusalem we read about in Scripture?
4. Chinese missionaries want to challenge the power of Islam from below, as underground missionaries, to prepare the way for the return of the Messiah. What do you think believers in your country can do to challenge the hold Islam has over people?
5. Do you think Islam should be challenged as a system, or should we focus on reaching individuals with the Good News? Or maybe both? What do you think and why?

DAY 57

THOUGHT CONTROL

———————

"In the course of my life, I have often had to eat my words, and I must
confess that I have always found it a wholesome diet."

—Winston Churchill

While chasing revival, I came to the conclusion that revival is sometimes delayed because of lack of confession. The Jewish leaders in
Jerusalem during the days of Jesus were notorious for this. Jesus gave grace
to those who recognized their need for salvation and rejected those who were
righteous in their own eyes.

Revival will never come unless we acknowledge our evil.

It is easy for us to say that
Mao Zedong and Hitler were

> **Revival will never come unless we acknowledge our evil.**

evil, but they didn't carry out their evil deeds alone. The cold, hard truth is
that those who executed tens of millions of people were just like you and me.

What evil do we harbor?

Maybe we have bought the lie that we are not sinners because we do not
commit big acts of sin, but the truth is, many of us do not commit a particular sin, not because we do not want to, but because it is kept from us.

Do we do good because God is alive in us or because we have been conditioned by society and the laws that keep us from sinning? If it is condi-
tioning, the kind imposed by outside reinforcements—meaning punishment

for bad and rewards for good—then our good behavior is not based on our relationship with God, but rather on self-preservation.

Many of us do not sin because we have not had the opportunity.

I had a couple who came to me for marriage counseling. They were looking at getting a divorce. We sat in their living room and discussed the challenges in their marriage. The husband, quick to defend his pious behavior during their marriage, proudly pointed out, "She doesn't trust me. Doesn't she know that I see beautiful women every day and haven't slept with any of them!"

"That doesn't count," I said before the wife could respond. "Brother, I have to be honest with you. You are the ugliest person I know. From my perspective we do not know if you haven't slept with these women because you do not want to or because they would not give you the time of day. You do not get brownie points for something you cannot do."

Jesus taught us that if we look upon a woman and desire her, then we are guilty in our heart. We are sinners, not just because of the things we do and do not do. According to Jesus, if our hearts desire sin, then we are sinners.

Let me put it another way: Do we refrain from stealing because we think that it is wrong, or do we refrain because of the punishments that come along with it in our society?

A mouse really wants cheese, but imagine a mouse being placed in a maze that zaps him every time he goes for the cheese. After a few zaps, will he eat the cheese even though he really wants it? If the mouse is conditioned through a system of punishments and rewards not to touch the cheese, he will not touch the cheese, but given the chance to eat the cheese without any punishments, then the mouse will eat the cheese.

> **Many Christians are confused about the ideas of desiring sin and committing sin.**

Many Christians are confused about the ideas of desiring sin and committing sin.

Our desires shape our thoughts, our thoughts create actions, and our actions form character. Our character is initially determined by our desires.

We must first desire before we sin. If we lack the desire, then we lack the action, but to lack the action does not necessarily mean that we lack the desire. If our desires are unholy, then our thoughts are unholy. It is possible to habitually have evil thoughts and not have evil actions if our society has conditioned us not to act on those desires, but it is not possible to habitually have evil actions if we do not have evil thoughts.

Revival is not just hindered because we do not repent from evil actions, but also because we

> **Revival has and always will be the work of the Holy Spirit.**

do not repent from evil desires. Evil actions are only a by-product of evil in our heart.

Christ gives us the most basic charge in confronting evil: start in the heart. "Ye have heard that it was said, . . . Thou shalt not commit adultery: but I say unto you, That every one that looketh on a woman to lust after her hath committed adultery with her already in his heart" (Matthew 5:27–28).

We must start with our thoughts because our actions do not say much about the conditions of our souls.

"It is written, This people honoreth me with their lips, but their heart is far from me" (Mark 7:6).

When praying for revival, we often look at the big dragons in our life and determine that they must be removed before revival can start, but that is not true. We have to start small. We have to face the little demons that are born in our thoughts. The everyday demons that germinate in our minds. Those thoughts are actually the big demons we must slay.

Maybe Westerners often fail to see revival because they are not looking low enough. They keep looking for the big, sinful actions to be destroyed in an announced dramatic fashion, when what is really needed is the small, quiet crucifixion of everyday thoughts.

Defeating evil in preparation for revival is as simple and as hard as denying ourselves the thoughts only we know we have. Not killing the actions, but the thoughts that create those actions. Therein lies the secret to defeating evil. Paul described it in Galatians 2:20 as being "crucified with Christ:

nevertheless I live; yet not I, but Christ liveth in me." And God said in Isaiah, "For my thoughts are not your thoughts, neither are your ways my ways" (55:8).

If we did that every day, if we combated evil in the smallest of things and we began to change our mind to focus on Christ in the minutia, then we could begin to get our minds and hearts in order. From there we could get our lives and families in order. From there we can help get our communities in order.

Revival has and always will be the work of the Holy Spirit. It will never come apart from Him. However, we are also called to follow Christ and to submit our lives to Him. And when we do that, we impact the world around us and create a more fertile ground for God to move.

Anyone who has been to New York City in the last few years might have experienced the world-famous skating rink, the Central Park Zoo, or even a romantic horse-pulled carriage ride.

New York City can be a great place to spend the day with your family, but that was not always the case.

In the 1980s, much of New York City was a horrible, dangerous dump. The famous Central Park was full of drugs, murder, and prostitution. Most of the city was a cesspool.

What changed? How did New York City transform from a bastion of crime to an enjoyable metropolis?

New Yorkers are politically liberal, but after the 1980s they were tired of the crime, so they brought in a tough mayor by the name of Rudy Giuliani. Rudy implemented a system that came to be known as the "Broken Windows Theory."

The Broken Windows Theory states that preventing small crimes such as vandalism, public drinking, or even citing broken windows on a building creates an atmosphere of order and lawfulness, thereby preventing more serious crimes from happening. It is the basic idea that big crimes can be prevented by stopping the small crimes.

After the first two years of Rudy Giuliani implementing the Broken Windows Theory in New York City, violent crime declined by more than 56 percent and property crimes tumbled by about 65 percent. Businesses came back, and the economy started to boom.

If we implemented the Broken Windows Theory in our lives, then maybe we could see a massive move of repentance that would spur revival in our lands all the way back to Jerusalem.

Many of us know that we have evil thoughts and want to eradicate them, but often we do not know how. James teaches us how to heal our hearts of evil thoughts: confess them. "Confess your sins to one another and pray for one another, that you may be healed" (James 5:16 ESV).

One of the tragedies in our Protestant church is that we have distanced ourselves from our Catholic brothers and sisters. As I have followed the footsteps of revival, I have come to the realization that Protestants and Catholics share the same history before the Reformation.

Until the sixteenth century, for better or for worse, Christianity was tied with the Roman Catholic Church. When we Protestants broke away from the church, we tried to break free of many of the bondages that had been added by men. In doing so, some biblical things were also thrown out. One of them is the idea of confession. I believe that we Protestants do not confess enough and that the lack of confession prohibits revival. Like the Jewish leaders in Jerusalem during the days of Jesus, we find reasons to defend the condition of our wretched hearts.

I am not advocating that we need to confess to a priest, but as James pointed out, we should find someone to confess our sins to. However, we should be wise to confess to someone who loves Jesus and is grounded in the Word.

We often reserve confession for our sinful actions, but this is a huge mistake. We should confess our thoughts as well so that they can be crucified before Christ.

It is not just spiritually heathy; it has been proven to be physically healthy to confess as well. Confession can benefit your spiritual life and your emotional life, and there are endless health benefits.

Confessions are contagious. That is why revival is usually sparked by people openly confessing their sins.

Why? Because when one person is open with his sin, the enemy is exposed, and others find strength and courage to confess as well.

At some basic level, confession cleanses the soul. They say that sunlight is the best disinfectant. Confession is directly connected to repentance and helps us establish the humble submission required to control our thoughts.

I think that is why we often hear about deathbed confessions. Individuals who have carried a heavy burden of secrecy their entire lives finally realize that they cannot carry the secret to their grave.

Whitey Bulger was a mobster on the run for sixteen years. He was living in hiding as a regular person. When the FBI finally caught him and put the cuffs on his hands, he looked at the officer who had arrested him with relief and asked what had taken them so long to catch him. It turned out that he desperately wanted to be arrested because he didn't want to live a secret any longer.

If we desire to be free from the burden of secret sins, we must cling to confession. Those who confess will find freedom, and the ripple effect confession can produce will be another spark to flame revival.

DISCUSSION QUESTIONS

1. When you think of Mao's Red Guards, Hitler's men, or maybe a famous preacher being caught with the wrong woman, do you ever feel worried about what you as a human may be capable of?

2. How do you think we can protect ourselves against being tempted by sin when the opportunity presents itself, or even worse, when the crowd actively tries to pull us in?

3. Have you ever practiced confession to another believer? Was it difficult to do? Do you think it was beneficial?

4. What do you think changes in our heart with confession?

5. What can we answer if somebody, or our own heart, tells us, "I may not be perfect, but I am okay compared to others"? Why would an attitude like that stand in the way of revival?

DAY 58

THE WRONG VICTIM

———◆———

"I, or any mortal at any time, may be utterly
mistaken as to the situation he is really in."

—C. S. Lewis

There is a prevailing thought in Christian charities that if you want to make the biggest impact on the mission field, you must first find the organizations with the most money or the agencies with the largest structure.

Those thoughts are birthed in fear, and fear cannot sustain the weight of the Great Commission in the final days. Charity will not bring about revival. Goodwill will not bring revival back to Jerusalem. Popular charity only appeals to our own selfish need to be accepted and have security.

What if God made a deal with you right now. What if He told you that you could do anything, go anywhere, and make the biggest impact for His kingdom, help the most people, end poverty and injustice forever—more than had ever been done in the history of man—but no one would ever know you were involved. Would you do it?

Let's take it one step further. What if the deal meant that someone else would get all of the credit?

Would you still do it?

Let's go even further. What if you could do anything, go anywhere, and start the world's largest revival, but no one would know it was you, someone who had nothing to do with it would get all of the credit, and those you love the most would never see you as anything but a loser and a hinderance?

Would you take that deal?

That scenario is actually almost every person ever used by God in the Bible. They did amazing things to help others, alleviate poverty, and bring about justice, but they themselves were lonely, persecuted, and even denied by those closest to them.

The road of a prophet is a hated one. It is a lonely one. The prophet is despised, and it is only in retrospect that they are recognized.

> # The road of a prophet is a hated one. It is a lonely one.

To see revival, we must accept that.

Be very wary of the path you follow if you grow popular for doing the work of the Lord. Be suspicious of a revival that is hailed by the secular world. It is out of character for those who are doing the work of the Lord to be liked and socially accepted.

Christians who seek to do charity without the Gospel do not help the poor or downtrodden. They contribute to it. Proper charity is impossible to implement without the Gospel message. Charity on its own does nothing and helps no one.

All of the resources in the world will not help the suffering or the poor. Only the unlearned and biblically ignorant believe that people suffer in poverty and pain because they lack resources.

Social justice without the Lord is growing in popularity among Christians, but it does not actually exist. The idea of social justice might sound cool and connect the church with popular secular figures, but it does absolutely nothing to bring about justice.

It contributes to the pride of man to think that he has evolved, apart from God, to be magnanimous. It is our audacity that makes us the judge and jury of God's Word and makes us think we get to determine what is fair and what is not.

The Bible has stood a million trials in the courts of public opinion of man, and it has been found guilty countless times for being unjust or inhumane.

Beware! Never make the mistake of thinking that we are more compassionate or just than God. You might just choose the wrong victim.

Do not think of your godless devotion to a cause as a worthy sacrifice to all mankind, because God is bigger than our anorexic charity.

Never boast of a righteous position that is founded in a successful short-term conquest, because Christianity consistently does what no other religion has ever done: it conquers in defeat.

If we are to see revival in Jerusalem again, we will need leaders who are courageous and strong and not swayed by the winds of the world. Holiness requires sacrifice and a willingness to take unpopular stances, and few stances have been more unpopular than supporting Israel.

In 2017, the president of the United States, Donald Trump, announced the recognition of Jerusalem as the Jewish capital of Israel.

There was widespread and aggressive opposition to this simple recognition of a historical fact. Jerusalem has been the capital of the Jewish people for more than three thousand years, but that did not stop the General Assembly of the United Nations from voting for a resolution condemning any nation that would formally recognize Jerusalem as the capital of Israel that was backed by 128 countries.

> Woe to those who call evil good
>> and good evil,
> who put darkness for light
>> and light for darkness,
> who put bitter for sweet
>> and sweet for bitter!
> Woe to those who are wise in their own eyes. (Isaiah 5:20–21)

The enemy knows that this perversion of justice is extremely effective, which is why it is like a nuclear weapon for him.

Humility and submission to the Word of God are the foundation of all other Christian virtues and lead to the best chance at understanding righteousness, love, mercy, and justice. Humility and submission to the Word of God are the most important when following the Word of God puts you in opposition to how the world defines those virtues.

God's Words are the building blocks to all holy virtues. Without humility and submission to God's Words, we have only the appearance of holy virtues. Let's looks at the example of Joseph when he was tempted by Potiphar's wife.

Do you notice the scripture where Joseph called Potiphar's wife a harlot for trying to seduce him? No? But surely he told her that she would be going to hell, right?

Joseph did not judge her according to God's Word, but he did judge himself. God's Word gave Joseph his holy virtues that kept him from falling into temptation. When tempted by Potiphar's wife to have a secret affair, Joseph responded with, "How can I do this thing against God?" (see Genesis 39:9). Joseph judged himself according to God's Word, but his actions judged Potiphar's wife.

Potiphar's wife was attracted to Joseph. She lured him in. She tried to entice him. She was using the sweetest honey known to man, and then she became enraged at Joseph's rejection of her advances.

How did she punish Joseph? Potiphar's wife became the victim, and Joseph became the victimizer. She cried out, "This Hebrew came in here and mocked me" (see Genesis 39:17). Some versions say that he "came in to me to laugh at me" (ESV).

Joseph did no such thing; he merely rejected her lifestyle for himself, but to her that was unacceptable.

Watch very carefully what happened here.

Potiphar's wife tried in every way to convince Joseph to join her in sin, but he could not. God's Word gave the boundaries of virtues he desired to live by. He did not judge her, but his refusal to participate at some level in her sin made her feel guilty, and she projected her feelings of rejection on Joseph, internalized them, and concluded that Joseph was mocking her and she was now a victim. Joseph was accused and convicted of being a victimizer because he would not abandon God's teachings.

In Potiphar's house there was a serious imbalance of power. Potiphar's wife was arguably the most powerful person in the house. Many would argue that she was more powerful at home than Potiphar himself was.

Joseph was on the opposite end. He was a slave. He was not an employee. He was property. They were not equals. He was the victim.

It was not enough for her that she thought that it was okay to have an affair; she saw a person who held sacred virtues that she needed to change.

We all have heard the words of Potiphar's wife: "Come and lie with me. It is not a sin. It is okay to put yourself first. That old, archaic book was written thousands of years ago. Don't be so closed-minded. Don't judge. Choose love, not hate."

The world doesn't just want you to violate your virtues. They want you, they need you, to celebrate their sin. To embrace it. And when you do not, they become the victims and you become the victimizer. You are labeled as judgmental, hypocritical, homophobic, bigoted, anti-human rights, anti-science, anti-etc.

> **The world doesn't just want you to violate your virtues. They want you, they need you, to celebrate their sin.**

The world is not merely satisfied with the idea of not recognizing Jerusalem as the capital of Israel; they demand it from you as well. They demand that you hope for the fall and destruction of Israel, and if you do not, then you become the victimizer and they become the victims.

Good intentions cannot lead the way for revival. Good intentions have paved a clear path to destruction. We cannot make eternal judgements with mortal hearts. Our emotions can be so easily twisted and tricked. Our hearts are easily misled. The world can twist and use good intentions against the church.

> A person's own folly leads to their ruin,
>
> yet their heart rages against the LORD.
>
> (Proverbs 19:3 NIV)

The heart is deceitful above all things,

and desperately sick;

who can understand it?

(Jeremiah 17:9 ESV)

If revival is to return to Israel, it must come through Christ and Christ alone. The perverse charity of men will only delay it.

DISCUSSION QUESTIONS

1. Have you ever been involved in ministries to the poor? Did you see long-term results?
2. What was the difference between those you were able to really help and those who remained poor?
3. Do you think Christians can/should be engaged in what is often called "kingdom work" without reference to the King? Why or why not?
4. This chapter states that we should be worried if the world is applauding our charitable efforts. Why do you think that is the case?
5. Is it possible for Christians to work together with secular organizations on alleviating poverty? Have you done that? What did you feel was helpful and what wasn't?

DAY 59

A CURIOUS CASE OF THE DIMINISHING MALE

"Only one man in a thousand is a leader of
men–the other 999 follow women."

—**GROUCHO MARX**

Living and working in China and seeing the history of the church throughout time, I am in awe at the constant work of women. Their leadership
in one of the world's largest revivals in China cannot be overestimated.

During the time I spent walking around the streets of Jerusalem, I was
always happy to see the active and necessary work of females in the Israeli
Defense Forces, keeping me and fellow visitors safe.

Without women, the world's
first announcement of the resurrection of Jesus would not have
taken place. Through my years
of revival research, I found that
women have played a vital role
in the continuation of revival
from Jerusalem to the rest of the
world, but as hard as I might try,

> **Without women,
> the world's first
> announcement of the
> resurrection of Jesus
> would not have
> taken place.**

there is one thing I cannot ignore: the necessity of male leadership.

Arriving back in Israel after traveling around the world following revival
has brought me to a place where my thinking is against social norms. The

inescapable truth that I cannot shake is that all the major spiritual break-throughs I witnessed in history and the shattering of normal standards necessary for revival to take place were all led by men of God.

When I think of every major revival, every major revolution, or even every country that has ever been started since the beginning of time, they were all started by men. They were all founded by men.

When I think of every new invention that disrupted societies and changed the way we live life, I cannot escape the reality that they were invented by men.

Abraham, Isaac, Jacob, and the twelve tribes of Israel—the foundation of the Jewish people—were all men. Moses, Joshua, and Caleb, who broke through and led God's people out of slavery and into the promised land, were all men.

All of the Levitical priests who were called into the Holiest of Holies to encounter God were men.

Even Jesus Himself and all twelve of His disciples—men.

The idea that men are essential to lead revival is extremely unpopular and sexist, but nonetheless is inescapable.

It is easy to find examples of women in history leading charges, inventing, and even helping start a country. I know because I have discovered many and shared them in this study, but I cannot help but come back to a major ingredient of revival that seems to be left out of many books about the matter and indeed even left out of our conversations today: the need for men to rise up.

One thing seems clear to me: the enemy's house is not run by women, or at least that is what I have found. When I study the house of Buddha, Hindu, or Islam in the land between the walls, I have discovered they are not run by women. Men are firmly in the leadership position. Is this coincidence? I think not. The enemy knows the power of male leadership and so has used that to ensnare women. In the house of Buddha, Hindu, and Islam I constantly find the victimization of women. They are persecuted and violated and can do nothing to prevent it because these religions are controlled by ungodly men who are not in submission to the Word of God.

The Bible is very clear that men are not better than women or more valuable than women, nor is that anywhere close to the conclusion I have come to. To ignore women is to deny half of God. To deny women a role in the leadership of the church is to handicap the body and miss the depth and width of God. Men and women are equal in value in the eyes of God, but could it be that their roles are undeniably different (and complementary), as is evident in their design?

I am afraid that if we ignore the design, then the implementation of any strategy we construct will be flawed.

Looking back at the history of the church to where we are today, I cannot help but believe that there is a feminization of men taking place in Christian countries, and it seems that it is being done on purpose. The feminization is not being forced; the enemy is not strong enough to do so. It is taking place voluntarily through guilt and pressure.

Satan treats men and women differently, and as Christians we need to recognize and learn from the different ways he tries to attack us. The difference tells us a lot.

There seems to be an increasing number of men missing from the church. They seem to be missing from the family. Is this the desire of the enemy?

> **There seems to be an increasing number of men missing from the church.**

Is it me, or does it seem that an alarming number of young boys are increasingly raised by single women in the West? Is it my imagination or are more young males increasingly shamed for showing signs of a masculine nature or displaying male virtues?

In the Bible, men are given a specific duty by God to protect and provide. What if the by-product of men being stripped of their nature is less protection and less provision in a society? Could the lack of male leadership translate to more bad guys doing bad things?

In Western Christian societies, maleness is being portrayed in a negative light. Male strength and aggressiveness are increasingly demonized, marginalized, and shamed. Those who merely point it out are quickly attacked as being misogynistic or anti-woman.

It seems that Christian men have been asked by society to socially castrate themselves and deny everything that makes them a man. By allowing this to happen, we have retarded revival.

It is not appropriate to voice these concerns in today's secular environment where everything is increasingly politically correct, but maybe it is a conversation we need to have if we long to see revival.

DISCUSSION QUESTIONS

1. Why do you think there are twice as many women in mission as men? Is there any connection with the fact that churches also often have more women than men members?
2. What do you think is holding men back?
3. How could a new generation of young men be set on fire for mission?
4. What is your best experience of working with brothers or sisters of the opposite sex in church/mission work?
5. Do you think women and men have ministries they excel in more than the other sex does? Why do you think that is?

DAY 60

LYING ABOUT WINNING?

———◆———

"Gambling is a disease of barbarians superficially civilized."
—Dean Inge

Are Christians actually making any progress on the mission field among the unreached or has Satan changed the game so that Christians only feel they are winning?

What if Christians are allowed to feel like they are winning when they are actually losing, like when a gambler is given a few small progressive wins in a casino thinking that he is going to be rich, only to walk away completely broke? Even if you don't lose every game, you still go home with less than you had when you came.

Gambling houses allow you to win some so that you will stay at their hotel, buy their drinks, watch their shows, eat their food, and pay their tips. But everyone knows that ultimately, the "house" always wins. It is like Aztek soccer that I mentioned earlier, where the winners were sacrificed to the gods. You think you win, but you actually lose.

When Christians are told that the main priority is their life, their ministry, and their fulfilment, then all focus and energy shifts to self and not to the mission.

How much should we celebrate our victories when what we are celebrating is completely different from what Jesus said we should be doing?

We are in a bit of a crisis in the church when it comes to missions.

It has been two thousand years since Jesus stood outside of Jerusalem on the Mount of Olives and gave us the Great Commission, yet the majority of the world's population lives in an area that is mostly unreached. The obvious question we should be asking is, "Why are so many people unreached?"

As I look at churches around the world, I am forced to look for the answer to this question.

I spend more than three hundred days a year traveling. I have been to churches big and small. I have attended mission conferences of all different shapes and sizes. I have studied many different courses and seminars on missions outreach. Though there are many good things taking place in missions, I believe that honesty might be one of our greatest weaknesses.

After walking through this road trip Bible study and following the history of the church all the way back to Jerusalem, I would like to ask you . . . do you think the church is winning or losing?

Maybe *winning* is not the right word. Christ is always the victor, but do you think the church is making progress on the mission field? I think the church is in crisis, and it is partially because Christians are not getting the full story.

Let me ask the question in another way. If you were to guess, what would you say is the number one missionary-sending country in the world today?

What if I told you that, per capita, the nation sending the most missionaries to the rest of the world is not a Christian nation; in fact, it is not even technically a nation. According to a 2013 study published by *Christianity Today*, Palestine sends the most missionaries per capita to unreached nations.

What if I were to ask you what the number one destination of missionaries is? Would you guess that it would be an unreached nation between China and Jerusalem, the area that needs missionaries the most?

Unfortunately, the top nine nations receiving Christian missionaries are all Christian nations. The number one nation, receiving more than 32,400 missionaries from other nations in 2016, was the United States. Only 13,300, less than half of those sent to America, were sent in total to non-Christian nations.

This is like some kind of missionary swap, where Christian nations just send missionaries back and forth to one another.

This is a crisis.

There are 5,626 unreached people groups living between China and Jerusalem, most of which do not have one single Christian living among them. There are 1.7 billion Muslims in the world with an average of only 1 missionary for every 500,000 Muslims.

The top ten unreached nations on earth make up 73 percent of unreached people globally but receive less than 9 percent of missionaries.

This is a crisis.

Perhaps one of the reasons why this is happening is because the church is not being told the truth. In the mission community, we have somehow been encouraged to sell ourselves, build ourselves up, and market our work, but not all of what is being said is true.

Even as I market this Bible study and the work our mission organization is conducting, I will undoubtedly share how amazing it is, how big of an impact it will make, and why you should join us. I will wrap it up in flowery Christian language, pepper it with Bible scriptures, and possibly present it with a humble cherry on top.

> **The top ten unreached nations on earth make up 73 percent of unreached people globally but receive less than 9 percent of missionaries.**

If you go to our website, we will tell you about all of the things that are taking place on the mission field, but what I am not going to tell you about are the many things I am constantly doing wrong on the mission field.

Have you read my glowing biography at the beginning of the handful of books I have written? If not, you should. It is good and will tell you exactly how amazing and qualified I am.

You know what the bio will not tell you? It will not tell you how many mistakes I made while writing those books. It will not tell you how little I pray on a daily basis or how little I know about the Bible compared to what

I *think* I know. It will not say anything about how I literally get into an argument at airport security in Uganda almost every time I travel there or how I recently have made really bad decisions that have cost the ministry a lot of money.

My bio says nothing about the fact that I lost my dad when I was a year old, grew up on welfare, and had a mother who got married and divorced three times to three different guys. Out of my four siblings, only one of them has the same last name as me. My bio says nothing about being put on probation at the age of fourteen and being initially rejected for military service because my probation officer said I was not worth the time of day.

I can keep going. I have done things so bad that I would not say them out loud if I were by myself in a dark room with the lights off.

Many of us who are in missions stand on stage and in pulpits week after week and share our virtues and victories, the love of our work and mission, but we hide our failures and vulnerabilities.

When we talk about missions, we often create a false narrative for the sake of making everyone feel good so they will pray for our work and give money to our cause, but it has clearly crippled missions.

We know deep down inside in places we don't talk about in prayer circles that we are completely incapable of controlling the outcome on the mission field, so in our state of desperation, dearly wanting to be accepted by others and also because we know we can't control the mission field, we control our image and our narrative. But the truth is, our narrative does not paint an accurate picture of us or our mission field.

We create a false image, and we lull the church into a false sense of security. We take away the feeling of the immediate need of sacrifice. We feed the monster of an egocentric church.

Our ego has outgrown our mission. Dr. Rick Rigsby once said, "Make sure your servant's towel is bigger than your ego. . . . Ego is the anesthesia that deadens the pain of stupidity."

Of course, revival tarries when we are not sharing the reality of what is happening on the mission field. The majority of the world is lost when we spend more time massaging the image of our mission organizations than we do on the mission. People die when mission organizations spend most of our time overselling their activities and presenting results that are massively inflated.

According to the World Evangelization Research Center, "250 of the 300 largest international Christian organizations regularly mislead the Christian public by publishing demonstrably incorrect or falsified progress statistics."

Could it be that it is even more difficult for the church to engage the most unreached when they are not even being given a correct report on what is happening?

Why does this happen? Why do missionaries and mission organizations continue to over-sell what is occurring on the mis-

> **Revival tarries when we are not sharing the reality of what is happening on the mission field.**

sion field? Why do we inflate our numbers? Why do we prance around in a missions masquerade wasting time and resources creating an image that is not accurate?

Because of one simple, sad truth: the church has lost sight of its mission.

Many churches are currently in a place where they have to be encouraged to support missions. Which is completely backward.

Missionaries are on the field, living in horrible conditions, haven't had steady electricity in years, can't remember what a warm shower feels like, and find sand in every little orifice known and unknown to man. These beaten-up missionaries and battle-weary mission leaders come to church hobbling, limping, skinny, and poor, and the church sits there wanting the missionary to encourage them!

The church wants to be entertained with a story of victory and told how they can make a difference by putting a few dollars and pocket lint into the collection basket.

You want to know why missionaries inflate their numbers? Because missionaries know that if they do not perform, if they do not motivate, if they do not make the church members feel that they are getting value for their money, then they do not get funding.

But Paul asked, how can they know unless they are sent (Romans 10:15)? What is the role of the church? Paul's letter to Romans was to the church in Rome, not to the missionaries. His letter was to the sender, not to the one being sent.

Missionaries paint elaborate stories, inflate numbers, and tell about huge revivals, but if you are to completely believe the words coming out of our collective mouth, Africa would have been saved a thousand times over.

But it isn't saved.

The church needs to embrace missionaries, encourage them, feed into the vision, and build them up. Churches need to be a place of recovery for the missionary and a place of encouragement for the mission organizations. When missionaries come and speak at a church, they need to be coming to a place of healing, life, and restoration for the battle-weary warrior.

If we are to see revival travel around the globe all the way back to Jerusalem, then it is important that the church know the truth about the mission field, and focus on sending and encouraging those they send.

DISCUSSION QUESTIONS

1. Do you think churches would still support missionaries if they didn't tell such great stories? Why or why not? Would you still support a missionary who is perhaps a bit too honest?

2. Should doing a great job at mission promotion and fund-raising really be a part of fulfilling the Great Commission?

3. Do you think mission is a cause that should be promoted, just like other causes that are promoted in the church? Or is it something that should grow in our hearts from the seeds the Spirit puts there? Why do you think so?

4. Do you think nations that have known revival but have lost this fire, be it by force or otherwise, "deserve" mission efforts, or should those efforts first be on lands that have never been reached with the Gospel?

DAY 61

CONCLUSION

———◆———

"If you're tired of starting over, stop giving up."

—Shia LaBeouf

Beware of those who claim that the movement of God is different this time.

It is never different. It happens over and over. Like clock hands that go around and around in a circle. If someone says that it is different this time, then that should be a sign that the person who is saying it might not be fully aware of history.

As I traveled around the world working on this road trip Bible study, I found that history always repeats itself.

The things that happened to Abraham are happening to us today. What happened with King David is happening today. The trials of Jesus' disciples are trials for us today. What happened with Communism in Russia and China in the early twentieth century is happening again today.

Over and over again we see that history repeats itself. There is nothing new under the sun (Ecclesiastes 1:9).

> **History always repeats itself.**

As we end our road trip Bible study, I think that it is vitally important to look back and interpret history through Christ.

There is a Christology to everything.

I think I began this journey believing that only Scripture is best interpreted through Christ, but now I believe that history too is best interpreted through Christ.

Christology is not anthropological. The modern mind might argue that theology is anthropology because man creates God in his own image. Think of the Greek gods—they looked like the men who created them. But a Christ-centered theology recognizes that man is created in the image of God, not the other way around. Christ is the center of the universe, not man. Jesus is the reason for history, not man. All that exists only exists because of Him and Him alone. All things come from Him, and all things will return to Him.

The study of history is altogether useless without the knowledge of the circumstances in which those events take place. Circumstances shed light on the events, and the circumstances are better understood through the lens of Scripture.

What better history is there to study than the move of God in the world of man? History is not the story of man, but the story of God, and God's history is still being made. It is all one continuous story that never began and will never end. He is ever present. Never hidden.

> **What better history is there to study than the move of God in the world of man?**

He never changes, yet He is always doing something new in me, through me, and to me.

I will always be a part of history because He lives in me. I live a dying life and die a living death. The same is true for you.

The sun rises in the east and sets in the west; it ever moves westward. Just as the earth is orbiting the sun, so does the history of revival orbit the Savior. The sun is motionless. From time to time, men forget, and from our own vantage point, it looks like the sun is going around the earth, because it's actually the earth that's turning.

The spread of the Christian church in its earliest centuries is one of the most amazing phenomena in all of human history. In the book of Acts 2:41, three thousand people came to Christ from a single sermon, and revival has continued to explode from there.

The new Christians faced a dark night and unexplainable persecution, yet they grew into the world's largest religion. But we still have much to do to complete the Great Commission.

This excites me. I know we are capable of doing so much more and are closer to the end than we have ever been before.

There has been a restlessness in my spirit. I feel the burden of not doing enough. I feel the anxiety of being so very close to a breakthrough, that I am just about to see on the other side of the wall and on the other side of the mountain.

Let the belligerent unbelievers who have access to the Gospel disbelieve. Don't waste time trying to convince them. Let the skeptics and the pious religious leaders know that what they fear the most is about to happen.

Right now it may seem the church of the West has so many spectacular comforts and such glorious apathy that we don't even need the devil to keep us from completing the Great Commission. But I believe a change is coming. A spiritual earthquake that will shake the world. It is time to move from defense to attack mode. God is calling His church to take the initiative once more.

We need to be a people who take chances again. We need to be a people who inspire the youth again. We need to be a people who make the old wish they were young again. We need to be a people who crave for the battles of Paul, Silas, and Peter.

Even though the disciples followed Jesus for three years, watching His miracles, hearing His teachings, being touched by His authority, I am positive they did not see His crucifixion coming. As He hung on the cross, I am certain they had to have been at a loss for words. Just as they couldn't have anticipated the humiliation and the pain of sorrow, so too are we blind to what may come, but we do know that everything is about to change.

When Jesus rose from the dead, I am certain that the disciples thought He would be with them in the flesh forever. Death could not hold Him; it had already tried to once. If He was resurrected once, He would be resurrected forever. They certainly did not foresee the road they would walk alone. But they also didn't know that He would send a Comforter who had never been known before. It was a change.

Paul preached a Jewish Gospel to a Gentile world. Men, women, and children began to follow after Christ without keeping the Jewish ceremonies, without being circumcised. It was a change.

For the last couple of hundred years, missionaries who have been sent out have been primarily Western; they have come from Europe, Canada, Australia, America, and other wealthy Western countries. But now God is choosing people from the nations of Asia and Africa to spread the Good News. They come from nations that are Communist and atheist. They are not white or Western. They are all the colors of the rainbow.

This new battle for the end of days will need a new strategy. Our Western strategies that have been printed in books will do little good in the future God has for us. We will not be able to rely on money from the Western church. We will have to rely on God and God only.

We will not be able to solely rely on our Western education, logic, and reasoning. We will have to dig deep, go back to the days of Acts and the apostles, and depend on the power of the Holy Spirit.

As things change, many will run in fear and be afraid. Do not be dismayed. Do not be anxious.

We have to embrace the challenge, thrive on the unknown, and be comfortable with the uncertainties of life.

In the last years we have seen great persecution, but there will be a final harvest, and it will be so abundant that there will not be enough workers to take it all in.

While in Australia in 2014, Brother Yun preached at a church and said, "Let us not build any more buildings, but let's take over mosques and temples."

There is a revival coming to the lands of Islam, Buddha, and Hinduism— all the way back to Jerusalem!

DISCUSSION QUESTIONS

1. When you think back on the stories of revival history that you have read, where is your life and your church in this picture?
2. Are you experiencing revival or are you part of a fizzled-out one? Are you longing to be part of God's continuing work and the new things He is doing?
3. Are you frightened of the disruption and the cost of revival? Do you feel longing or resistance? Are you ready to run or ready to jump in?
4. Have you heard the voice of God in any way speaking to your heart as you learned about revival history?
5. Where do you think your place is?

NOTES

Day 2: What Is the Gospel Message?

1. http://docplayer.net/95990-The-mission-has-a-church-an-invitation-to-the-dance-stephen-bevans-svd.html

Day 6: Revival Night: An Oxymoron

2. F. W. Boreham, "The Land of the Midnight Sun," in *A Reel of Rainbow: A Collection of Essays*, Kindle Edition, 2013, Published by Chariot e-books.

Day 7: Revival and the Rise of Free Nations

3. http://www.christianitytoday.com/ct/2014/january-february/world-missionaries-made.html?paging=off
4. Ibid.

Day 8: Where It All Began

5. http://www.christianitytoday.com/edstetzer/2014/january/my-inter-view-with-tabletalk-magazine.html, emphasis added.

Day 11: Discovering Revival on Pentecost

6. Rabbi Moshe Weissman, *The Midrash Says: Shemot* (New York: Benei Yakov Publications, 1980), 182.
7. Rick Deadmond, *The Betrothed Bride of Messiah* (Salem Publishing Solutions, 2007), 88.

Day 24: A Failed Missionary Travels to Africa

8. http://www.tertullian.org/fathers/apocryphal_acts_04_philip.htm
9. http://www.mcah.columbia.edu/courses/medmil/pages/non-mma-pages/text_links/gl_matthew.html
10. http://www.mappingthemartyrs.org/items/show/66
11. https://www.britannica.com/biography/Saint-Bartholomew

Day 25: The Holy Ghost Welcomed in Africa

12. http://www.tertullian.org/theology.htm
13. http://www.tertullian.org/works/de_praescriptione_haereticorum.htm

Day 27: The Bastardization of a Continent

14. https://theglobalchurchproject.com/augustines-influence-calvin-luther-zwingli/
15. http://www.islamreligion.com/articles/4996/viewall/first-migration/
16. http://www.historytoday.com/eamonn-gearon/arab-invasions-first-is-lamic-empire#sthash.u9RQUlF2.dpuf

Day 38: Shipwrecked in a New World

17. http://www.history.com/topics/exploration/leif-eriksson
18. http://www.christianitytoday.com/history/issues/issue-63/greenland-father-son-saga.html

Day 43: America and the Bible

19. Cornelius Dyck, *An Introduction to Mennonite History* (Herald Press, 1967), 45.
20. Dialogue available at https://www.plough.com/en/topics/faith/anabaptists/the-martyrs-of-alcatraz

Day 47: A Pressure Cooker for Revival

21. https://blacklivesmatter.com/about/what-we-believe/

Check out other books published by
BACK TO JERUSLEM

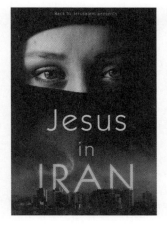

JESUS IN IRAN

The Bible contains many stories specifically from the region of ancient Iran, among them the story of Esther. By studying the Bible more closely, we can understand the heart of Iran better, and by studying the history of Iran, we can understand the Bible better.

Through reading *Jesus in Iran* you will also become intimately familiar with the aspects that China and Iran share and learn how the Chinese are playing an instrumental role in reaching the Muslim world. This book is not written with a Western perspective, but with a Chinese perspective. As such, you will be encouraged and challenged to support our Chinese missionaries as they are tasked to go where few others are able to go.

Iranian missionaries were, in fact, active players in founding the first churches in China a long time ago. Now it is time for the Gospel to go in the reverse direction—from China back to Iran.

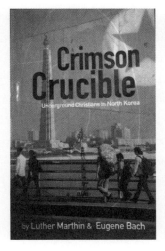

CRIMSON CRUCIBLE
Underground Christians in North Korea

North Korea is a country shrouded in mystery for most people. It brings to mind barbed wire, famine, and Kim Jong Il's nuclear shenanigans, and this book touches on some of the negative aspects of the nation. But it also focuses on what God has done in North Korea in the past and the new work He is doing there today.

Most outsiders think the church in North Korea has been destroyed, but this couldn't be further from the truth. There is a body of believers there that has held out for generations, even after years of persecution and attempts to destroy Christianity. On top of this, sparks of revival are flying all over the country as thousands of North Koreans quietly give their lives to Christ. How can this be? Be prepared to see a side of North Korea you've never seen before.

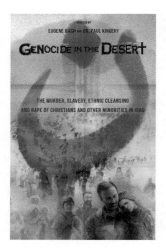

GENOCIDE IN THE DESERT

The Murder, Slavery, Ethnic Cleansing, and Rape of Christians and Other Minorities in Iraq

There are few places on earth where Christianity is as old as it is in Iraq. And according to the Bible, Iraq's geographical location is central to both the creation of man and the end times. Iraq is in the heart of the Middle East and represents the country with the most insane persecution against Christians in the world today. For Christians who take the Great Commission seriously, Iraq is in the center of the final frontier for the Gospel message.

During three months in 2014, nearly one million people from ancient Christian communities were targeted in a deliberate campaign of hate. This book captures many of their untold stories for the first time. What is taking place in Iraq must not be ignored by the universal church. The same group that is attacking Christians in Iraq is also launching attacks in the Middle East, Africa, Europe, and even America. This book boldly shows how Islam was forced on the Iraqi people to imprison them and delay the return of the Messiah. We must sound the alarm to collectively take the Gospel message into the heart of one of the last unreached regions on earth before it is too late.

THE UNDERGROUND CHURCH

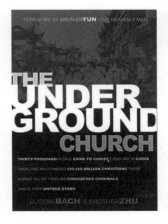

The Chinese house church is one of the most misunderstood and controversial subjects in Christian world missions today, and house churches in China are growing at a phenomenal rate. Never in the history of the world have so many people in such a short time left one belief system for another without a hostile revolution. Lives in China are being transformed daily by the Gospel of Jesus Christ and the display of His miraculous power.

The Underground Church demystifies the Chinese house church movement with real-life examples and personal testimonies from Chinese Christians. The movement's unique characteristics—both good and bad—are addressed, as well as how they have led to the church's astonishing growth.

Read and be amazed at what God is doing in China!

TALES FROM FUFU'S FOREST

True Stories Told by Fictional Characters

As you step through the swaying arch into the bamboo forest, you enter the warm, welcoming home of a rotund panda and a few quirky friends. There

in FuFu's Forest you will always find a bottomless cup of tea and true tales brought back from missionaries in the field.

BOOK 1: THE COURAGE TO OBEY

Shan gets a little spooked while staying home alone and ventures out for a walk. That's when he discovers the enchanting bamboo forest and some very interesting new friends. But it's there in FuFu's Forest where Shan finds exactly what he needs: the encouraging story of a real-life missionary in Tibet, with the courage to go wherever God may lead.

BOOK 2:
THE MIRACLE OF SPRING

When a baby bird falls from its nest in the bamboo forest, Shan and his friends gather around, hoping for a miracle. Yang, seeing Miss Fay's sadness, reminds her of a real-life miracle that she had witnessed in Saudi Arabia not too long ago. That's when Miss Fay proceeds to tell them all about a true miracle of spring, about a girl who saw Jesus in the bottom of a well and was raised up again, to a new life in Him.

BOOK 3:
THE HEALING HAND OF GOD

When Shan's father becomes very sick, Shan keeps watch by his bedside all through the night. Feeling worried and helpless, Shan finally steps away to get some fresh air and wanders into the lush bamboo forest. That's where he bumps into Old Red and hears the miraculous true story of a Chinese missionary touched by a power much greater than him, a power that sets him free: the healing hand of God.

BTJ PRAYER BEAR

This prayer bear, FuFu, the main character in our children's book series Tales from Fufu's Forest, has no special powers; it has not been prayed over or blessed. It is simply a reminder to pray for the BTJ missionaries, as a prayer card or calendar would. This is a great gift or tool to help children learn to enjoy praying for missions.

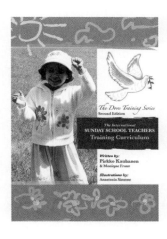

DOVE

In China, it is illegal to evangelize children under the age of 18. Dove was started out of the concern that by that age the Communist party would have infiltrated the hearts and minds of children, and it would be impossible to reach them. The focus of this study is to provide teachers simple, basic training on how to teach young children to know Jesus and receive salvation.

This curriculum is created for children ages 3-12. It is divided into 12 books, one for each month. Each month has a theme and a memory verse. The weekly lessons contain a lesson aim, a memory verse, a sample schedule, activity directions, and a sample script. There is a fifth week included each month that is dedicated to exposing children to missions work. You can use as much or as little of the material as you see fit for your group, and it is easy to incorporate your original ideas into the lessons.

Because of its success in China and in an attempt to reach as many children as possible, Dove has been translated into over 12 languages and is still growing.

WHAT IS BACK TO JERUSALEM?

Many mistake the idea of Back to Jerusalem as a movement of the Chinese church to evangelize Jerusalem. However, Back to Jerusalem is the goal of the Chinese church to evangelize the unreached peoples from eastern provinces of China, westward toward Jerusalem. The vision was birthed among the Chinese in the 1920s, and since that time, the churches of China have strove and even suffered persecution to fulfill what they believe is their integral role in fulfilling the Great Commission. Our organization partners with the church of China not only to evangelize the religiously oppressed areas of Asia but also to train and send Chinese missionaries into the unreached regions of the globe, including Muslim, Buddhist, and Hindu nations.

For more information about Back to Jerusalem,
please visit their website: https://backtojerusalem.com